D0645499

A Survey of Linguistic Theories

Mildred L. Larson, Editor in Chief

Volume Editors

Mary Huttar
Rhonda L. Hartell
Marilyn A. Mayers

Production Staff

Laurie Nelson, Production Manager, Compositor
Bonnie Brown, Managing Editor
Hazel Shorey, Graphic Artist

A Survey of Linguistic Theories

Jerold A. Edmondson
Donald A. Burquest

Third Edition

The Summer Institute of Linguistics
Dallas, Texas

© 1992, 1994, 1998 by the Summer Institute of Linguistics, Inc.
Library of Congress Catalog No: 98-89616
ISBN: 1-55671-068-2

Printed in the United States of America
All Rights Reserved

First edition 1992
Second edition 1994
Third edition 1998

06 05 04 03 02 01 00 99   10 9 8 7 6 5 4 3 2 1

No part of this publication may be reproduced, stored in a retrieval system, or transmitted in any form or by any means—electronic, mechanical, photocopy, recording, or otherwise—without the express permission of the Summer Institute of Linguistics, with the exception of brief excerpts in journal articles or reviews.

Copies of this and other publications of the Summer Institute of Linguistics may be obtained from

International Academic Bookstore
Summer Institute of Linguistics
7500 W. Camp Wisdom Road
Dallas, TX 75236-5699

Voice: 972-708-7404
Fax: 972-708-7433
Email: academic_books@sil.org
Internet: http://www.sil.org

Contents

Abbreviations and Symbols

A	adjective		LFG	Lexical Functional Grammar
ACC	accusative		M or Mo	modal
Adj	adjective		MAP	Morphosyntactically licensed Argument Positions
ADV	adverb			
Aux	auxiliary		Mar	margin
COMP	complementizer		N	(common) noun
Cl	clause		Neg	negation
CR	current relevance (perfect)		NOM	nominative
DAT	dative		NP	noun phrase
Det	determiner		Nuc	nucleus
DO	direct object		P	preposition
DS	deep structure		P&P	Principles and Parameters Theory
e or Em	empty (node)			
ECM	exceptional case marking		Perf	perfect
Emp	emphasis		PP	prepositional phrase
EPP	Extended Projection Principle		PreS	pre-sentence
			Prog	progressive
GB	Government and Binding Theory		Prt	participle
			PS	phrase structure
GEN	genitive		Q	question symbol
GPSG	generalized phrase structure grammar		QP	quantifier phrase
			S	sentence
GR	Grammatical Relations		SC	structural change
GTG	generative transformational grammar		SD	structural description
			SS	surface structure
iff	if and only if		State	state aspect (progressive)
INFL	inflection		t	trace
IO	indirect object		Tns	tense
IP	inflection phrase		U	union
LF	logical form		UG	universal grammar

V	verb	1	subject relation
VP	verb phrase	2	direct object relation
		3	indirect object relation
*	not well-formed	/ /	phoneme
?	well-formedness	[ ]	phone
	questionable	// //	systematic phoneme
!	meaningless or false	{}	set
		∈	element of a set
		∪	union of two or more sets
		→	rewrite as

Preface

This book is intended to be used in connection with the course Linguistics 5332 'A survey of linguistic theories', which we have regularly taught at the University of Texas at Arlington since 1981. It is not intended to be a comprehensive account of everything that is happening in linguistics today but rather a sample of the more popular approaches to linguistic theorizing.

The authors wish to thank those colleagues and students who have already commented on this work, in particular our colleagues Ilah Fleming, Shin Ja Hwang, Sydney Lamb, Robert Longacre, Stephen Marlett, William Merrifield, Evelyn Pike, Kenneth Pike, and Harry Reeder. We urge future readers to give their reactions to style, presentation, and content.

Jerold A. Edmondson
Donald A. Burquest
April 1992

Preface to the Third Edition

This revised edition continues the intentions of the first and second editions in presenting a sample of the more popular approaches to linguistic theorizing. We have chosen in this edition to eliminate the chapter on phonology since this subarea of linguistics has developed toward homogeneity in the last years in a manner that grammar and discourse studies have not. At the same time, we have expanded and updated the chapters on Principles and Parameters Syntax, Relational Grammar, and Functionalist Models.

The authors wish to add to the list of colleagues mentioned in the earlier editions who have aided us by reading and commenting on versions of the manuscript the names of Susan Herring, Marlin Leaders, Ken McElhanon, John Paolillo, and David Silva. We wish also to thank many of our students who have given us comments on various versions, especially James Hafford, Mike Bryant, Jim Hudson, Teresa Jade, C. J. Searsy, and Michelle Miller. Any remaining errors are, of course, our own.

1

Linguistic Theorizing

1.1 Of surveys and theories

Since this book is entitled *A Survey of Linguistic Theories*, it is incumbent upon us to make clear what we mean by a survey, what we mean by a theory, and particularly what we mean by a linguistic theory. We begin with the first of these by arguing that SURVEYS are not the same as HISTORIES. Moreover, we contend that comparison of theoretical proposals in linguistics is possible despite some counterclaim (cf. the question of incommensurability in Kuhn (1962)). After a discussion of the notion of survey, we turn to the characteristics of theories in general and linguistic theories in particular. In the closing section of this chapter we present the schema that will be used for the comparative presentation to follow.

1.1.1 The nature of a survey. In the context of this book, we use the term survey in the same manner as it is used in land measurement. Specifically, we intend to examine the BOUNDARIES, AREA, and ELEVATION (the three notions that form the concerns of the surveyor) of a number of linguistic theories. We regard these three notions as the essential traits that need to be discussed, as there is no unanimity about the boundaries, the dividing lines between linguistic investigations, and the investigations of researchers in other disciplines; it is also a contentious matter what linguistic terrain or area is to be covered, and by what means; and, finally, there is no agreement about which aspects of the covered area are central and thus "elevated" in importance in relation to those aspects which are peripheral.

BOUNDARIES are important because not all investigators agree about limits. The language behavior of humans is indeed a complex

1

phenomenon and, as a consequence, it may be unclear whether gesturing, the AFFECTIVE INTONATION we use to indicate attitude (e.g., sarcasm, anger, sadness, etc.), or the individual and unique qualities of voice of a specific speaker belong to linguistic study or to psychology or to anthropology. And even in relation to such matters as text structure and pragmatics, when these topics are incorporated within a linguistic theory, it is not always clear precisely how they are to be handled, what domain of language they belong to, and how they relate to other domains.

One is reminded of a similar problem found in natural science. While chemistry is primarily interested in COMPOUNDS, i.e., matter at the molecular level, there is growing interest in the chemistry of submolecular units, extending the subject matter of chemistry into new domains such as nuclear chemistry. Nor is there overlap in this direction only. For example, solid state physics is encroaching on the subject matter classically included within chemistry, for it is concerned with the nature of crystal structure in compounds. In fact, very similar kinds of experiments can be performed by physicists and by chemists on very similar kinds of materials and yet each gets different results and each investigator has a strong sense that this study is physical or chemical, respectively.

In the case of language and speech, there are a great many neighboring disciplines that count either as linguistic periphery or as something quite different from the proper domain of linguistic study. A sampling of some of these related areas includes: (a) psychology of language—the perception and comprehension of verbal signals; (b) sociology of language—language in large groups; (c) speech pathology and neuropsychology—language pathology; (d) post-modernist, critical theory—the properties of verbal texts and the interpretations given to them by readers; (e) history of a given language—the accumulation of borrowed words and language change; (f) biology of communication—the biosystems subtending language; (g) physics of language—the acoustics and aerodynamics of sound production and perception; (h) mathematics of language—mathematical properties of language systems; (i) computer science—artificial intelligence; (j) archaeology—the bearing of fossil hominids on questions relating to language origins; and (k) animal behavior—capacities of subhuman primates, dolphins, birds, bees, and other organisms for communication. With the overlap of domain between linguistics and these neighbors we may speak of psycholinguistics, neurolinguistics, sociolinguistics, etc. But the relationship of related areas to a particular approach to linguistics proper can be quite different. For example, generative transformational linguistics regards language as a system quite different in nature than the system that underlies some kinds of nonverbal behavior and therefore looks only for DIFFERENCES in kind not SIMILARITIES; tagmemics takes just the opposite position. Thus, in many cases, different theorists establish different boundaries, and a great deal of the manifest divergences among linguistic theories follow from that.

When speaking of AREA, a similar need to distinguish arises. Does the theoretical proposal claim to encompass the entirety of speech and language, or is it more modest in scope? Even if only a limited subarea is the aim, can the principles developed be applied to other areas? For example, in the theoretical proposal known as RELATIONAL GRAMMAR, the grammatical relations (e.g., subject, direct object, indirect object, etc.) are paramount, and such considerations as word order, verb morphology, and constituent structure are useful in developing arguments for the grammatical relations in a particular language; one does not expect grammatical relations in every language to be manifest in the same way. These latter areas are to be dealt with by means of rules external to relational grammar, presumably because principles derived from the study of grammatical relations cannot be extrapolated to all other kinds of relations. On the other hand, the theoretical proposal known as TAGMEMICS regards all-sized pieces of language to be analyzable into the same number and kinds of subunits, whether sounds, words, sentences, or texts; in fact, as mentioned above, tagmemics claims that the same principles and category types can be applied to verbal and nonverbal behavior alike.

The definition of areas can involve more than just differences of comprehensiveness. Whether one part of the language system depends upon another can be the subject of disagreement; in the post-1965 period, for example, one group of linguists (the interpretive semanticists) advocated that sentences, as strings of symbols, could be analyzed syntactically independent of the semantic interpretations assigned to these strings. Others (the generative semanticists) saw the interpretation as primary and the structure of symbol strings as dependent upon them. (We return to this discussion in chapter five.) Thus, linguistic theories differ not only in regard to what is encompassed in language study, but also how the parts are related.

The third task of the surveyor, the determination of ELEVATION, we will take to be prominence in a theory. Theorizing about language differs in the prominence given to particular aspects. The structuralist linguists, for instance, were concerned first and foremost about the notion contrast. Generative transformational linguists regard contrast as less central and regard the linguistic rule that captures generalizations across languages as primary.

1.1.2 Surveys are not histories. For the purposes of this work, we will regard a survey as something not identical with a history. Therefore, we will not chronicle the development of ideas and the contributions of various personalities as a primary aim, though some of this is also included. For instance, we have chosen not to discuss American or European structuralism in any detail, because—despite their contentions to the contrary—much of contemporary theorizing builds on what was important in structuralism. Nevertheless, the influence of pure structuralism of vintage 1930 or 1940 is waning, as a glance at most international journal articles will tell. We will rather concentrate on approaches that are currently being practiced—what Kuhn (1962:23-34) calls NORMAL SCIENCE, the pursuit of solving problems arising from observation—and experiment within the assumptions of a given pattern or accepted model. The history of linguistics is a discipline worthy of study by specialists, but in linguistics as in other fields, comprehensive knowledge of the history of linguistics is not a requisite of every linguistic practitioner.

1.1.3 Surveys can be comparative. We propose to make this survey of linguistic theories a comparative one. There is, however, an inherent danger in the comparison of theories. *The Structure of Scientific Revolutions* (Kuhn 1962) has taken the position that competing scientific theories are radically incommensurable, and thus cannot be compared. This incommensurability is the result of the fact that theories (Kuhn calls theories of this type PARADIGMS) define for themselves what the interesting problems in a discipline are, what methods will be used to solve them, what standards will be expected of a solution, what role argumentation will play, how much the theory is to be under-determined by the data, and other such questions. Thus, two competitors differ so radically that one cannot engage meaningfully in any sort of comparison.

> In the first place, the proponents of competing paradigms will often disagree about the list of problems that any candidate for paradigm must resolve...More is involved, however, than the incommensurability of standards. Since new paradigms are born from old ones, they ordinarily incorporate much of the vocabulary and apparatus, both conceptual and manipulative, that the traditional paradigm has previously

employed. But they seldom employ these borrowed elements in quite the traditional way. (Kuhn 1962:148–9)

From the philosopher Stephen C. Pepper (1942) we hear a similar warning. For him there are two fundamentally different sorts of theories. WORLD HYPOTHESES reject nothing as irrelevant and are thus defined as "unrestricted products of knowledge." These contrast with THEORIES concerned with restricted fields of knowledge exemplified by works such as Euclid's *Elements* and Darwin's *The Origin of Species*. World hypotheses result from ROOT METAPHORS, which are attempts to understand the world by using knowledge of one area as a pattern for understanding other areas. These root metaphors perform three functions: (a) they connect world hypotheses to common sense; (b) they illuminate the nature of hypotheses; and (c) they can be an instrument for evaluating hypotheses. Since a world hypothesis is determined by a root metaphor, and since root metaphors differ from one world hypothesis to another, world hypotheses cannot be compared. It also does not strengthen one world hypothesis if one exhibits the shortcomings of another.

> ...a great proportion of philosophical—and not only philosophical—books give a large part of their space to polemic, finding the faults in rival theories with an idea that this helps to establish the theory proposed. The cognitive value of a hypothesis is not one jot increased by the cognitive errors of other hypotheses...If a theory is any good it can stand on its own evidence. The only reason for referring to other theories in constructive cognitive endeavors is to find out what other evidence they may suggest, or other matters of positive cognitive value. (Pepper 1942:101)

According to Pepper, it is also "confusing" to mix world hypotheses. World hypotheses are "mutually exclusive."

Two comments must be made about Pepper's suggestion. First of all, as mentioned above, he has specifically excluded restricted fields of knowledge from consideration, because they—unlike world hypotheses (e.g., Plato's *Republic*, Aristotle's *Metaphysics*, and Hume's *Treatise*)—can "reject facts as not belonging to their field if the facts do not fit properly within the definitions and hypotheses framed for the field" (1942:1). Linguistic theories, however, are presumably an example of such restricted theories, not world hypotheses. It should not be surprising, therefore, if Pepper's suggestions do not apply to language theorizing. Secondly, it seems to us that Pepper takes a rather optimistic view of the potential role of evidence in persuading a practitioner to give up his world hypothesis in favor of another. Max Planck once sadly remarked:

> A new scientific truth does not triumph by convincing its opponents and making them see the light, but rather because its opponents eventually die, and a new generation grows up that is familiar (sic) with it. (Kuhn 1962:151)

Kuhn's position on comparing theories (paradigms) has made its way into the arguments of linguists. Thus, Jones abandons any attempt at comparison saying:

> Ultimately choice of theories is a question of values, of choice of axioms. At best, one theory can hope to win through "conversion," but never by "proof"...
>
> Ultimately, then, each theory must be evaluated for its own merits, and NOT by comparison with other theories. In particular, how successfully a theory meets its stated purposes and goals, and the general usefulness or applicability of the theory, are what is to be evaluated. (1980:88)

Yet, such claims of radical incommensurability—both in natural science and in linguistics—are based on a view that scientists are totally irrational and dogmatic; that linguists are incapable at any level of seeing the world or possible world described by a linguistic paradigm in competition with their own. As Laudan argues, however, this logic is flawed and, in fact, there are ways of comparing without seeing other worlds.

> But *its central flaw*, for our purposes, *lies in its presumption that rational choice can be made between theories only if those theories can be translated into one another's language or into a third "theory-neutral" language*...I shall maintain, to the contrary, that even if we accept the view that all observations are theory-laden to a degree that makes their contents inseparable from the theory which is used to express them, it is still possible to outline machinery for objective, rational comparisons between competing scientific theories and research traditions...What this approach ignores is that *neither* correspondence rules *nor* a theory-free observation language are necessary for comparing the empirical consequences of competing theories. For even *without* correspondence rules and without a purely observational language, we can still talk meaningfully about different theories being *about the same problem*, even when the specific characterization of that

problem is crucially dependent upon many theoretical assumptions. [His emphasis] (1977:142)

As Laudan goes on to point out, Kuhn and other radical non-comparativists such as Feyerabend have concluded that since some empirical problems are theory-laden, that all such problems are (Feyerabend 1978). But most linguists, of whatever school, feel this is not so.

In linguistic theorizing, for example, are we to believe that the morphology of English plurality is theory-laden even at the level of observation? There are the three odd types of encoding: (a) the S-ADDITIVE strategy (e.g., *boy* vs. *boy-s* or *key* vs. *key-s*); (b) the MODULATORY or umlaut strategy (e.g., *foot* vs. *feet* or *goose* vs. *geese*); and (c) the NONICONIC and unmarked plural (e.g., *deer* vs. *deer* or *fish* vs. *fish*). While different analysts may differ as to whether forms such as *feet* or *deer* contain two morphemes each, how can it be said that the observations themselves are influenced by one's theoretical perspective? As long as the low-level theoretical assumptions needed to characterize an observation are not crucially dependent upon the high-level assumptions in a paradigm, then the problem to be solved by each of the theories can be said to be the same. In Laudan's terms the two sets of assumptions in such a case are disjoint.

It is true that in linguistics many problems cannot be stated in a theory-independent fashion, e.g., what is the role of meaning in determining form or what is the role of function in determining form? But, according to Laudan, one can discuss these issues comparatively as long as one is talking about the same problem. Moreover, failing to attempt a comparison or an evaluation and relying only on how successfully a theory meets its own stated aims makes linguistic theorizing a matter of whim. Only dogged, irrational loyalty and careful "crank turning" is required, so if a good technician can properly churn through the chosen axioms to the ultimate theorems of a theory and do so in a manner attracting popularity, then the theory based on these axioms must be judged satisfactory. But from this point of view there would be no sense to the term "progress of knowledge."

In addition, according to this reasoning, there would have been no motive to retreat from Ptolemy's view of the universe. His geocentric view was accepted for over 1,500 years. He could correctly predict the motion of the planets and understood the precession of equinoxes. The planets in his view were fastened to giant invisible spheres with the earth at the center. Instead of being pinned in fixed fashion to these spheres, however, each planet was attached to an off-center wheel that was said to account for the meandering paths each took in the night sky (Sagan 1980:52–3). When the Copernican heliocentric model of the universe appeared in 1543, it was equally good at predicting planetary motion but offended many who held that man is in the image of the Divine and that his planet should be the center of things; moreover, it disrupted the notion of the "music of the spheres." Nevertheless, heliocentric astronomy did ultimately dislodge Ptolemy's theory when an increase in the accuracy of measurement of planetary orbits allowed Kepler to discover the elliptical and not circular path of Mars.

In light of this case history from astronomy, we conclude that comparison and evaluation of theories with regard to problem-solving capacity may not be fruitless endeavors. Once problems can be stated in terms of low-level theoretical concepts, and once such problems can be characterized as being solved, then we begin to approach an evaluation of the effectiveness of a given research tradition. If a tradition can solve all the problems it sets for itself and thereby create no anomalies, and if it can expand its domain of explained problems, reducing the important unsolved and previously anomalous ones, then one can speak of scientific progress (Laudan 1977:146). In this view, comparison and evaluation can thus be seen as possible. Therefore, our survey will seek to be a comparative and evaluative view of the topology of current (post-1965) linguistic theorizing.

1.2 Scientific progress and the logic of research

In the traditional view, scientific progress was regarded as a cumulative process. Like the filling of water into a bathtub, generations of scientists toiled in the vineyards of observation and experiment, each adding through this normal science to collective knowledge. From the experience of observation and experimentation one could, by virtue of the method of induction, arrive at the regularities. From these regularities, in turn, there remained the second inductive step to natural laws, the generalizations that underlie the observed behavior. These laws were timelessly valid and revealed something about the nature of things.

In this section, we discuss various alternatives that have been advanced regarding the progress of science. We discuss inductive and deductive approaches, and the question of discovery, making reference to ideas of various philosophers.

1.2.1 Induction and irrationality. Consider as an example of discovery, the work of Isaac Newton. From the observation of objects in motion and at rest, Newton discovered the law of inertia. Yet, this law came into conflict with the motion of the moon. From the failure of the moon to fly out of its circular orbit around the earth, he further concluded that an unknown force must bind the moon to the earth and that it was that very same force that caused an apple to fall to the ground. This discovery led to positing the laws of gravity. But, according to David Hume, no rational justification can be provided for the induction from observations to such laws. That is, just because the sun has risen every morning of our lives and every morning of human history, this doesn't allow us to conclude that it will rise tomorrow morning. To go from observations, which are formulated as singular statements (those true of individual cases or times), to laws, which are formulated as universal statements (those true in general), an induction principle is needed. But, induction principles are themselves universal statements and demand support in their own right (Popper 1962, Stegmüller 1969, 1975:488). Thus, Hume concludes that empirical sciences proceed inductively but irrationally in the sense that their underlying principles are ungrounded and unjustified.

1.2.2 Induction and rationality. Hume's conclusions resulted in numerous attempts at justifying INDUCTIVE INFERENCE as a method. This striving became especially intense in the twentieth century. Carnap attempted to construct an inductive logic to parallel the long-established methods of deductive logic. This undertaking—had it succeeded—would have changed the empirical sciences into inductive but rational pursuits. The philosopher Reichenbach made an important distinction in the inductive procedure. He speaks of induction in the CONTEXT OF DISCOVERY and in the CONTEXT OF JUSTIFICATION. Hume and Carnap had two different contexts in mind when speaking of induction; Hume the former context and Carnap the latter.

1.2.3 Deduction and rationality. In opposition to the solutions of Carnap and Reichenbach to the dilemma of irrationality in induction as posed by Hume, the Viennese philosopher Karl Popper claimed that induction cannot be used either in a context of discovery or in a context of justification. Popper says the methods of discovery are not conscious ones and in principle they remain clouded in speculation. One might cite in confirmation of Popper the words of discoverers about their discoveries. According to Sagan (1980:69), Newton is supposed to have said that he discovered the foundations of a theory of universal

gravitation "by thinking upon them." Einstein, the man called the Newton of the twentieth century, was as mystified by the birth of an idea as
the rest of us. Of the time that led to that magical year 1905, in which
he punctuated a decade of preparation with the proposal of The Special
Theory of Relativity, his biographer Peter Michelmore says:

> He worked on and on through 1904. One puzzle led to another.
> His brain was on fire. His body exhausted. He could not eat. He
> could not sleep. The speed of light never varies. When people
> spoke to him, he did not hear. He wandered in a daze. At times,
> he wondered if this was the way to insanity...
>
> Perhaps because of the sudden relaxation after months of in-
> tense brain work, that night the missing pieces fell into place.
> Relativity yielded and came scrambling into the world...This
> had come from the inventive element of human reason that
> Kant had written about. Einstein had proved his creativity.
> He was ecstatic. (1962:44–45)

Einstein says in his own words in the Kyoto lecture of 1922:

> Unexpectedly a friend of mine in Bern then helped me. That
> was a very beautiful day when I visited him and began to talk
> with him as follows: "I have recently had a question which
> was difficult for me to understand. So I came here today to
> bring with me a battle on the question." Trying a lot of dis-
> cussions with him, I could suddenly comprehend the matter.
> Next day I visited him again and said to him without greet-
> ing: "Thank you. I've completely solved the problem."
> (quoted from Pais 1982:139)

Or a more recent story is equally enlightening. A Stanford University
graduate student in 1979, Alan H. Guth, proposed a brilliant new account of the universe before the 'big bang'. He has posited a kind of cos-
mic 'inflation' for one-trillionth of a second just before the explosion. Of
the germ of the idea he has said that he had no idea why the equations
began to come to him just when they did. "Without my knowing it the
ideas were already in my head, and they seemed to come together in
one fell swoop" (Waldrop 1984).

These accounts sound little like the experiences of persons wrapped
in cool inductive thinking but rather of men possessed by their own cre-
ative intuition. Moreover, a *post hoc* reconstruction of the inductive
steps that led to discovery is probably not possible since some kinds of
noncontinuous, catastrophic (in the sense of René Thom) development

seems to be involved. Nor does it seem very important to the involved person to confirm the intervening steps that led to breakthrough.

In addition to this claim regarding discovery, Popper also baldly asserts that a grounding or justification of theories or hypotheses does not exist. Nevertheless, such theories differ from pure metaphysical speculation because they must be put to the test of rigorous deductive confirmation. One proceeds by tentatively assuming a hypothesis and then trying to falsify it. According to Popper (1962:32–34), four tests are involved: (a) The conclusions of the theory are compared logically; (b) the logical form of the theory is considered (e.g., is it tautological?); (c) in comparison with competing theories it must count as a scientific advance; and (d) the theory must be tested with regard to its derivative empirical applications. The results of this last test are what Popper calls PREDICTIONS. If the predictions are confirmed or verified, then such a positive result is only temporary support, for subsequent negative results will always be able to overthrow the prediction and the corresponding theory that has led to it. Should a theory stand up to the four tests and exhibit no negative predictions, then it counts as corroborated. Therefore, Popper sees progress in science as noninductive (the theories are assumed and not induced logically from observation) but rational (the theories are testable with explicitly defined tests).

We have already mentioned Thomas S. Kuhn's *The Structure of Scientific Revolutions* in connection with the comparison of theories or PARADIGMS. This book is, in a sense, the most radical of proposals about the philosophy of science, because Kuhn advocates that research employs procedures that are neither inductive nor rational. He agrees with Popper in testing hypotheses but differs in hypothesis abandonment, because he pleads that progress—just like discovery itself—occurs in a discontinuous, catastrophic manner. Knowledge does not accumulate like water in the bathtub but instead through periods of perturbation, which he calls SCIENTIFIC REVOLUTIONS. It is as if the plug in the bathtub were pulled out and new water put in; the same observations must be accounted for but they are accounted for in such a way as to give them a newly-shaped interpretation. These new containers represent developments "sufficiently unprecedented to attract an enduring group of adherents away from competing modes of scientific activity. Simultaneously, [they are] sufficiently open-ended to leave all sorts of problems for the redefined group of practitioners to resolve" (Kuhn 1962:10). Such achievements which Kuhn calls paradigms have names like Ptolemaic, Copernican, Newtonian, Einsteinian, or Maxwellian. He further asserts that falsification of predictions should not be equated with anomalous experiences.

...no theory ever solves all the puzzles with which it is confronted at a given time; nor are the solutions already
achieved often perfect. On the contrary, it is just the incom-
pleteness and imperfection of the existing data-theory fit, at
any time, that define many of the puzzles that characterize
normal science...But falsification, though it surely occurs,
does not happen with, or simply because of, the emergence of
[such] an anomaly or falsifying instance. (Kuhn 1962:146)

In Kuhn's view, scientific progress can be characterized as follows.
After a new paradigm has established itself, then normal science, problem solving, takes place. During this initial phase, few textbooks are
written; the literature is mostly found in highly intricate journal articles. This is the period of paradigm articulation. As long as a paradigm
holds sway, the basic assumptions, methods, and standards for solutions
are not questioned by its practitioners. This stability is necessary for the
articulation. A mature paradigm is recognized by the appearance of textbooks for the indoctrination of an upcoming generation of scientists. A
paradigm in decay can be recognized by the buildup of anomalous problems in the course of normal science. At some point, a relatively young
scientist, usually an outsider, enters the picture to propose a new paradigm. If he or she is successful in turning anomalous problems into
solved problems and thereby winning adherents, then the next catastrophic event is at hand. In science, evolution is by revolution.

For the nonempirical sciences Lakatos (1976) refines many of Kuhn's
concepts, including replacing Kuhn's term PARADIGM by RESEARCH
TRADITION. In light of the distinctions Lakatos makes, we should change
the title of this book to "Survey of linguistic research traditions." What
we discuss and compare is namely these broadly defined mixes of ontology, methodology, and specific proposal. Such "super-theories" are
composed of three subparts: (a) a hard-core of fundamentally unchal-
lengeable assumptions called the NEGATIVE HEURISTIC; (b) a belt of
POSITIVE HEURISTIC that admits of modification without repudiation of the
research tradition; and (c) a number of COMPOSITE THEORIES that recapit-
ulate the general macrotheory in the microcosm of a specific domain.
Lakatos expresses a less radical stance than Kuhn on the comparison of
theories, agreeing that such is possible. While Lakatos represents an im-
provement over Kuhn, he still maintains the tenet of scientific
irrationalism; he persists in the view that at least the negative heuristic
aspects of research traditions (like Kuhn's paradigms) cannot be
changed without overthrowing them completely and he claims that the
"accumulation of anomalies has no bearing on the appraisal of a

research tradition" (Laudan 1977:78). Yet some of these ideas are strongly refuted by the history of science and each also extracts a certain methodological and metaphysical commitment on the part of practitioners. Each goes through a series of formulations with a relatively long history even though theories themselves may be short-lived. From Lakatos we take the useful distinction between the general methods for solving problems and a general ontology of nature; these are part of the research tradition. A theory, on the other hand, provides a particular ontology of nature and gives the practitioner a number of specific and testable laws about nature. In the upcoming chapters, we will use these two divisions, general ontology and specific ontology, as two of the three pillars upon which the various linguistic research traditions and theories are presented. We will also examine the ability of theories to solve problems.

1.3 A brief history of the axiomatization of mathematics

Up to this point we have discussed theorizing in empirical sciences and have had little to say about linguistics. As distant a point as it might seem, we now begin to turn our gaze more toward the ultimate object of this work. We will not, however, do so directly but rather circuitously by looking first at some of the major landmarks in pure mathematics over the course of the last one hundred years. As we hope to show, there is a direct linkage between some of the developments in this neighboring discipline and the development of system linguistics since 1965.

In his classic work on the history of mathematics, Ball (1906) claims that "the history of mathematics cannot with certainty be traced back to any school or period before that of the Ionian Greeks." That is not to say that older cultures had no sense of practical mathematics. Indeed, many cultures such as the Egyptians, Chinese, and Phoenicians were capable of practical calculation involving numeration, mechanics, and land-surveying. While the Greeks themselves saw the origins of geometry in Egyptian culture—the word itself means 'earth measure'—still the Ionian mathematicians specialized in discovering the lawlike, gnomic, immutable behavior of figures, independent of any particular instance of them. Ball says:

> Now the Greek geometricians, as far as we can judge by their
> extant works, always dealt with the science as an abstract

one: they sought for theorems which should be absolutely
true... (1960:5)

The crown of classical mathematics was achieved in Euclid's *Elements*
which was so successful that Ball reported in 1906 that this book had
been supplanted on the continent only about one hundred years earlier
but that the version based on Simson's 1758 edition was still in active
use in England at that time. The feature of Euclid's *Elements* held in special esteem was the method of presentation. Propositions were arranged
in a chain from the most obvious to results of considerable complexity.
These most obvious starting points are known as POSTULATES or AXIOMS.
The five postulates of Euclid are found in (1).

(1)   a. A straight line segment can be drawn joining any two
            points.

        b. Any straight line segment can be extended indefinitely in a
            straight line.

        c. Given any straight line segment, a circle can be drawn hav-
            ing the segment as radius and one end point as center.

        d. All right angles are congruent.

        e. If two lines are drawn which intersect a third in such a way
            that the sum of the inner angles on one side is less than
            two right angles, then the two lines inevitably must inter-
            sect each other on that side if extended far enough.

The methods of inference, ways of proceeding from one axiom or a combination of axioms to statements that could be shown to follow from the
axioms, was a tradition established by the Greeks. These latter-named statements are known as THEOREMS and the demonstration that a theorem follows from an axiom or axioms by a rule of inference is known as a
DERIVATION or PROOF. This technique as a whole is called the AXIOMATIC
METHOD. Generation after generation of mathematicians have been im-
pressed with the rigor and elegance of this kind of device.

Toward the end of the nineteenth century, it was discovered that
quite interesting and fruitful results could be obtained by altering or
giving up Euclid's fifth postulate, the parallel axiom. It had generally
been assumed that the abandonment of any one of the postulates—since

no one had been able to show that any one postulate was a consequence of any of the other four postulates—would result in the destruction of the entire system. Such proved, however, not to be the case. Instead, abandonment of the fifth postulate yielded a new geometry, hyperbolic geometry. In similar fashion, abandonment of other postulates produced elliptical geometry. In other words, if the axioms were altered, then the set of theorems derivable was simply a different set of theorems, not chaos. In this insight, mathematicians of that age saw the opportunity of redefining all of mathematics axiomatically. By taking different axioms and different rules of inference, much previous work could be recast in a more rigorous, elegant, and ultimately more simple mold. It was in this sense that Bertrand Russell answered the question "What is mathematics?" by saying in *Mysticism and Logic*:

> Pure mathematics consists entirely of assertions to the effect that if such and such a proposition is true of *anything,* then such and such another proposition is true of that thing. It is essential not to discuss whether the first proposition is really true, and not to mention what the anything is of which it is supposed to be true...Thus mathematics may be defined as the subject in which we never know what we are talking about, nor whether what we are saying is true. (1910:75)

The axiomatic theory held much promise of ridding mathematics of any internal inconsistency and of becoming the forge for new, more powerful subareas of the discipline. The mathematician who was most influential in pushing the axiomatic method instead of informal methods, which came to be known as naive methods (cf. for example Halmos (1960) *Naive Set Theory*), was David Hilbert. To accomplish this end, Hilbert proposed eliminating any meaning from expressions of a system and constructing a calculus, rules for producing all the sign strings, theorems, in a formalized way. Thus, the added difficulty of formalism would pay the dividend of "naked clarity" (Nagel and Newman 1958:27) of allowing testing for consistency. Because symbols were purged of their meaning, one could see whether strings of these symbols were put together according to the precisely stated rules of the calculus and whether the strings of symbols were well-formed according to the rules of the system. Any interpretation of these symbols was not part of mathematics but part of "meta-mathematics," the language about mathematics.

1.4 Chomsky's definition of a grammar

Now that the groundwork has been laid we proceed to discussing the common basis upon which the grammar theories to be discussed will be compared. As Laudan (1977) has stated, it is not necessary to translate one research tradition into a language used by another for the purposes of comparison. While this is, however, not a formal requirement, it may be useful to establish some sort of common frame in order to trace the specifics of a particular theory. This is not the same as eclecticism (mixing of theories), nor does it have to lead to the error of comparing incommensurables. The common frame to be used here is Chomsky's formal definition of a grammar.

A specific subtype of axiomatic system that leads to Chomsky's definition of a grammar is the SEMI-THUE SYSTEM. An in-depth description of the relationship of semi-Thue systems, Thue systems, and other axiomatic systems that might be relevant to linguistic theory is beyond the scope of this discussion. See Wall (1972) for a good account of these matters. For our purposes, it is sufficient to note that such a semi-Thue system contains three parts: (a) the axioms, sometimes called the START SYMBOLS, because all derivations must begin with an axiom; (b) rules (of inference), sometimes called PRODUCTIONS; and (c) THEOREMS, the strings of symbols produced from the axioms via the rules of inference. The specific aspect which characteristically determines a semi-Thue system is a restriction on the kinds of productions allowed. In the semi-Thue system, A and B stand for the vocabulary of the language, classes of symbols that are allowed to occur. The symbol $(A \cup B)^*$ is called a FREE MONOID and stands for the set of well-formed strings formed over the vocabulary sets A and B, and means all the properly constructed sequences of 'words'.[1]

(2)   Definition of a semi-Thue system

A semi-Thue system is an extended axiomatic system (A, B, S, P) so that each rule of inference (production) fits the mold:

$$XxY \rightarrow XyY,$$

where x and y are strings from $(A \cup B)^*$ and X and Y are variables from the set $(A \cup B)^*$ as well.

---

[1] A free monoid is the set of strings that includes all the terminal strings and all the strings that can be built up by these rules that contain terminal, nonterminal, or combinations of them, e.g., in decimal arithmetic a string ACA = 4 belongs to the free monoid, as does 5CA = 4, etc.

One reason that Chomsky's definition of a grammar may be capable of aiding comparison without distortion is that his conception is a very general—and for that reason vague—definition.

Bearing in mind the preceding discussion, one can conceive of a natural language as a set of strings of symbols, the words of the language, that have been put together by rules. Of course, any real human language is more than just the strings themselves. These strings also have interpretations, i.e., they are meaning-bearing. This viewpoint emphasizes the similarity of natural languages to other kinds of language. For example, the language called arithmetic would be just the set of strings combined from the natural numbers and the two-place operators: $+$, $-$, x, $\div$, and $=$. For English and for arithmetic, some strings would be well-formed, for example, *the King was in the countinghouse* and for arithmetic *2 + 2 = 4*. Some conceivable strings would not be well-formed, such as **The was King in the countinghouse* and **2 + = 2 4*. These illustrate that WELL-FORMEDNESS is a judgment about the SYNTAX or GRAMMAR of languages. In addition to being unacceptable because they are not well-formed, strings can also be unacceptable because they have no meaningful interpretation. Thus, the following strings from English and decimal arithmetic are well-formed but meaningless or false. (There are other accounts of the relationship of well-formedness and meaningfulness—the one discussed here is the usual one assumed by linguists.) *!the Confucianism was in the countinghouse* and *!2 + 2 = 5*. Notice that strings may have to be interpreted with respect to a given context or set of circumstances; absolute context-independent meaninglessness may not be valid. For example, the string *1 + 1 = 10* evaluated in decimal arithmetic will be false but true in binary arithmetic, in which *10* corresponds to *2* in the decimal system. This point will be argued again below.

Chomsky (1956) claims that a formal model of a grammar can be formulated as:

> The grammar G of a language L consists of four kinds of things, i.e.,

$$G = \{V_T, V_{NT}, \{S\}, P\}.$$

> V_T and V_{NT} are together the vocabulary (sets) of TERMINAL and NONTERMINAL strings respectively. Moreover, V_T and V_{NT} must be disjoint (i.e., not overlap in membership). S is the START SYMBOL. P is the set of RULES or PRODUCTIONS, which must be finite in number and conform to the scheme

$$\alpha x \beta \rightarrow \alpha y \beta,$$

where x and y are from the vocabulary, i.e., V_T or V_{NT} and the symbols α and β come from the free monoid $(V_T \cup V_{NT})^*$.

This definition certainly needs some illustration. Consider an example of a grammar in which the following values of V_T, V_{NT}, S, and P occur.

(3) V_T = the set of natural numbers N and $+$, $-$, x, $\div$, and $=$
        V_{NT} = A, B, C, and S

The set of start symbols contains just the symbol S

$P = \{S \rightarrow A B A, A \rightarrow A C A, A \rightarrow a \, e \, N, C \rightarrow \{+, -, x, \div\}, B \rightarrow =\}$
N is the set of natural numbers.

The symbol $\rightarrow$ is to be read "rewrite as." Some of the derivations that this grammar produces are shown in (4)–(6).

(4)   S
                            A   B   A
                    A   C   A   B   A
                    2   +   2   =   4

(5)   S
                            A   B   A
                    A   C   A   B   A
            A   C   A   B   A   C   A
            2   +   2   =   3   +   1

(6)

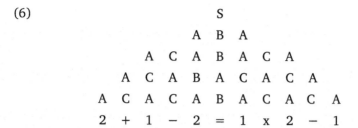

```
                              S
                        A   B   A
                    A   C   A   B   A   C   A
                  A C   A   B   A   C   A   C   A
                A C   A   C   A   B   A   C   A   C   A
                2 + 1 - 2 = 1 x 2 - 1
```

More useful to linguists than derivations such as the above are phrase markers, which are merely enriched IMMEDIATE CONSTITUENT DIAGRAMS of the structuralists. In phrase markers, one can see the overall structural relationship of the rule applications more clearly. On the other hand, the order of application of rules is no longer evident. The phrase marker equivalents of the above are shown in (7)–(9).

(7)

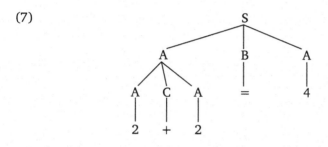

(8)

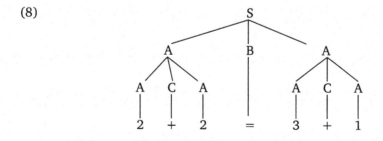

(9)

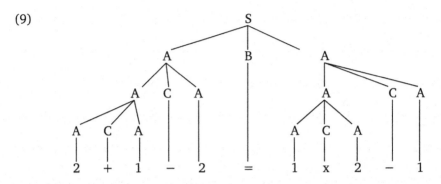

The collection of well-formed strings produced by the grammar, i.e., all those that are formed from the rules or productions and contain only items from the vocabulary, are called THE LANGUAGE OF G. In the above example, the set of strings included not only the strings whose phrase markers have been exhibited but an unlimited number of additional ones, a great many of which will be false in arithmetic. For instance, the grammar will generate symbol concatenations such as: 2 + 2 = 7,213; 6 − 0 = 8; 15 x 3 = 0; etc. These still need an interpretation before one can speak of an INTERPRETED LANGUAGE, such as arithmetic. We see, however, that one property of a grammar is that it conforms to Chomsky's definition of a grammar stated above.

Another important property of a grammar is RECURSION. If the productions (which are equivalent to the rules of inference in an axiomatic system) contain the same symbol on both the right and left side of an arrow, then the rules are recursive. The grammar portrayed in (3) above is recursive, because in the second rule of P the symbol A appears on both sides of the arrow. (Another type of recursion involves a pair of rules such that, for each rule, a symbol on the right side of the arrow in one is on the left side in the other.)

Chomsky showed in early work that languages generated by formal grammars have different properties according to restrictions put onto the productions or rules. In the descriptions of grammar types that follow, the central concept is the string; strings can be null (meaning that there is no string there) or nonnull (meaning that there is a string there).

(10)   A TYPE 0 or UNRESTRICTED REWRITING SYSTEM has no further restrictions beyond those of formal grammars.

(11)   TYPE 1 or CONTEXT-SENSITIVE GRAMMARS have the restriction that ev-
       ery rule must conform to the scheme

$$\alpha A\beta \rightarrow \alpha B\beta$$

       alternatively

$$A \rightarrow B \: / \: \alpha \: \_ \: \beta$$

       in which the unspecified strings α and β, but not the single non-
       terminal symbol B, may be the null string.

(12)   TYPE 2 or CONTEXT-FREE GRAMMARS have the restrictions of Type 0
       and Type 1 grammars and additionally the condition that all
       rules have the form

$$A \rightarrow \Omega$$

       Contrary to Type 1 grammars, α and β must be the null string;
       moreover, the single nonterminal symbol A must be replaced by
       some unspecified string Ω that is not the null string.

(13)   TYPE 3 or FINITE-STATE GRAMMARS have the conditions of Types 0
       through 2 plus the additional constraint that each production
       must conform to the scheme $A \rightarrow xB$ or $A \rightarrow x$, where x is not the
       null string and A and B are single elements from the set of
       nonterminal symbols.

It is especially important to observe that a Type 1 grammar (context-
sensitive) is more powerful than a Type 2 grammar (context-free), because a Type 1 grammar contains a Type 2 grammar as a special case.
One should not, for instance, believe that a Type 1 grammar is more
"constrained" because it "requires a context," but instead note that the
context "required" can also be null.

In order to become familiar with grammar types, the reader should
consider the following languages and try to devise grammars for them:
the language called $(ab)^n$ which is the set {ab, abab, ababab,
abababab,...} and the language $a^n b^n$ which is the set {ab, aabb, aaabbb,
aaaabbbb,...}. What kind of grammar is the following and what strings
does it produce? {V_T = {a, b}, V_{NT} = S, S = S, P = {S→(S)ab}}.

The terminology and concepts just introduced will turn out to be general enough to characterize most of the types of linguistic theorizing to

be discussed below. There will, however, also be examples that do not conform to these principles. Nevertheless, this scheme will help us to classify the proposals as to grammar types and thus estimate their expressive (generative) capacity. Some very interesting results have been obtained concerning capacity and these results will have bearing on the individual approaches.

1.5 Linguistics: A natural science, a social science, or a human science?

Linguistic theorizing reflects to a great degree the most central of all questions in linguistics: what is language? Depending on how this question is answered, linguists may regard their occupation as one of the humanities, one of the social sciences or, perhaps, one of the natural sciences. The most important factors in the equation are: (a) the role of the utterance object, as Bloomfield said "the noises we make with our faces;" (b) the role of the individual human speaker and talker or hearer and listener; and (c) the role of groups of individuals, speech communities at one time or over time. Earlier we presented Chomsky's definition of a formal grammar and its corresponding account of a formal language as the set of symbol strings produced by a grammar. By viewing language as a system of objects whose properties are reflected in the on-paper construct, it is clear that a natural science view of language is being favored. Most of the approaches to be compared in this book will be of this type. Of course, the human behind the system will not be totally excluded, because genetically transmitted constraints of mind (universal grammar), human behavior as a unity, and/or neural circuitry may figure in this or that paradigm. Nevertheless, the complexity of utterance objects of humans dictates that these formal factors receive the most attention in normal science practice even if the investigator may occasionally do or say otherwise.

In one sense, linguists who study utterance objects exclusively still may be studying the human animal behind them. In the language system, many dimensions show a characteristic bias that reveals a prototypical speaker. Vowel height (distance between tongue and palate) in many languages, for example, correlates to the deictic categories in the demonstrative system; if there are two positions on a scale, then the ego-distal demonstrative form is likely to have a low (distant) vowel and the ego-proximal the high vowel. Cf. French *ici* versus *la bas*; Chinese *zhei* versus *na:* Amis (an Austronesian language) *kiya* versus *koya* and Mayerthaler (1981) for many more examples. Still another illustration of the prototypical speaker's shadow cast in the language system is the order in irreversible pairs of the type *day and night, now and then, sight and sound.* The first seems to be the perceptually more accessible of the two. Our senses are predetermined for light not darkness, for the temporally near, and for the sight sense to dominate over others.

A branch of linguistic theorizing that is currently enjoying a burst of popularity puts the emphasis on the speaker-and-talker and hearer-and-listener. These investigators are stressing the importance of CONVERSATIONAL ANALYSIS. Conversational analysts concentrate on aspects of language other than form, grammatical function, and meaning (i.e., on things other than noun phrases, subjects, agents). Instead, they stress that the speech act is the crucial category. They, therefore, study what Goffman (1959) calls FACE WORK, the expression of solidarity, the gaining and saving of face, the maintenance of conversational floor, the negotiation of turns, and frontstage versus backstage exchanges (Esau 1981). In this sense, spoken language is quite different from written language; reading is not the same as acting out verbally. While the exchange of propositional information is doubtless important, it is not prototypical language behavior. From earliest childhood on, our language experience is interactional and multipolar; monologue is restricted almost exclusively to the rather atypical world of the classroom, lecture tours, government, and the stage. Most humans rarely practice it. Nevertheless, we are forced to deal mostly with utterance objects in this book, because there is at present no real alternative within linguistic theory of an articulated proposal despite some promising beginnings.

There is finally the perspective of language as the product of humans in large groups. These linguists study phenomena such as PIDGINS and CREOLES, LANGUAGE ATTITUDES, BI- and MULTILINGUALISM, and LANGUAGE PLANNING. Through the work of sociolinguists such as William Labov (1972a, 1972b), much has been learned regarding the influence of PRESTIGE in language variation and change. People tend to speak like those they admire. Moreover, this linguistic envy may be overt admiration for a group of leading citizens, the upper class, the educated class, or those living in the capital city of a country. The admiration may, however, also be covert, e.g., imitation of lower class speech as a sign of masculinity (Trudgill 1974).

We plan to focus primarily on language as utterance objects. Nevertheless, we hope to have emphasized sufficiently that these human and social aspects of language deserve equal weight in an ultimate account of human verbal behavior even if high-level theoretical proposals are not as advanced in these areas.

1.6 Verbal and nonverbal behavior, a unity?

In a sense, this section treats a matter similar to the one above. Some approaches to linguistic theorizing regard language (verbal) behavior to be distinct from some other kinds of nonverbal behavior. At least one, however, explicitly advocates a unity. Pike (1971) argues at length that humans engage routinely in nonverbal behavior that supports and supplants speech. We can sing songs replacing some of the words with gestures; deaf people can be taught to use a sign language such as AMSLAN as their primary means of communicating; verbal and nonverbal elements can substitute one for another in some cases. In other words, verbal and nonverbal behavior evidence the same kinds of units, functions, semantic roles, and context dependency, and, therefore, should be subsumed under the same kind of descriptive apparatus.

An opposing position is held by Chomsky. He has argued in many places that human language is quite different from other human abilities. Human languages in particular have two properties that distinguish them from other forms of behavior: their richness and their manner of acquisition. If one counts the number of distinctive sentences in English, for example, this number would be in principle unlimited. While it is somewhat unclear that the nonverbal equivalent of sentences—perhaps gesture sequences—are less numerous, such seems likely. At least, it is unlikely that a preschooler without special training can effortlessly produce and comprehend an infinitude of distinctive nonverbal messages as he or she obviously does with sentences. Perhaps, the nonverbal channels are simply underexploited by humans. It is not natural for us to rely on these means so much. And, the sign language of the deaf does in fact have the requisite limitlessness so characteristic of spoken communication. There is, however, yet another sense in which verbal behavior differs in richness from nonverbal behavior. It is a characteristic of sentences to be STRUCTURALLY RICH. They can have RIGHT-BRANCHING:

(14)   There's a flea on a hair on a frog on a bump on a log in a hole at the bottom of the sea.

LEFT-BRANCHING:

(15)   Dad's sister's husband's brother is running for Congress.

and INTERSENTENTIAL RELATIONSHIPS:

(16)   You can lift 500 pounds.

(17)   Can you lift 500 pounds?

Of course, AMSLAN also has these properties, but gesturing largely fails to have them. In more recent work, Chomsky (1980) has claimed that cognitive abilities such as vision will differ from language (grammar) abilities in significant ways.

With respect to the second area, acquisition, verbal behavior seems quite unique. Chomsky has always stressed the POVERTY OF STIMULUS ARGUMENT in speaking of the uniqueness of human speech. A child is able to acquire language not by stimulus and conditioning from the sentences heard. Very soon after the onset of speech the child will produce sentences that were NEVER heard. A Skinnerian model of language acquisition is clearly inadequate to account for this striking occurrence.

This question will be discussed again in the appropriate place. In summary, however, it seems to us that these two approaches are emphasizing different types of things. Specifically, Pike looks at the large manifest units of verbal and nonverbal behavior seeing the doubtless parallels, whereas Chomsky stresses the microscopic and technical dissimilarities. The scope of the observations is certainly part of the competing world views involved; the interests are simply different.

1.7 Formal versus functional models

In the last ten years or so, there have been some noteworthy developments in linguistic theory in reaction to a natural language being only a collection of well-formed strings (sentences) and ignoring the function of such strings within a larger discourse or context. Considering languages to be only collections of well-formed strings is to deny that a natural language has any communicative function. A group of linguists such as T. Givón, P. Hopper, S. Thompson, and others in the neofunctionalist camp have been emphasizing that the communicative function of language isn't sufficiently considered in approaches concerned only with rules of sentences. As they might say it, some substantial structures are determined or codetermined by discourse features. For example, the constraints on the distribution of aspect- and tense-marking in sequences of sentences must refer to textlinguistic patterns of organization and cannot be analyzed solely in terms of the structure of a single sentence. Moreover, there are rules of discourse organization such as Longacre's concept of PEAK, often corresponding to the point of highest tension in a discourse, that must refer to all the sentences within a discourse. Both of these topics are considered in detail in §3.6.2.

While the functional orientation is especially clear in some specific models (see especially the discussion in chapter nine), it should be stressed that Tagmemics (see §1.6, and chapter three) and stratificational linguistics (especially in the Fleming tradition, see chapter four) both make significant use of this notion as well.

It is a commonly held assumption that the purpose of language is COMMUNICATION, and it is this position that lies behind functional models of language. Given such an orientation, the motivation and explanation for various linguistic facts is sought in text structure above the sentence level (where it is assumed that factors involving information structure influence the organization and the sorts of syntactic structures found) and in various interpersonal pragmatic patterns of behavior (especially conversation, cf. §1.5). For example, the article by Hopper and Thompson (1980) demonstrated that the linguistic category TRANSITIVITY could be motivated from its USE in a sentence.

By contrast, there is another view that emphasizes the formal properties of sentences over their functional properties. Chief among these is transformational-generative linguistics in its various forms. While formal linguists do not deny the importance of function in influencing the linguistic forms which are found in a given instance of language, they do take the position that there are formal constraints and rules independent of considerations of textual organization. They would agree that language is commonly used in a social context, and that it has a pragmatic function, but they would argue that to look ONLY at the pragmatic functions of language is to miss important organizing forces in natural languages. Formal theories commonly take the position that the goal of linguistics is to account for the facts of language acquisition, and that it is the definition of the formal characteristics of language, and the attributing of the knowledge of such characteristics to the language acquisition capability of human beings, which makes language acquisition possible.

Two sorts of facts may illustrate the discussion here. First, note the following examples:

(18)   a. *John ate dinner after he went home.*
       b. *After he went home John ate dinner.*

(19)   a. *He ate dinner after John went home.*
       b. *After John went home he ate dinner.*

Clearly the (a) and (b) sentences in each pair represent alternative manifestations of the same syntactic structure. We note further that in each there is a noun (*John*) and a pronoun (*he*) which agree for the features of person, number, and gender. We might expect that discourse factors play a role in determining for sentences like these whether the adverbial clause or the main clause occurs first; or viewed from another perspective, we might expect that the alternatives have slightly different semantic interpretations in terms of focus or relation to surrounding linguistic context.

But there is an important fact involved in the sentences in (18)–(19) which has nothing at all to do with text structure or pragmatics, and which is of a purely formal nature, true—presumably—for all languages for all time. Note that in (18a) the pronoun *he* may refer either to *John* or to someone else in the context. The same holds also for (18b), and again for (19b). But (19a) is different; the pronoun *he* cannot refer to *John* but must in fact refer to someone else. That is, the difference in (19a) and (19b) is not a function of discourse or pragmatic considerations, but simply a function of formal grammar. In particular, it is proposed that if pronominal forms like *he* are to find their reference within the same sentence, the NP to which they refer must either precede the pronoun (as in (19b)) or be in a main clause to which the clause containing the pronoun is subordinate (as in (18b)), or both (as in (18a)). In (19a) these conditions are violated, with the result that *he* cannot refer to *John*, but must find its reference elsewhere within the larger context. What is important to note here is that this difference is not a function of text structure, pragmatics, or information structure, but rather a function of the nature of the structure of sentences; by focusing on the formal characteristics of languages, such universal constraints on the possible forms and possible interpretations of natural language structures become clear, a result which is not likely if formal properties are ignored.

Take as a second example patterns like those in (20) (again we use examples from English, but the proposed account is claimed to be universal):

(20)   a. *John saw him.*
       b. *John saw himself.*
       c. *John said that Bill saw himself.*

We know three things immediately from such sentences: in (20a), *him* cannot refer to *John*; in (20b), *himself* must refer to *John*; in (20c) *himself* must refer to *Bill* not *John*. But once again, these constraints on coreference are not in any way related to text structure or pragmatics, but rather result as a consequence of the formal properties of languages, in particular the relationship holding between the noun *John* and the pronouns in the three sentences. In each of these instances, the relationship between the nominal in subject position preceding the verb and that in object position following the verb is one of C-Command coupled with the notion of binding (the nominal subject position binds that in object position, see chapter five). Reflexive pronouns must be bound within the simple clause, nonreflexive pronouns must not be. Thus, *him* cannot refer to *John* in (20a) (because then *John* would be binding *him*), *himself* must refer to *John* in (20b) (because otherwise it would receive no interpretation), and *himself* in (20c) must refer to *Bill* not *John*, because *Bill* is the closest subject and, in fact, the one within the minimal clause in which *himself* occurs. But once again, there is no account of such facts outside the domain of the simple sentence itself, much less the context of a full discourse or a pragmatic speech situation.

Formal approaches, then, insist that there is value in studying the formal properties of languages, because by defining such properties, it is possible to identify constraints governing languages which then can be attributed to the hard-wired innate language acquisition capability of human beings, thus providing a beginning understanding of how language acquisition becomes possible.

One way to characterize the opposing view of functionalists versus formalists is that functionalists might say that in describing grammar at all levels, whether concerned with discourse, sentences, phrases, or some other category, that there is only one "grammar" and grammar is determined by function. The formalists, on the other hand, might say that there are basically two "grammars" to discover: one to organize the computational-representational aspects of language and one to organize the functional-informational aspects of language. The choice between these two views continues to be debated with the outcome still uncertain.

2

The *Aspects* Model

We have picked Chomsky's *Aspects* model (1965) as a point of departure for the discussion of linguistic research traditions even though it is not chronologically the earliest of the proposals we intend to report on. It occupies this position as point of reference because supporters and nonsupporters all agree that it and its successors have had the most influence on the greatest number of linguists. Moreover, in this work, Chomsky explicitly pleads for a particular research logic and is quite concerned about methods. As already stated, the presentation of this model and subsequent models as well first center on the general aims, methods, and philosophy before moving on to discuss the specifics of individual theories. The final area to be discussed is the problem-solving capacity of a particular approach. Because we feel this particular feature of a theory needs illustration, we have chosen the English auxiliary system as an example to be used in the discussion of each theory. We note, however, that the details of the treatment are not to be regarded as adequate in the empirical sense. In many instances, advocates of a particular position might reject them partially or totally. We are more interested in the manner of presentation, kind of evidence, methods of argumentation, and interests than in the validity of the specifics.

The book *Aspects of the Theory of Syntax* (1965) is reputed to have been written in a few short weeks. Whether this is true or not, it bears the marks of a piece composed in the heat of discovery. Important points or points that became important are found in footnotes. Judged even by today's standard, there are paragraphs still demanding exegesis and interpretation. Nevertheless, it has probably sold more copies than any other linguistic book to this day. The current editions of the paperback exceed twelve. It is divided into four chapters: METHODS, THE BASE, THE TRANSFORMATIONAL COMPONENT, and RESIDUAL PROBLEMS.

2.1 World view

Chomsky's interests, as stated in the first chapter, are in a historical position he calls RATIONALISM in which he includes such men as René Descartes and Wilhelm Von Humboldt. He identifies himself with them and contrasts himself with the EMPIRICISTS Willard Van Orman Quine and B. F. Skinner. The crucial point of disagreement is the notion of INNATE IDEAS. Children in acquiring their mother tongue are involved in "drawing out what is innate in the mind" (1965:51). The empiricists and modern linguists before 1965 maintained that children learn by conditioning, by drill and explicit explanation from their caregivers, or by elementary 'data-processing'. In these passages, Chomsky pleads for a universalist (language universals play a significant role in language acquisition and language structure) and platonic view of knowledge. The interest in language universals and child language has, since this period, enjoyed a flourishing interest unlike anything in the periods before Chomsky.

Chomsky clearly is interested in language as utterance objects. Indeed, throughout much of his work, he has shown more concern for the notion GRAMMAR than for the notion LANGUAGE. This tendency becomes much more dominant in later work. In *Aspects* (p. 3), he claims he will be concerned with the syntactic component of a GENERATIVE GRAMMAR that specifies the WELL-FORMED STRINGS of a natural language and also assigns a STRUCTURAL DESCRIPTION to these strings. He also points out that strings which are not well-formed will also be structurally characterized. Language will thus be that set of well-formed strings produced by a system of rules, a grammar. The strings which are not well-formed will be of interest—perhaps of even greater interest than the well-formed ones—because they help to establish the need for a particular rule. This is a similar kind of argument to the old saw that the exception proves the rule; by being able to recognize what the rule must not do, one gains knowledge about how to refine the rule toward avoiding strings which are not well-formed. Chomsky claims, moreover, that "a generative grammar must be a system of rules that can enumerate or generate an indefinitely large number of structures" (pp. 15–16). This set of strings must be sentences. For Chomsky, the grammar is to produce a set of sentence strings, each of which begins with the symbol S, i.e., the grammar will be a sentence grammar. No other-sized piece of structure larger or smaller serves as the starting point for any derivation. In terms of the formal grammar model of chapter one, the start symbol will always be S. Notice, however, that there is no nonempirical reason whatsoever that the start symbol could not be a larger or smaller piece of structure, for example, a discourse level unit, or that multiple start symbols could not have been chosen. It is part of the *Aspects* model that sentences and syntax receive the greatest emphasis, that all structural pieces, irrespective of ultimate shape and scope, must begin as sentences. This is a specific ontological assumption of the *Aspects* model.

Chomsky takes a position not only on the nature of grammars but also on the area to be covered by a linguistic theory. As he says in a famous quote:

> Linguistic theory is concerned primarily with an ideal speaker-listener, in a completely homogeneous speech-community, who knows its language perfectly and is unaffected by such grammatically irrelevant conditions as memory limitations, distractions, shifts of attention and interest, and errors (random or characteristic) in applying his knowledge of the language in actual performance. (1965:3)

This interest in an ideal instead of real speaker-listener corresponds to what, in other branches of science, is called ESSENTIALISM, the claim that natural laws are observed in experiments only in imperfect states because of the disturbing qualities of reality (Popper 1950). Ideal gases do not behave in every way as real gases do; bullets in the real world do not follow a parabolic arc when fired out of a gun because of air resistance. The essences of nature must be seen through the imperfections of reality to posit laws. The danger of essentialism, as Popper points out, is the immunization of a proposal from refutation. If counterexamples can be dismissed as the distortion of reality, then the law becomes irrefutable, and as a result, empirically incapable of explaining or predicting anything.

Chomsky also makes a distinction between knowledge of a grammar and the use to which a speaker puts this knowledge in performing sentences. The former is called COMPETENCE, the latter PERFORMANCE. It is, of course, obvious that real speakers fail to have the properties required of an ideal speaker. Chomsky, nevertheless, feels that the important characteristics of grammars can be discovered by studying an ideal.

The assumption of a HOMOGENEOUS SPEECH COMMUNITY has especially come under criticism. The assumption of homogeneity is made because it allows linguistic research to proceed most efficiently, and Chomsky's rejoinder (1980:25–6) is that critics of such a point of view must be wedded to one of two alternatives which must be true to demonstrate that the idea of homogeneity is not a useful one.

1. People are so constituted that they would be incapable of learning language in a homogeneous speech community; variability or inconsistency of presented evidence is a necessary condition for language learning.

2. Though people could learn language in a homogeneous speech community, the properties of the mind that make this achievement possible do not enter into normal language acquisition in the real world of diversity, conflict of dialects, etc.

But, he adds that either seems "hopelessly implausible." Nevertheless, it is far from evident that these are so implausible. One may hope that such finely stated hypotheses might be the subject of empirical testing for validity.

Another notion from the *Aspects* model that has frequently been misunderstood is that of production and reception vs. knowledge. In essence, this is the same distinction as competence and performance. A generative grammar is not to be taken as a model for humans; there is no real equivalence to the rules to be proposed with the mechanisms in the brains of English speakers. Rather, the rules of the grammar are intended to be constructs or models that exhibit the same properties as an ideal speaker (viewed, of course, through the imperfection of his or her performance). Other approaches to be considered in this book will claim to be models of actual linguistic performance in real time. This point of difference has often led to unnecessary misunderstanding in discussions across paradigms.

2.2 Ontological primitives

As should have become clear, Chomsky stakes his grammar on the notion SENTENCE. Defined, sentences are nothing more than strings of words. Because he employs a formal grammar to produce or generate an unlimited set of such strings, and because this grammar manipulates an uninterpreted inventory of symbols—an alphabet—these strings themselves are uninterpreted. Therefore, the keystone of Chomsky's generative transformational grammar is the syntactic sentence, not words, not phrases, not sentence sequences, not discourse pieces, and also not interpreted (meaning-bearing) sentences, phrases, words, or discourse pieces. For this reason, some have called this approach AUTONOMOUS SYNTAX, because of the key role of sentences to the exclusion of semantics and to the exclusion of other structural levels (larger or smaller structural pieces). In terms of the formal grammar, every derivation (proof) uses the start symbol S, every phrase marker grows downward from the ubiquitous sentence. A grammar is a "blueprint for a sentence factory" (McCawley 1980:169).

A second primitive involves the organization of a grammar model. Chomsky sees a generative grammar as being compartmentalized into a number of subcomponents that are separated by levels with no overlap. There is, moreover, a correlation of syntactic subcomponents with types of rules (cf. the discussion of rule types in chapter one). There is, first and foremost, a division into a SYNTACTIC COMPONENT, a SEMANTIC COMPONENT, and a PHONOLOGICAL COMPONENT. The syntactic component sets itself off from the other two by being the only generative component. Framed in terms of the definition of a formal grammar, it alone has a start symbol; it alone can initiate a derivation. The remaining two types have, according to the definition, only vocabulary and productions, which is the same as saying no axioms. They can map one string onto another if the syntactic component has already provided such a string. By virtue of lacking the capacity to initiate a derivation or to generate structure, these components are not generative, only interpretive. Moreover, every syntactic string must be interpreted in these two ways: semantically (it must be assigned a meaning) and phonologically (it must be assigned a manifestation as a sound sequence). We indicate this arrangement by means of the diagram in (21).

(21)   The components of a generative grammar

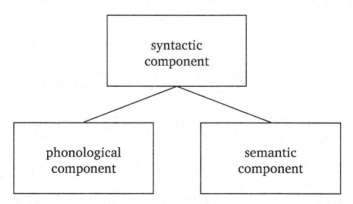

There is a further subdivision of the syntactic component into two subcomponents: the BASE and the TRANSFORMATIONAL COMPONENT. Just as in the case of the phonological and semantic components, one of these fails to be generative. In the *Aspects* model, the transformational component is only interpretive. It contains a body of rules that only map one string onto another string. No string may originate here. The base, as its name suggests, represents the derivational pedestal from which all strings ultimately arise. The transformational subcomponent reshapes it, and the remaining components assign it meaning and give it phonetic form to produce a final sentence string cast as sounds.

At the interface of some of these components, Chomsky has seen linguistically significant levels. Since the transformational component carries out the task of syntactic repackaging, the form of a string before it and the form of a string after it constitute two different and linguistically significant levels. These are known as THE SYNTACTIC DEEP STRUCTURE LEVEL and THE SYNTACTIC SURFACE STRUCTURE LEVEL, respectively. The global picture of the *Aspects* model is then seen in (22).

(22)   The *Aspects* model of Chomsky (1965)

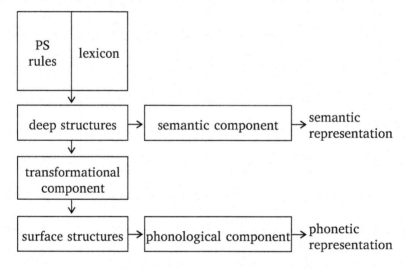

As can be seen in the overall picture of the organization of a generative grammar, the syntactic deep structure (or simply deep structure) forms the boundary between the base, the transformational component, and the semantic component. Note that each of the components and all others as well are integral and homogeneous; there is no level mixing or mixing of rules from one into strings at a derivational stage belonging to another. That a formal grammar intended to describe and ultimately explain human languages can be so organized is one of the two carrying hypotheses of the *Aspects* model. It is known as the DEEP STRUCTURE HYPOTHESIS (Partee 1971). Notice, furthermore, that the semantic component, the only source sentences have for interpretation, has access to symbol strings at only the deep structure level. Since the transformational component will perform many changes of structure, it must be the case that these changes in form DO NOT change meaning, for the interpretation comes from only one source, the deep structure, and that level has already been passed. This second carrying hypothesis of the *Aspects* model, that transformations do not change meaning, is known as the KATZ-POSTAL HYPOTHESIS (Katz and Postal 1964). The two hypotheses, together with the organization of a grammar portrayed in (22), are the assumptions of the *Aspects* model.

We have said in passing that different components have different rule types. We now wish to make explicit what this entails. Chomsky assumes that the base component is composed of two subparts: the PHRASE STRUCTURE RULES and the LEXICON. The need for these two rests in a fundamental difference between words (usually linguists call these LEXICAL FORMATIVES because the concept "word" is a difficult one to define in some languages) and category symbols. These two together, the V_T (terminal) and V_{NT} (nonterminal), form the composite vocabulary of the grammar. Natural languages have the property that sentences divide without residue into two or three category symbols. We represent this splitting into two with the production S → NP VP. It is stated as a phrase marker in (23).

(23)

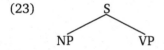

The symbols mean that a sentence is rewritten as a noun phrase followed by a verb phrase. This is part of the phrase structure of English. While these symbols have no inherent interpretation, the dichotomy in the split corresponds to the traditional notion that a sentence is composed of two things, subject and predicate, even if NP and VP are not the same as subject and predicate. In other words, this phrase structure rule breaks down a category into subconstituents in a strict hierarchical manner, i.e., in a manner reminiscent of biological classification. Consider the TAXONOMY, in particular the system of classification, of the Siberian tiger among great cats in (24).

(24) KINGDOM   animalia

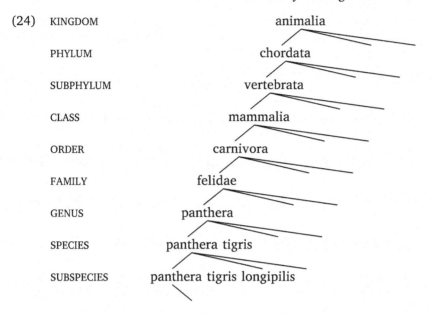

       PHYLUM   chordata

       SUBPHYLUM   vertebrata

       CLASS   mammalia

       ORDER   carnivora

       FAMILY   felidae

       GENUS   panthera

       SPECIES   panthera tigris

       SUBSPECIES   panthera tigris longipilis

In Linnean fashion, each example of a lower classification must be an example of a higher classification; each panthera is also a felida, though other examples at the same classificatory level are also felidae. In such a taxonomic system, one can always describe an organism by taking a pathway that only goes downward. But, in the classification of words of English this is not the case. Consider the case of the classificatory levels COMMON NOUN versus PROPER NOUN and COUNT NOUN versus MASS NOUN. Notice first of all that these categories have grammatical consequences. Proper nouns cannot generally be preceded by articles, e.g., *the William, *the Mt. Everest. There are a few exceptions such as, for example, the Sudan or the Malay Peninsula. Also, mass nouns cannot be preceded by numbers or appear in the plural, e.g., *two flours, *informations. There are, however, nouns of English that are proper and countable, common and countable, and common and mass. Though there may be no nouns that are simultaneously proper nouns and mass nouns, there is still no way to organize the classification of word categories, such as common and proper and mass and count, into a hierarchical classificatory scheme. Therefore, Chomsky cleaves the base into two components, one for phrase structure which is hierarchical and one for lexical items (formatives) which are not. These are known as the PHRASE STRUCTURE RULES and the LEXICON. The first of these base subcomponents is made up of intrinsically ordered context-free rules. The lexicon is composed of context-sensitive rules. It resembles in many ways a kind of dictionary that contains details about a particular word's context of use.

2.3 Methodology

Chomsky is particularly explicit in his justification of models. In particular, he writes at length on the adequacy of competing proposals. On gathering data he says that "There are...very few reliable experimental or data-processing procedures for obtaining significant information concerning the linguistic intuition of the native speaker." Even though we lack many operational procedures, still "investigation of the knowledge of the native speaker can proceed perfectly well" (1965:19). The problem is not insufficient data but inadequate theories. The data required comes from introspective evidence and elicited native speaker intuition. And these are to be "the ultimate standard that determines the accuracy of any proposed grammar, linguistic theory or operational test" (p. 21). He, moreover, argues that the native speaker's intuition about sentences may be of little value in constructing a theory as such. When confronted with ambiguous sentences such as in (25), the native speaker may give only a single interpretation and even deny that there are two or more.

(25)   *Visiting relatives can be a nuisance.*

Yet, all, after an illustration, will admit the ambiguity. Therefore, native speaker intuitions about the analysis of sentences must be employed with great caution. Instead, his or her intuition should be used primarily to test predictions.

Chomsky also distinguishes three kinds of adequacy: OBSERVATIONAL ADEQUACY, DESCRIPTIVE ADEQUACY, and EXPLANATORY ADEQUACY. The lowest level, observational adequacy, involves the accurate observation, collection, and recording of data. This data may need to be arranged in some order or classification. Observational adequacy is not discussed at length in *Aspects of the Theory of Syntax* (1965). Descriptive and explanatory adequacy are discussed, however. A descriptively adequate theory, according to Chomsky (1965:30), has the properties in (26).

(26) a.   It has a technique for representing input signals.

b.   It has a way of representing structural information about these signals.

    c.   It has some initial delimitation of a class of possible hypotheses about language structure.

    d.   It has a method for determining what each such hypothesis implies with respect to each sentence.

A descriptively adequate grammar of a natural language must, in other words, make available for each sentence of the language a structural description that corresponds with the linguistic competence (knowledge) of the native speaker.

An explanatorily adequate theory is subject to much more stringent conditions and has the properties in (27).

(27) a.   It has a universal phonetic theory that defines the notion 'possible sentence'.

      b.   It has a definition of 'structural description'.

      c.   It has a definition of 'generative grammar'.

      d.   It has a method for determining the structural description of a sentence, given a grammar.

      e.   It has a way of evaluating alternative proposed grammars. In particular, it has a method for selecting one of the (presumably infinitely many) hypotheses that are allowed by (26c) and are compatible with the given primary linguistic data.

While it is clear that items (27a)–(27c) are all requirements of definitions of terms used in descriptively adequate theories, the statements (27d) and (27e) are quite different. (27e) in particular needs illustration and justification. It has been claimed by some, e.g., Jones, that there is no difference between description and explanation. She states:

> Tagmemics does not distinguish between description and explanation, and I am skeptical that any substantive difference between description and explanation can be maintained. It seems to me more a matter of different degree of adequacy along a single scale. (1980:86)

From this quote and from her statement that "there is no insistence that there is only one correct grammar, or one correct theory" for each set of data (1980:79), it is clear that she is using the words DESCRIPTION and EXPLANATION in a different way than Chomsky has used them here. Let us, however, take under consideration the issue of a difference between descriptions and explanations as Chomsky is using the words. Is it, for example, possible to have more than one descriptively adequate grammar for a given language or set of data? Consider the following two grammars and the language that each produces.

(28)   A grammar G is defined as: $V_T = \{a, b\}$, $V_{NT} = \{S\}$, the start symbol (axiom) is S and the production or rule is $S \rightarrow (S)\ a\ b$.

The language produced by this grammar has these strings among others.

(29)   a.   ab
       b.   abab
       c.   ababab
       d.   abababab

This language is sometimes called $(ab)^n$. Now, compare the grammar in (30).

(30)   A grammar G is defined as: $V_T = \{a, b\}$, $V_{NT} = \{S, S'\}$, the start symbol is S and the rules are $P = \{S \rightarrow S'b,\ S' \rightarrow (S)\ a\ /\ \_\_\ b\}$ (from Gazdar 1980)

The formalism $S' \rightarrow (S)\ a\ /\ \_\_\_\_\ b$ is to be interpreted as S' IS REWRITTEN AS AN OPTIONAL S FOLLOWED BY A WHENEVER S' IS FOLLOWED BY B. It is a notational variant of $S'\ b \rightarrow (S)\ a\ b$. The grammar in (30) also produces the language, i.e., set of symbol strings $(ab)^n$. This is a clear example of a particular language, $(ab)^n$, that can be generated by two different grammars. Notice, however, that the grammars assign different structural descriptions (phrase markers) to each, i.e., (31) is produced by the grammar in (28), and (32) is produced by the grammar in (30).

(31)

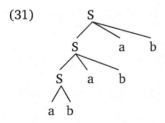

(32)

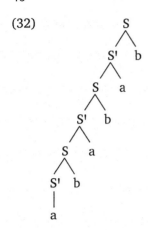

Note that these grammars assign different structural descriptions to strings (sentences) of the language. The choice between these two may be a question of descriptive adequacy. In addition, there are languages with strings possessing the same structural description that are still generated by different grammars. Consider the grammars in (33).

(33) a. S → A B A
      b. A → {1, 2, 3, 4, ... }
      c. B → =
      d. A → A C A
      e. C → {+, −, x, ÷}

In chapter one this grammar was used to generate arithmetic. Now note the grammar in (34).

(34) a. S → A B A
      b. A → {1, 2, 3, 4, ... }
      c. B → =
      d. A → A C A
      e. C → {+, −, x, ÷} / {1, 2, ... } ____ {1, 2, 3, ... }

This grammar produces exactly the same set of strings with exactly the same structural description.[2] It differs only in regard to rule e, which is, in one case, context-sensitive and, in the other case,

---

[2] In generative transformational grammar the following notational conventions apply. The brace { is used for choice of an element, and parentheses (indicate optionality. Thus, the grammar A → {a, b, c} will signify that A is to be rewritten as a or as b or as c. And A → (B) C is to signify that A is to be rewritten as B C or as C.

context-free. The phrase marker family generated by these grammars contains the member shown in (35).

(35)

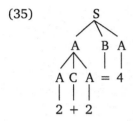

This phrase marker could have been arrived at in different manners. The context-free grammar allows the symbol C to be rewritten as $+$, $-$, x, or $\div$ any time it appears. In the context-sensitive version, this operation is not permitted until the neighboring symbols have already been rewritten as natural numbers. It seems to be a clear-cut case in which two descriptively adequate but different grammars exist. It also seems clear that principles that decide which of the two above should be favored are located at a level distinct from writing the grammars themselves. In the case of natural language, explanatory principles from the inventory of species-specific language universals would presumably decide. In treating specific grammatical phenomena it will often be necessary to search for such principles. From these and other examples, it is evident that explaining and describing statements, as Chomsky has defined them, certainly are different things.

Because of the distinction between descriptive and explanatory adequacy, Chomsky has quite a surprising attitude toward coverage of data. He points out that even if a proposal is capable of accurately predicting large amounts of observed phenomena, this may not be relevant in evaluating its descriptive or explanatory adequacy. For example, it is possible on the basis of observation of the tide heights at some point—say the berth of the Queen Mary in Long Beach harbor—to develop a predictive account of the water's depth, and the cyclic changing of more or less water. It may not even be recognized that from time to time the predictions are slightly—sometimes not so slightly—incorrect. These could be seen as insignificant disturbances of unknown source; troublesome anomalies but usually not sufficient to ground a ship. Names could be assigned to the values of high and low water: MEAN LOW WATER, MEAN LOWER LOW WATER, etc. (Chapman 1942). Yet, none of these observations and classifications would ever be capable of producing the explanatory account, for the ultimate explanation of the tides lies outside the data.

In fact, nothing resembling the explanation—the gravitational influence of the earth's only natural satellite—can even be observed in water height.

It is examples such as the tides that well illustrate the statement that a theory is underdetermined by the data. A theory is definitely more than just a statement capable of producing all of the relevant data upon demand. For example, a theory of multiplication must do more than simply be capable of yielding all the right answers to each conceivable 'a times b'. The action of the moon at a distance cannot be observed immediately in the measurements at the wharf. At the same time, the formalism is itself no explanation. When the equations of Einstein or Guth turn up anomalous solutions with unexpected properties, the result in itself does not constitute an explanation. In many cases, a theoretical prediction made by virtue of the formalism alone yields counterintuitive results and leads us in directions where the intuition cannot follow. The explanation of this gravitational collapse requires the construction of new intuitions such as black holes.

Since data coverage is not a sufficient test of theories, i.e., theories aren't regarded as falsified by just one anomalous result, how is one to evaluate? Chomsky answers that the major problem is to discover which generalizations about a language are the "significant ones" (1965:42). For grammars, he feels significant generalizations occur when distinct rules can be replaced by a single one or if a natural class undergoes a particular rule as a whole. The difficulty is to decide which is the most highly valued if natural classes compete. Chomsky suggests two ways out of this dilemma: (1) to place greater restrictions on formal grammars, which would limit what could be an acceptable basis; or (2) to refine evaluation metrics. While it is not quite so clear in this early work, Chomsky generally prefers the first approach, in particular capturing a phenomenon by regarding it to be a universal property of language rather than by regarding it as a language-specific property.

2.4 The specific assumptions of the *Aspects* model

As we have already mentioned, the *Aspects* model is a model of a generative grammar that is divided into a number of components: the base, the transformational component, the semantic component, and the phonological component. Since the book *Aspects of the Theory of Syntax* (1965) has very little to say about the semantic and phonological components, we will not spend much time on these points either. The remaining parts of the grammar will be discussed in the order listed above.

2.4.1 The base. Chomsky (1965:63) begins by asking what information traditional grammar supplies in its analysis of sentences. He mentions three things: (1) category information, (2) grammatical relations, and (3) lexical restrictions.

(36)   *Little Miss Muffet sat on a tuffet.*

(37)   **Epilepsy sat on a tuffet.*

In sentence (36), *Little Miss Muffet* is a noun phrase (NP), *sat* is a verb (V), *on* is a preposition (Prep), *a* is a determiner (Det), and *tuffet* is a noun (N). Moreover, *a tuffet* is a noun phrase (NP), *on a tuffet* is a prepositional phrase (PP), and *sat on a tuffet* is a verb phrase (VP). This analysis shows expressions and their syntactic categories. The functional relationships of parts are: *little Miss Muffet* is the subject of the sentence and *sat on a tuffet* the predicate. The phrase *on a tuffet* is an adverbial modifier of the verb *sat*. There are also lexical restrictions on sentence composition. *Little Miss Muffet* is a proper name and therefore, cannot be preceded by a definite article. The verb *sat* requires a concrete noun as its subject (except in bizarre circumstances). A sentence such as (37) would not be well-formed except in some sort of a morality play where characters had the names of diseases or afflictions. These three aspects of traditional grammar are not the only things grammarians have dealt with. For Chomsky, they are, at this point in generative transformational linguistics, the only significant ones.

In the definition of a formal grammar, we have distinguished between terminal and nonterminal symbols. In the same way, in the *Aspects* model, Chomsky will deal with the categorial aspects and the lexical aspects of language in different subcomponents of the base. The categorial part will be handled by rules like the ones in (38).

(38)   S   →   NP VP
         NP →   (Det) N {(PP) (S)}
         N   →   (Adj) N ({Adj PP S})
         VP →   V (NP) (PP)

These rules are called PHRASE STRUCTURE RULES and can produce the phrase markers for sentences as in (39).

(39)

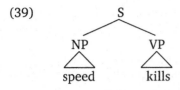

For English, there are many structures that cannot be generated by this limited inventory of syntactic symbols. For example, a sentence like (40) lies outside the capability.

(40)   *Mary wanted John to come over for a visit.*

Nevertheless, these rules could be expanded in principle to include just those structures that occur and exclude just those that do not.

In order to deal with the lexical properties of words as they influence their ability to combine with other words, a second rule type is needed in the base. Each terminal symbol, which for a natural language can be called a LEXICAL ITEM, will have an entry in a lexicon. The entry will contain two kinds of distributional information: (a) those syntactic properties of the environments in which it fits are called STRICT SUBCATEGORIZATION RESTRICTIONS; and (b) those semantic properties with syntactic consequences for the environment are called SELECTIONAL RESTRICTIONS. Note the sentence in (41).

(41)   *John smokes a pipe.*

In this sentence, the verb *smoke* has strict subcategorization restrictions that demand either a subject NP and no object NP, or that demand animate subject NPs such as *John, the man, the lady in the red hat,* etc. The selectional restrictions will stipulate semantic restrictions of the surrounding environment. For the verb *smoke*, the object NP must be the name of a tobacco product, narcotic, or a smoking device. In another case, a verb such as *pour* will require an object NP that is the name of a liquid or a liquid-like substance. The claim Chomsky wishes to make is that with the combination of a generative categorial component—the set of PHRASE STRUCTURE RULES, and a lexical restriction component—the LEXICON, exactly the set of deep structure phrase markers of English or any other language for which the grammar is written will be produced.

2.4.2 The transformational component. The transformational component of a grammar will be a set of potentially context-sensitive rules that operate to map one phrase marker onto the next in a sequence until the syntactic surface structure is produced. These transformational rules will be strictly LOCAL. By that Chomsky means that the rule will be able to have access only to the last phrase marker and not, for example, to previous phrase markers in a long derivational history, should this be the case. Rules that could look backwards or forwards more than locally he calls GLOBAL. We will discuss a number of transformational rules below.

2.4.3 The semantic component. The semantic component will make use of SEMANTIC PROJECTION RULES. These rules take deep structure phrase markers as input along with the dictionary meanings of individual words. The projection rules then produce interpretations of word complexes working hierarchically up the deep structure tree. From the lexical meanings of *speed* and *kills,* and from the phrase marker of the sentence *speed kills,* the interpretation of the whole can be calculated. The technical requirements of the rules will be discussed in the next section.

2.5 The problem-solving capacity of GTG

As we have previously stated, one good way to become acquainted with linguistic theorizing is to examine in detail the manner in which a given theory solves problems. In the upcoming chapters, we discuss the accounts provided by a number of theories or research paradigms in solving the problem of the English passive and the English auxiliary complex. The discussion of the generative transformational grammar (GTG) paradigm presented here is taken largely from Chomsky (1965) and Culicover (1976).

We begin by briefly examining the example of the English passive. First of all, note that the active and passive surface forms show identical restrictions in regard to what kinds of NPs may cooccur with a given verb. For instance, let us say that the verb *to square* has selectional restrictions that permit only one direct object NP, namely *a circle.* If we compare the active and passive forms of sentences with this verb as in (42):

(42)   a.   *John squared this circle.*
       b.   *This circle was squared by John.*
       c.   *?John squared his little sister.*
       d.   *?His little sister was squared by John.*

The common behavior of the pairs suggest that (42a) and (42b) are derived from a common source or deep structure.

In *Aspects of the Theory of Syntax* (1965) Chomsky suggested that the underlying structure for active and passive sentences are as follows:

(43)   a.

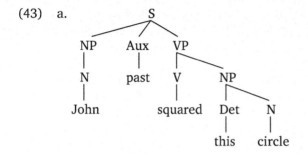

b.

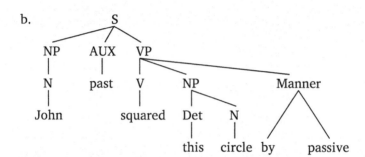

Note that the base component produces (43a) and (43b), which share a great deal in common while still differing. These two differ namely in that (43b), the source structure for *This circle was squared by John,* possesses a VP constituent Manner dominating *by + passive. Square this circle* occurs in both structures with the same relationship between the two parts, and that is why the two surface sentences share the same selectional restrictions.

In order to arrive at the surface structure form of (43b) the PASSIVE transformation must be applied to (43b). It will move *John* to replace *passive* and move *this circle* to the subject NP position. Although we will not formulate transformations explicitly just yet, we can see that care must be taken to identify which NPs are to move and how they are to attach to the new locations once moved.

If the sentence were *This circle was squared,* then the deep structure would be again very similar to (43a) and (43b). Looking at it, however, gives us a chance to examine yet another piece of theoretical apparatus that will be of later use.

(44)

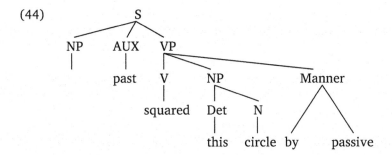

In (44) the deep structure contains a dummy element , which occupies the subject NP position at DS. After *this circle* has been moved to the left and replaces *passive,* then the Manner node must be deleted.

English exhibits not only simple verbs as in the sentence *Speed kills,* it also has forms such as *will come, has seen, might know, didn't care, must have been hanging,* and many more. Traditional or school grammar calls such forms PERIPHRASTIC, meaning that they are made up of more than one part. Traditional grammar also calls forms such as *have, can, might,* and *do* auxiliary verbs. More systematic grammar notes that these auxiliary verbs or auxiliaries (if one believes that they are perhaps no longer true verbs) have the same distribution.

(45)   *John   can   come.*
       John   must   come.
       John   will   come.
       John   is going to   come.

In the sequence *John ____ come,* each of these words or sequences can be substituted. They have the same DISTRIBUTION and, therefore, these forms should be regarded as being in the same syntactic category. The result is that a place in phrase markers will have to be made for the auxiliaries. We will assume that the auxiliary relates to surrounding structure as in (46).

(46)

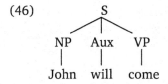

Correspondingly, we will need a phrase structure rule of the type S →
NP Aux VP.[3] Notice, moreover, that the auxiliary and verb complex can
appear in a variety of forms, e.g., *be, being, been* in sentences such as *He
is coming, He has been coming, He is being difficult.* The so-called MODAL
VERBS *can, could, must, will,* and *shall* may also occur with various combinations of *be* and *have.* Moreover, *come* sometimes appears as *come,*
sometimes as *coming.* For other verbs, an even wider variety of forms
can be seen. For instance, *sing* is realized as *sing, sang, sung, singing.* The
crucial observation to make is that a special kind of context dependency
exists among these forms. In particular, *have* conditions a past participle
form on its right; whenever *have* appears, the form to its right is always
a participle; similarly with *be,* which conditions an *-ing* form to its right.
Such DISCONTINUOUS DEPENDENCIES are characteristic features of the English auxiliary system. The lines of connection in (47) show this
dependency.

(47)

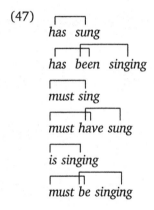

Modal verbs are followed by the zero form (infinitive form in school
grammar), *be* by the *-ing* form and *have* by the past participle form.
Therefore, we conclude that such things always occur together. We may
insure that they always appear together by having them generated

---

[3]Note that this assumption is the same as saying that auxiliaries are not part of the
predicate, that they belong to an independent syntactic category and that they are on the
same level as NP and VP. Many empirical assumptions are being made at this point. Arguments would have to be provided to justify this choice. One could, in principle, claim
that the auxiliary is a separate category but that it belongs to the VP. Such an assumption would require phrase structure rules like S → NP VP, VP → Aux VP. The recursion
in the rule would allow for multiple embeddings of auxiliaries. Many other possibilities
could be chosen as alternatives. Because our purpose is to illustrate the approach of the
theory, rather than to argue for a specific analysis, we take over the assumption here
without grounding it.

together by the phrase structure rules and by using the transformational rules to position them correctly in surface structure. Sentences with auxiliaries like those above are produced in the *Aspects* model with phrase structure rules as in (48).

(48)   Base rules of *Aspects* model (1965)

S→ NP Aux VP

$$\text{VP}\rightarrow \left\{ \begin{array}{l} \left[\begin{array}{l} \text{Copula Predicate} \\ \\ \\ \end{array} \right. \\ \text{V} \quad \left\{ \begin{array}{l} \text{(NP) (PP) (PP) (Manner)} \\ \text{S'} \\ \text{Predicate} \end{array} \right. \end{array} \right\}$$

Predicate → {Adjective, (like) Predicate Nominal}
PP → Direction, Duration, Place, Frequency, etc.
NP → (Det) N (S')
Aux → Tns (M) (Perf) (Prog)

$$\text{M}\rightarrow \left\{ \begin{array}{l} \textit{must} \\ \textit{might} \\ \textit{should} \\ \textit{will} \\ \textit{may} \\ \textit{can} \\ \textit{could} \end{array} \right\}$$

Perf → *have* + Prt
Prog → *be* + ing
Tns → {pres, past}

Here the auxiliary structure is produced by the Aux phrase structure rule, which gives to it the internal structure of tense (Tns), an optional node of Modal (M), Perfect (Perf), and Progressive (Prog). The modals are then specified by a phrase structure rule, Perf is given the internal structure of *have* + *Prt*, and Prog is given the internal structure of *be* + *ing*. Tense in this model is treated formally only and can be either present or past. With an appropriate lexicon and a transformation to be discussed these rules will produce sentences such as in (49)–(51).

(49) *I see the house.*

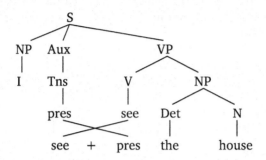

(50) *I am visiting the house.*

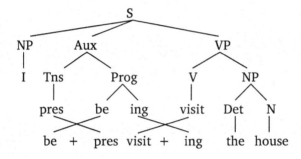

(51) *I have visited the house.*

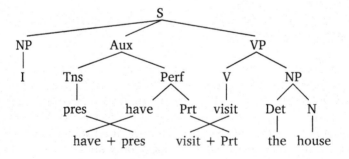

Phrase markers produced by the rules in (48) clearly show that the affixes *pres*, *past*, *Prt* and *ing* must be moved from their original positions to a position behind the verbal element that follows them. We might show the result of this movement with the phrase markers in (52).

(52)   *I have been visiting the house.*

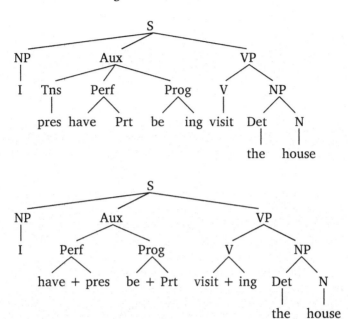

That is, *ing* is moved onto the following V, *Prt* is moved onto the follow-ing *be*, and *pres* is moved onto the following *have*. In order to carry out the reattachment of affixes, a transformation is needed.

2.6 The AFFIX-HOPPING transformation

In §2.5 we demonstrated how periphrastic forms of the English verb could be derived by first generating a sequence of symbols with ele-ments that always appear in the same environment, as sister nodes, and then reattaching them to the element that was immediately to the right. Moving branches of a phrase marker tree constitutes an entirely new kind of rule, the transformation. Transformations, specifically this affixation transformation, are written as in (53).

(53)   AFFIX-HOPPING

         SD: X - A - B - Y
             1   2   3   4

                                    obligatory ⇒

         SC: 1 # 3 + 2 # 4

    Conditions: 2 is one of the symbols *pres, past, Prt, ing* and 3 is a
                verb or a verbal element.
                # represents a word boundary.

    As can be seen in this transformation, a somewhat different formal-
ism is employed. SD stands for STRUCTURAL DESCRIPTION, SC for
STRUCTURAL CHANGE, X and Y for a VARIABLE STRING (i.e., any single symbol or string of symbols), A and B for CONSTANTS (i.e., some one particular symbol). The cardinal numbers below the strings, which are called
the INDEX, give the relative position and changes of elements. This rule
operates on a structure of an affix (as listed in the Condition) and a
verb, surrounded by any other elements (the variables), and it moves
the affix to a position following the verb and attaches it to the verb as
one word (indicated by the word boundaries). Note that, instead of a
single-shafted arrow, transformations use a double-shafted arrow to
keep them distinct from phrase structure rules. Transformations may
also have conditions such as those listed in (58) (specification of constants) and condition of application, e.g., obligatory. Lastly, there may
be ordering relationships among transformations whenever more than
one is involved in a derivation.
    Notice that this particular transformation will sometimes have to op-
erate more than once. There is, however, a danger in multiple application, because there must be a way to prevent this transformation from
applying to a string to which it has previously applied. Culicover in con-
fronting this problem says:

    However, if Affix Hopping may or must apply more than
    once in the same sentence, then there must be some way to
    guarantee that once an affix has been hopped, it will not hop
    again. For if this were not done, a situation could arise in
    which an affix that had been moved over a verbal element
    could then be moved over the next verbal element, and then
    over the next, until it ended up attached to the last element
    of the sequence...

There does not exist any clear evidence that transformations must be able to apply a number of different times to a single simple sentence. Thus, the convention that will be adopted here will be that the transformation applies simultaneously to all of those parts of the tree that meet the conditions for its application. (1976:54)

The notion of obligatory application needs a word of explanation. This rule will apply obligatorily whenever its structural description is met. In order to see if this is the case, we will illustrate application of the rule in (54) and (55) by drawing a phrase marker candidate and the structural description below it, and also the result of the application of the rule. This is done here only to demonstrate that the SD does, in fact, apply to this candidate phrase marker. Usually, this step is omitted. (Here, and in the following, we employ triangles instead of showing the internal structure of constituents when this detail is irrelevant.)

(54) *I see the house.*

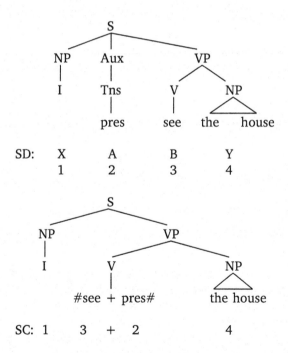

or:

(55)   *I am visiting the house.*

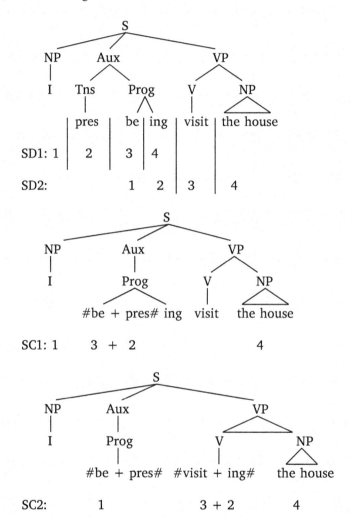

As the reader should demonstrate for himself or herself, the order of application of the SD and SC, i.e., whether change 1 or change 2, is immaterial. The result is the same in both cases. Finally, we note that the rule AFFIX-HOPPING is an example of a transformation using the elementary transformation ADJUNCTION because it adjoins one constituent to another.

Since the transformations in generative transformational grammar are to create well-formed sentences in a fashion that is co-extensive with the sentences produced by native speakers, it must be capable of producing the complexes of auxiliaries no matter how long. Notice that the phrase structure rules and transformations, moreover, fail to produce unacceptable strings such as *he is musting come, *he must be having sung, *he is having sung* because the sequence generated by the PS-rules is constrained to TENSE-MODAL-PERF-PROG. The first element must be tensed; modals must precede perfect; perfect must precede progressive, etc. The transformation moves the affix irrespective of its neighbor as long as it is a verbal element. Most importantly, these rules are better than a list of the cases. They intend to capture the LINGUISTICALLY SIGNIFICANT GENERALIZATION. A list captures no generalization; it is nothing more than a recapitulation of the data itself. Moreover, the rules—base and transformational—must be capable of producing ALL but ONLY the well-formed strings (sentences) of English and in this case English auxiliaries in particular. The ALL guarantees that the grammar is sufficiently strong to produce each well-formed sentence and the ONLY guarantees that the grammar is sufficiently weak to produce no ill-formed sentences as well. As Chomsky argues in *Aspects* and throughout his work, the latter is the more difficult.

2.7 The DO-SUPPORT transformation

One of the very characteristic rules of English involves the auxiliary *do* which must be present in negation, questions, and emphatic assertions when no other auxiliary is present.

(56)   a. *John came. / John didn't come.*
       b. *John knows the answer. / John doesn't know the answer.*
       c. *John is coming. / John isn't coming.*
       d. *John has known the answer. / John hasn't known the answer.*
       e. *John came. / Did John come?*
       f. *John knows the answer. / Does John know the answer?*
       g. *John is coming. / Is John coming?*
       h. *John has known the answer. / Has John known the answer?*
       i. *John came. / John DID come.*
       j. *John has known the answer. / John HAS known the answer.*
       k. *John came. / John came, didn't he?*
       l. *John knows the answer. / John knows the answer, doesn't he?*
      m. *John is coming. / John is coming, isn't he?*
       n. *John has known the answer. / John has known the answer, hasn't he?*

It is the presence and kind of auxiliary that determines whether *do* must be added. In older varieties of the language the *do* was not obligatory. Shakespeare writes: *Do not for ever with thy veiled lids, Seek for thy noble father in the dust* showing its occurrence, but then he says also *Then saw you not his face?* both from Hamlet.

Chomsky (1957) offered an analysis of *do* that can be considered a breakthrough over school grammar analyses. He not only provided an analysis that vindicated the rules previously developed, but offered for the first time a motivation, a PRINCIPLED BASIS, for the appearance of *do*. The crucial claim comes in the form of the DO-SUPPORT rule.

(57)   DO-SUPPORT transformation

                DO-SUPPORT

SD: X - Tns -   A - Y

              1   2   3   4

                                      obligatory $\Rightarrow$

SC: 1 -   #do+2# - 3 - 4

Condition: 3 $\neq$ a verbal element

The force and importance of this rule must not be lost in details of the formalism. DO-SUPPORT INTRODUCES A *DO* INTO THE STRING OF ELEMENTS JUST IN CASE THE TENSE MARKER IS NOT FOLLOWED BY SOMETHING THAT CAN BEAR THE TENSE MARKER IN SURFACE STRUCTURE. The configuration of elements is important and if some foreign element intervenes to prevent the AFFIX-HOPPING rule from doing its job, then a *do* is introduced to support that tense element which would otherwise be left stranded.

We now turn to illustrating the DO-SUPPORT rule. To do so, however, we need to discuss negation because—as stated—the *not* is one of the elements that blocks tense from its natural support. We assume the phrase marker must have a place for a syntactic symbol to indicate NEGATION, QUESTION, and IMPERATIVE. This can be done conveniently with a PRESENTENCE NODE. The position in the phrase marker and the corresponding PS-rule are seen in (58) and (59).

(58)

(59)   S → (PreS) NP Aux VP
       PreS → {Neg, Q, Emp}

These rules are to replace the rule *S → NP Aux VP* in the original set of PS-rules. In order to derive a sentence such as *John doesn't know the answer,* we assume a phrase marker and movement of the negation as indicated in (60).

(60)   *John doesn't know the answer.*

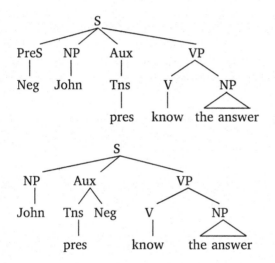

The symbols Neg and Emp are moved into this position by a rule NEG-EMP PLACEMENT.

(61)   NEG-EMP PLACEMENT

$$\text{SD: X - A - Y - B - Z}$$
$$ 1 \quad 2 \quad 3 \quad 4 \quad 5$$

obligatory $\Rightarrow$

$$\text{SC: 1} \quad \emptyset \quad 3 \quad 4+2 \; 5$$

Conditions: 2 = Neg or Emp

$$4 = \text{Tns} + \{\text{have, be, can, must, ..., } \emptyset\}$$

Now, consider the second phrase marker in (60). As can be seen, the transformation AFFIX-HOPPING can no longer apply to it, because Tns no longer stands immediately next to a verbal element; it is blocked off from the verb *know* by Neg. Therefore, in exactly this environment no hopping is permitted. But, also this environment satisfies exactly the SD for the rule DO-SUPPORT. After the symbol *do* has been inserted, the phrase marker that results is shown in (62).

(62)   *John doesn't know the answer.*

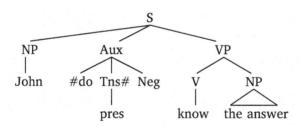

If Emp had been chosen instead, the results would have been the same except, of course, Emp would have occurred instead of Neg.

Whenever an auxiliary is present, however, we have the phrase marker as in (63). Parallel results would have been obtained if a modal verb had been used.

(63)   *John hasn't known the answer.*

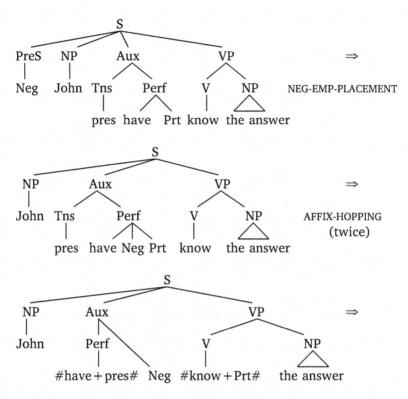

While it cannot be said that the English auxiliary has been adequately treated as yet, still a sizable body of cases are describable. We note, moreover, that the actual lexical form, e.g., *known, come, dreamt,* and *dreamed* remain to be derived. Here we have dealt only with the syntactic behavior of these, not with their surface morphological shape; the latter are handled by lexical rules (where generalizations exist) or by morpheme-specific lexical information (for idiosyncratic forms).

2.8 Generative transformational theorizing

In summary, we can say that the GTG research tradition is oriented on language universals not language particulars, grammars not languages, ideal not real speakers and hearers, and the knowledge of a speaker not his or her use of that knowledge. For purposes of comparison, we now give a summary of some further properties of the *Aspects* model.

Summary of the *Aspects* model

1. Levels: GTG assumes two levels, an abstract syntactic deep structure level and a more concrete syntactic surface structure level.
2. Primitive symbols: Small in number, consisting of such things as S, NP, VP, etc.
3. Rules produce: A constituent order, a constituent structure, a constituent distribution, category symbols.
4. Rules do not produce or reference directly: Grammatical relations, such traditional categories as subject, direct object, etc. These are defined configurationally, e.g., subject is the left daughter of S.
5. Context sensitivity: Found in lexicon and in the transformational component.
6. Only one generative component, the phrase-structuer rules of the base component.
7. Sentences, e.g., statements and questions, related by (context sensitive) transformations.
8. Separation of components of grammar. The generative component, the base, does not overlap with the structural repackaging component, the transformational component, nor with the computation of meaning, the semantic component, nor with the idiosyncratic lexical part of grammar, the lexicon.
9. Different components employ different kinds of rules, e.g., the PS rules make up a special kind of context-free grammar.
10. The grammar is monodirectional. There are no explicit procedures for language analysis (model of reception), the putting together of parts toward creating a whole. This is not needed since the *Aspects* model is not supposed to be a model of actual language production or processing, only of our implicit knowledge about our languages.

3

Tagmemics

3.1 Introduction

Because we were able to consult tagmemic work with two of its major advocates, we have decided to include a statement of the views of each of them in this chapter. Thus, the positions of Kenneth L. Pike and Robert E. Longacre will be articulated. In describing Pike's tagmemics model of linguistic theorizing, we have relied primarily on Pike 1971, 1982, and 1987 as well as Pike and Pike 1982. A slightly different perspective has come from Longacre 1964, 1976, 1981, 1983, and 1996. Unlike the *Aspects* model, we have cited some of the newest work of Pike and Longacre because the changes from earlier work strike one as not being so extreme as is the case between Chomsky 1965 and later works (which later developments are discussed in chapter five). Here, as before, we will proceed with a three-pronged attack, discussing first the general world view, ontology, and methodology, then going to the specifics of the proposal in the linguistic microcosm. Finally, we will illustrate the problem-solving capacity of the proposal by giving an analysis of the English auxiliary complex.

3.2 General ontology, methodology, and world view

While Pike is less explicit about his philosophical roots, it is not too difficult to see connections to the philosophy of the later Wittgenstein, to the behavioristic and pragmatism theories of meaning of Peirce, William James, Charles Morris, and John Dewey, as well as to the positivistic ideas that human knowledge is made up of the POSITIVE THINGS, the OBSERVABLES. This last-named area, however, comes more from Pike's tie with structuralist linguistics. We will now try to illustrate these connections with quotes from the written work.

3.2.1 The world view. The basic assumption that determines much of tagmemic theorizing is the notion that human behavior is a unity. This idea is so important that it found its way into the title of Pike's mammoth *Language in Relation to a Unified Theory of the Structure of Human Behavior* (762 pp.). As Pike says:

> The approach here is designed to serve in a very wide range of circumstances. The principles have been applied, for example, to football games..., party games..., church services..., a breakfast scene..., and—briefly—to society...as well as to language. Human emic experience is the target, not merely linguistics. (1982:xv)

The character of the human is to be found in all these because, for Pike, we always inject ourselves into the things we are trying to define.

> What is a chair, if there is no man to sit on it? A flute, with no player? A concert, with no listener? A saw, with no carpenter? The relevance or intended use of a thing is part of its nature as experienced by us—a component added to it by its designer or user or deduced by an observer. (1982:3)

Therefore, it is obvious that Pike agrees very much with the views of Kuhn (1962) that all, or at least a great deal, of data is theory-laden. These reactions to data must be added to the structure of the language. In this sense, a theory is a tool, a window on the world. By changing the window we change what we can see, how clearly we can see it, and the aspect it presents to us to perceive. Theories are, in other words, choices we make. There may be different reasons to adopt a theory: because it is exciting, because it allows us to reach a goal, or because it is helpful to understand oneself, others, or one's environment. Because 'theory' is being used in this very broad manner, it might be wise to regard the previous discussion of Chomsky in a new light. When Chomsky speaks of a theory, he is speaking of 'explanatory theories of language' rather than a theory that interests a particular observer. Or, at least, he would say we should strive to develop the most explanatorily adequate theory. Pike, on the other hand, is more interested in allowing the shape of the theory to be determined by the particular linguist's goals.

In statements such as Pike's above, one can see a view that there is no basis for distinguishing between ego (the observer) and the world, no knowing subject and known object. The two form a unity. Moreover, it is also clear that the observer is exposed to a continuum of sense impressions within which there are regularities. This two-faced view of reality, the division into

> a persistent, perceptual unit...termed an EMIC one (drawn from the linguistic term PHONEMIC)—an entity seen as "same" from the perspective of internal logic of the containing system, as if it were unchanging even when the outside analyst easily perceives that change. (Meanwhile, the term etic, from the linguistic term phonetic, labels the point of view of the outsider as he tries to penetrate a system alien to him; and it also labels some component of an emic unit, or some variant of it, or some preliminary guess at the presence of internal emic units, as seen either by the alien observer or as seen by the internal observer when somehow he becomes explicitly aware of such variants through teaching or techniques provided by outsiders.) (Pike 1982:xii)

If one adds that distinctive (emic) categories must be perceivable, largely by contrast, then one has an almost perfect fit with the tenets of positivism.

The linkage to the elder Wittgenstein is evident in Pike's HOLISM and in his insistence that there are multiple (to be precise three) PERSPECTIVES of 'things'. The holism we speak of is the notion that each linguistic level can potentially influence every other level, that linguistic units must be understood in a context. One of the amazing facts about Wittgenstein's *Philosophische Untersuchungen* (1971) (Philosophical Investigations) is its near total rejection of the views expressed in his *Jugendwerk* that had already put him in a class with Bertrand Russell, *Tractatus logico-philosophicus* (1961). In particular, he overthrows his earlier view that language can be described in terms of a CALCULUS, a system of rules describing how, from each linguistic atom, one can build up linguistic molecules and compounds according to well-defined rules.

> Aber welches sind die einfachen Bestandteile, aus denen sich die Realität zusammensetzt?—Was sind die einfachen Bestandteile eines Sessels?—Die Stücke Holz, aus denen er zusammengefügt ist? Oder die Moleküle, oder die Atome?—'Einfach' heißt: nicht zusammengesetzt. Und da kommt es darauf an: in welchem Sinne 'zusammengesetzt'? Es hat gar keinen Sinn von den 'einfachen Bestandteilen des Sessels schlechtweg' zu reden. (1971: para. 47)

But, what are the simple components from which reality is assembled? What are the simple components of an armchair?—The pieces of wood from which it is put together? Or the molecules, or the atoms?—'Simple' means: not put together. And in exactly that point it matters; in what sense 'put together'? It makes no sense to speak of the 'simple components of a chair' at all. [Our translation]

Pike, after Wittgenstein, claims that there is no context-independent manner to characterize linguistically simple and linguistically complex units. Each is itself context-dependent. Even in apparently unambiguous test cases of description, such as a chessboard, more than one perspective of its makeup is possible. One can say it is composed of thirty-two red and thirty-two black squares. Equally well, however, one could say it contains three elements: the color red, the color black, and the scheme of organizing the colors.[4] For Pike, the multiple perspectives result from treating the observer as an element of the theory. He can view the chessboard statically as PARTICLES, blotches of red and black discretely separated into rows of alternating colors; or equally as a rapidly rotating board, as a WAVE, a dynamic pattern of stripes of red and black as units merge and overlap. The third perspective is that of the FIELD, the principles of organization behind a chessboard, that colors alternate in each row and column so that the board could in principle be enlarged indefinitely. Here the opposition to Chomsky's view is bared most tellingly. Whereas Chomsky follows the tradition of ANALYTIC PHILOSOPHY in his demand for a description that is as complete and accurate as possible, Pike would claim that each unit is a member of a hierarchy of units

---

[4]Note the following from Wittgenstein (1971: para 47):
Aber ist z.B. nicht ein Schachbrett offenbar und schlechtweg zusammengesetzt?—Du denkst wohl an die Zusammensetzung aus 32 weissen und 32 schwarzen Quadraten Aber könnten wir z. B. nicht auch sagen, es seien aus den Farben Weiß, Schwarz und dem Schema des Quadratnetzes zusammengesetzt? Und du dann noch sagen, das Schachbrett sei 'zusammengesetzt' schlechtweg?—Ausserhalb eines bestimmten Spiels zu fragen "Ist dieser Gegenstand zusammengesetzt?", das ist ähnlich dem, was einmal ein Junge tat, der angeben sollte, ob die Zeitwörter in gewissen Satzbeispielen in der aktiven, oder in der passiven Form gebraucht seien, und der sich nun darüber den Kopf zerbrach, ob z. B. das Zeitwort "schlafen" etwas Aktives oder etwas Passives bedeutet.
But isn't a chessboard clearly and absolutely put together? You may well think of the composition of 32 white and 32 black squares. But, can we, for example, not say it is composed from the color white, black and the scheme of a network of squares? And if there are quite different ways to view things, will you still say that the chessboard is 'put together'? Outside of a particular game to ask the question "Is this object put together?" that is similar to that which a youth once was asked; whether a verb in a particular example was used in the active or the passive form, and who then thought over it till his head burst, whether the verb 'sleep' meant something active or passive. [Our translation]

of its type and that each unit is subject to change in a context. In this context, it makes no sense to speak of the meaning or well-formedness of sentences (or other structural pieces) aside from the use that they are put to.

Another similarity with Wittgenstein's philosophy of language as espoused in *Philosophical Investigations* rests in the low priority assigned to formalism.

> In this volume PERSON (and relation between persons) is given theoretical priority above formalism, above pure mathematics, above idealized abstractions. (Pike 1982:xi)

Like *Philosophical Investigations*, the books *Grammatical Analysis* (the part on theory at least) and *Linguistic Concepts* are written in very simple everyday language. There is little formalism. Moreover, in *Grammatical Analysis* the introduction contains a list of axioms and their explanations written very much in the manner of Wittgenstein's *Tractatus* (1961), in that each is given a number, e.g., 1, 1a, etc. This is not to say that Pike advocates linguistic theorizing totally without formalism. In an important paper of his own, he makes use of the techniques of GROUP THEORY to analyze turn-taking in conversation. The most important point of this essay is to demonstrate that not all solutions presented by the formalism, in this case the group theory, may be interpretable or applicable in solving the linguistic problem. Here Pike and Chomsky see eye-to-eye, since the formal definition of a grammar, in Chomsky's view, is bound to be too vague. Linguistically based restrictions must be added to the concoction to guarantee descriptive or explanatory adequacy.

We see a linkage between Pike and the philosophical direction known as pragmatism and behaviorism because of the concept of behavior as a unity. Von Kutschera describes the commonality of James, Dewey, Morris, and Peirce as:

> Speech is a form of human behavior that has its place in the general course of human life. Therefore its function is always to be analyzed with this context as a background. The realistic account, according to which the semantic function, the meaning, of a linguistic expression can be defined independently of the context of use, is therefore false. Language is used in the course of various activities, for various purposes, in various situations. Therefore, one cannot ascribe to language just one semantic function, but there are as many semantic functions as there are contexts of activity in which

language is used. Semantics can consequently not be pursued independently of pragmatics. (1975:59)

BEHAVIORISTIC theories of language constitute an initial group within what we have called pragmatic theories of meaning.

3.2.2 Ontological primitives. The underlying principles of tagmemics, as stated in *Grammatical Analysis*, are:

(64)   1. Unit

      a. contrastive-identificational features

      b. variation, and physical manifestation

      c. distribution

          1. in class

          2. in sequence

          3. in system

   2. Hierarchy

      a. referential

      b. phonological

      c. grammatical

   3. Context

      a. form-meaning composite

      b. change via shared element

      c. universe of discourse

   4. Perspective

      a. static (particle)

      b. dynamic (wave)

      c. relational (field)

These will be commented on in what follows.

By UNIT Pike means that language (and other things) comes in pieces or constituents. It may, however, not be possible to recognize them overtly. Segmentation procedures have to be applied. These make use of the contrastive-identificational features of a unit. In order to recognize a unit two things are needed: discrimination and identification. These involve two different kinds of perception. As Pike (1982:42ff) says "We do not know what something is unless we know something about what it is not." This is in essence the operation of discrimination. We can tell that two notes struck on a piano are different by listening to them. Even quite fine distinctions can be discriminated. As Pike points out, however, defining units only by contrast is tiresome in practice and impossible for some cases. For example, using the negative for a definition of a thing raises the FIGURE AND GROUND PROBLEM. In his book *Gödel, Escher, Bach* Hofstadter writes:

> So far, the only way we have found to represent prime numbers typographically is as a negative space. Is there, however, some way—I don't care how complicated—of representing the primes as a positive space—that is, as a set of theorems of some formal system?

> Different people's intuitions give different answers here... 'How could a figure and its ground not carry exactly the same information?' They seemed to me to embody the same information, just coded in two complementary ways. What seems right to you?

> It turns out I was right about the primes, but wrong in general. This astonished me, and continues to astonish me even today. It is a fact that:

> There exist formal systems whose negative space (set of nontheorems) is not the positive space (set of theorems) of any formal system.

> This result, it turns out, is of depth equal to Gödel's Theorem—so it is not surprising that my intuition was upset. I, just like the mathematicians of the early twentieth century, expected the world of formal systems and natural numbers to be more predictable than it is. (1980:72ff.)

In spite of these difficulties, the notion of contrast remains an important component in identifying units in most linguistic theories, including tagmemics.

Pike notes, moreover, there will always be VARIATION in behavior. Units will have different manifestations, but these will not be in contrast.

Variation, as a property of language, is the factor that introduces heterogeneity in behavior while, at the same time, maintaining recognizability. Within variation will fall the uniquely recognizable units that will be nonuniquely realized. This variation can arise from stylistic changes, individual idiosyncracies, or environmentally conditioned alternations. Pike (1982:55) gives as an example of variation the positions of *yesterday* in sentences such as (65).

(65)   a.   *I came from Detroit yesterday.*
       b.   *Yesterday I came from Detroit.*

Within a larger discourse context these sentences may not be in free variation but in conditioned variation dependent on their function in that context. This view considers positional variants as well as sociolinguistic (regional, stylistic, sociolectal) variants as manifestations of comparable significance, the nonidentity of repetitions of behavior. Chomsky's theory, on the other hand, regards some of these as competence (conditioned variation) and some as performance (sociolinguistic).

By DISTRIBUTION Pike means that a unit is characterized or identified by the company it keeps, its GRAMMATICAL CONSTRUCTIONS. Thus, for example, the sentence *is the square root of two a rational number?* is in part identified by the response that can follow it, which—except in noninformation (rhetorical) questions—requires the answers *yes, no,* or *I don't know.* We can at times identify a thing by describing its membership in a class of replaceable units, i.e., its DISTRIBUTION CLASS. Mutually substitutable units are therefore in one distribution class. Thus, *sleeps* would be in the same class as *runs every day*, since both can follow *John* and both have the PREDICATE function.

HIERARCHY is termed to mean that smaller units are themselves organized in larger encompassing ones. In particular, three kinds of hierarchies are distinguished: grammatical, phonological, and referential. These three evidence parallel, but not totally parallel, structures. In a way they may be compared and contrasted to Chomsky's syntactic, phonological, and semantic components though much is different. The grammatical hierarchy, for example, will be organized into 'levels', the same word used by Chomsky in 'deep' and 'surface structure levels'. Yet, 'level' in a tagmemic context refers to the size of a piece of the grammatical hierarchy, e.g., root, stem, word, phrase, clause, sentence, and paragraph. Each major level will, however, include information not only about the FORM OF THE UNITS AT THAT LEVEL BUT ALSO ABOUT THE FUNCTION AND GENERAL IMPACT ON THE HEARER. Thus, a hierarchy is more than just the inclusion of lower-level chunks within the next higher-level chunk. Each unit in a hierarchy has a function, a structural arrangement or form, and a meaning or general impact on the hearer. At the highest level of the grammatical hierarchy—the conversation—the meaning, i.e., the general impact on the hearer, is that of social interchange, because language is rooted in human behavior and "takes its meaning from social settings, intents, and reactions" (Pike 1982:73).

Another major difference with the *Aspects* model is the relationship among hierarchies. In tagmemics, grammatical and phonological hierarchies are not sequenced derivationally one after the other. Instead, they have overlapping borders. For example, in *I'm* the 'word border' occurs between *I* and *am* grammatically, whereas phonologically no 'syllable border' occurs within *I'm*. It is evident from this kind of example that the grammatical hierarchy doesn't count as derivationally prior to the phonological hierarchy. Rather, the two address different substance. The phonological hierarchy is made up of phonological units, for example, syllables and phonemes, whereas the grammatical hierarchy is made up of grammatical units, for example, morphemes and words. Moreover, in tagmemics, the phonological hierarchy at each level has information about form, function, and other things to be discussed presently. In totally parallel fashion, the referential hierarchy possesses multiple kinds and levels of information as well. The referential hierarchy differs from the grammatical by allowing PARAPHRASES under maintenance of referential identity. Thus, an identifying description of *the man who drank the hemlock* will be identical with the name *Socrates*. The units of the referential hierarchy are, therefore, not ISOMORPHIC with the units of the grammatical hierarchy, i.e., there is no one-to-one mapping of one into the other. In other words, the relationship among them should be represented as in (66).

(66)

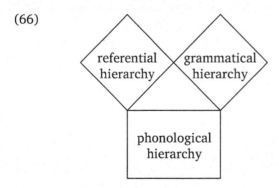

3.2.3 Methodology. Pike, in a manner comparable to others, notes that more than one account may be advanced for covering a given set of data. And, furthermore, that there is no discovery procedure for theories.

There is no algorithm (a fail-safe mechanically-applicable set of steps for arriving at the one correct result) for the segmentation of a stretch of speech into words. The judgment of two analysts in weighing the importance of segmentation criteria for any one language may differ. If so, then (ideally) they should be expected to publish different descriptions that are mechanically convertible into each other (i.e., by a set of rules one should be able to change the one description mechanically into the other). In such instances, practical goals of making an alphabet, or of writing a grammar, or of the preparation of language lessons, may be well served by both. Usually, however, one description will be slightly more economical for one part of the description, and the other slightly more economical for another part—or for another purpose. (Pike and Pike 1982:98)

It is quite evident here that Pike and Pike are speaking of NOTATIONAL VARIANTS, by which one means descriptions that contain exactly the same information in different form. They quite rightly note that notational variants are for all intents and purposes identical accounts. One should, however, not think that notational variants means the same thing as WEAKLY or STRONGLY EQUIVALENT GRAMMARS (Wall 1972:209). This is apparently the misunderstanding in Jones (1980:89), "Hence, tagmemics assumes neither that there is only one correct linguistic theory nor that there is only one correct grammar for each set of data." To make this difference clear let us examine an instance of notational variants. The information in a phrase marker (67) can also be rendered by means of labelled bracketing (68) as one can show by drawing projection lines from each category and terminal symbol, e.g., NP, and then connecting it to its node as in (69).

(67)

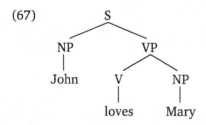

(68)   [s [NP John NP][VP [V loves V][NP Mary NP] VP] s]

(69)

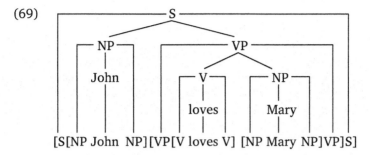

[S[NP John NP][VP[V loves V] [NP Mary NP]VP]S]

Examples (67) and (68) are thus shown to be notational variants of one another since either can be mapped to the other with no loss or gain of information, as the projection lines show.

It is, however, another matter entirely when one begins to compare grammars.

(70)   a.   S   →   A B A
          b.   A   →   {1, 2, 3, 4,...}
          c.   B   →   =
          d.   A   →   A C A
          e.   C   → $\{+, -, x, \div\}$

(71)   a.   S   →   A B A
          b.   A   →   {1, 2, 3, 4,...}
          c.   B   →   =
          d.   A   →   A C A
          e.   C   → $\{+, -, x, \div\}$ / {1, 2,...} ___ {1, 2, 3,...}

In chapter two of this volume, the grammars (70) and (71) were shown to generate exactly the same set of strings with the same set of structural descriptions, i.e., they are strongly equivalent. Yet, even though the rules a–d are identical, the rules in e cannot be mapped one onto another without change of information. For this reason the grammars in (70) and (71) are not notational variants. In other words, two grammars may be strongly equivalent and still not be notational variants of one another and thus not "mechanically convertible" into one another. This state of affairs will call for additional criteria for evaluation; the value of a grammar depends upon more than just the data it generates.

Pike and Pike employ methods of analysis that we have already encountered. At least this is true for their general strategy.

> In our insistence that workcharts and formulas should be a
> part of the initial states of linguistic analysis, we are building
> on the fact that *man is a pattern-seeking creature.* He cannot be
> happy with, nor operate efficiently within, chaos and ran-
> domness. A good analytical research procedure (a *heuristic*)
> for linguistics requires that a student (1) *start with probable
> norms*—and so do the easiest things first, (2) *make quick
> guesses* (right or wrong), and (3) *check them* rigidly and sys-
> tematically, revising as necessary and checking again.
> (1982:64)

The deductive method from hypothesis is clearly what is being advocated here. Once the pattern has been discovered, then FORMULAS can be
written. These should then be used to test "for adequacy of formulas by
generation of acceptable constructions" (Pike and Pike 1982:70). In
other words, tagmemicists and transformationalists do not differ in regard to the descriptive adequacy of grammars, for both require that the
description be tested against the data. They do use different names for
the generalizations captured by the grammar. Transformationalists
speak of RULES and tagmemicists of FORMULAS.

> Formulas of a tagmemic construction are designed to be a set
> of obligatory and optional choices which, when followed out
> successively through descending layers of structure, result in
> the producing of *all*—and *only*—the specific clauses, phrases,
> or other constructions of the languages implied by the for-
> mula. When the linguist plugs members of morpheme classes
> into formulas at places designated by the formulas, units re-
> sult which are *predicted (generated)* by that set of formulas.
> (Pike and Pike 1982:70; emphasis theirs)

Although much more needs to be said, we are rapidly approaching a
point at which specifics must be used.

3.3 The specific assumptions of the tagmemic model in Pike and Pike (1982)

The major unit (type) and the entity from which this model gets its
name is the TAGMEME, which Pike (1982:75) terms "the unit-in-context."
It is said to have four features that are in part independently variable, in
part dependent upon each other. These features are intended to answer
for a specific token the questions: *where, what, why,* and *how* the unit is

tied to its surroundings, in a manner to be illustrated below. For the grammatical hierarchy, there are also minimal units, termed MORPHEMES. The formulas of tagmemics produce CONSTRUCTIONS, which may be represented as TREE DIAGRAMS. Taking reference to the definition of a formal grammar, we would count tagmemes as quadruples of nonterminal symbols with the actual morphemes as terminal symbols, the formulas the productions, and the constructions the set of well-formed structured strings, i.e., the language.

(72)   A tagmemic formal grammar
        1. NONTERMINAL symbols: the quadruples composed of SLOT, CLASS, ROLE, and COHESION
        2. TERMINAL SYMBOLS: the morphemes of the language (for the grammatical hierarchy, at least)
        3. PRODUCTIONS: the formulas
        4. START SYMBOL: Since Pike and Pike (1982:20) give the highest level as conversation (others are exchange, monolog, paragraph, sentence, clause, phrase, word, morpheme cluster, and morpheme), at least that one would be a start symbol. There would be others for the phonological and the referential hierarchies.

Let us begin to discuss the details of some of these terms by examining the tagmeme. As mentioned above, the tagmeme is itself a complex made up of four components or features. The information in each of the parts is supposed to answer the questions: where, what, why, and how tied to context? The names assigned to each of these are respectively: STRUCTURAL SLOT, SUBSTITUTION CLASS, ROLE, and FRAMEWORK AND CONTROL (COHESION). "The item in a class fills a slot which performs a specific role (or function) in a stream of speech. (In *Bill hit Joe, Bill*, which is a member of the class Proper Noun Root, fills the slot of subject which has the role of ACTOR, whereas *Joe*, a second member of the class Proper Noun Root, fills the slot of ADJUNCT which has the role of UNDERGOER" (Pike and Pike 1982:33).

The first of these, SLOT, is that grammatical function that expresses the syntagmatic relationship between this item and surrounding items at this level. It expresses the wave, dynamic merging, and overlapping aspect of language, that one unit is on the leading or trailing edge of a construction and another is the center. Examples of slots at the clause level are: NUCLEUS and MARGIN, with nucleus filled by a clause root whose slots are (if transitive) SUBJECT, PREDICATE, and ADJUNCT with other slots being marginal. We believe margin and nucleus closely resemble the concepts made reference to by other linguists such as: NUCLEUS and SATELLITE, HEAD and COMPLEMENT or ATTRIBUTE (Bloomfield 1933:195), or INDEPENDENT and DEPENDENT ELEMENT, which in DEPENDENCY and VALENCE GRAMMAR means hanging the dependent element onto the independent one (Tesnière 1969). According to Pike and Pike (1982:25), the nucleus is the more independent item of a pair; it is more frequent in representing the whole unit; it is a member of a larger class; it occurs in more kinds of grammatical slots; and it has a more central semantic role to play. By way of comparison, Bloomfield says of ENDOCENTRIC CONSTRUCTIONS, those that have a subordinate member,

> the resultant phrase (after combination—jae & dab) belongs to the same form-class as one of the constituents, which we call the HEAD: thus, *poor John* belongs to the same form-class as *John*, which we accordingly call the head; the other member, in our example *poor*, is the ATTRIBUTE. (1933:195)

We shall meet this distinction between syntactic centrality and syntactic periphery again in our discussion of X-bar syntax in chapter five.

The feature, CLASS, is very similar to what Chomsky would call syntactic (for the grammatical hierarchy only, of course) categories and subcategories. It expresses a general set of items substitutable appropriately in a slot. It, furthermore, captures PARADIGMATIC RELATIONS, the relationship between things that can appear with the same function at the same place in a sequenced string, e.g., *John* and *the owner of the dog* can both appear in front of *died* as subject. Examples of such a class include: subject pronoun, verb phrase, count noun phrase, location phrase, mass noun phrase, limitation word, possessor phrase, numeral phrase, adjective phrase, restricted noun phrase, relative clause, and many more.[5]

ROLE is basically a functional characterization of some item. For example, for nominals it includes labels such as: ACTOR, UNDERGOER, SCOPE, and ITEM. In the sentence *he handed me the books,* *he* is the actor, *me* is scope, and *the books* is undergoer. There are many more role labels depending upon the level. Role properly expresses some semantic characteristic of the class as it relates to surrounding classes.

The final feature is COHESION. The tagmemic model views this unit as a member of a field, its sensitivity to the context in which it occurs. Formally, arrowheads are used to indicate whether a particular item

---

[5]Notice that much information that Chomsky assigned to the strict subcategorization/selectional restrictions of the lexicon are contained in the class name itself. In other words, this rich inventory of the class features amounts to splitting the larger syntactic (for the grammatical hierarchy) categories into subcategories. This tendency is also found in successors to the *Aspects* model.

determines or is determined by those that surround it. Examples of cohesion are the categories: STORY TIME (the base line for time margins of verb, clause), NUMBER in subject (governs number within predicate), GENDER (gender of noun root governs the pronoun used as referent), etc.

3.4 The specific assumptions of the tagmemic model of Longacre (1983)

The SYNTAGMEME is "a structurally contrastive type on a given level of hierarchical structuring, e.g., a word type...a discourse type. More explicitly: a syntagmeme, as a functionally contrastive string on a given level, has (1) closure and internal coherence; (2) a minimal structure (a nucleus at least part of which is obligatory) and usually an expanded structure (the entire nucleus plus the optional periphery); and (3) contrast, variants, and distribution" (Longacre 1983:275). According to Longacre, two of the fundamental interrelationships between tagmeme and syntagmeme can be represented as in (73).

(73) $(\Sigma) = \{T^1, T^2,...T^n\}$
      $T^f : \{(\Sigma)\}$
      Where (Σ) is the syntagmeme, T^i the tagmeme, and the equal sign may be read as 'composed of', and the colon may be read 'is expounded as'.

It seems to us that there is very little difference in this definition of syntagmeme or formula from the rule concept in Chomsky. The LAW OF COMPOSITION as Longacre calls the above representation, if viewed in the generative sense quoted by Pike and Pike above, could be conceived of with an arrow instead of the equal sign. As Longacre adds, however, elements of the set $\{T^1, T^2,...\}$ typically "occur in linear order," just as in Chomsky's rewrite notation. Therefore, the formula and syntagmeme corresponds to a production or rule in the sense of the definition of formal grammars.

A second 'law' of tagmemic theorizing is Longacre's LAW OF PRIMARY EXPONENCE, which he formulates as in (74).

(74) $T^n : \{ (\Sigma)^{n-1} / (\Sigma)^0 \}$

It means

> that the function of a tagmeme on any given level is expounded by a set of syntagmemes from the next lower level (descending exponence) and/or syntagmemes from level zero (level skipping to zero). To illustrate the above formulization take, for example, a sentence type (i.e., a sentence-level syntagmeme) in such a language as English. We can expect the constituent tagmemes of a sentence to be expounded by clauses, in that clause is the next descending level below the sentence. We do find, however, that there are bits and pieces of sentences, in fact, essential parts of their framework, which are composed of functional morphemes, i.e., syntagmemes of level zero...What we say in this formulization is that the primary elements of constructions are elements from the next lower level of construction and such functional morphemes. (1983:278)

Since this law applies to any level, there is a proportion that discourse is to paragraph, as paragraph to sentence, as sentence to clause, as clause to phrase, etc.

A third 'law' is the LAW OF SECONDARY EXPONENCE. Longacre (1983:279) formulates this law as in (75). He interprets it to mean that the function of a tagmeme on any level may be expounded by a set of syntagmemes on the same level as itself. This kind of structure results in nesting instead of strings.

(75) $T^n : \{(\Sigma)^n\}$

Having now mentioned most of the terms, we turn to illustrating the use of the tagmemic approach in problem solving using the case of the English auxiliary.

3.5 The problem-solving capacity of Tagmemics

In at least two places, Pike and Pike have analyzed the English auxiliary complex: In Pike and Pike (1974) and in *Grammatical Analysis* (1982:204–7). In the first account, which we sketch only briefly, there are the classes: MODAL, CURRENT RELEVANCE, STATE, and NUCLEAR VERB. The interpretation of the first of these is evident from the name. The second corresponds to a syntagmeme, CURRENT RELEVANCE, equivalent to Perf in the *Aspects* model. The third unit, STATE, correlates to Prog in the *Aspects* model treatment.

(76) Act(ive)Indic(ative)Nonemph(atic)V(erb)P(hrase) = ±iMar:MoV ±n^1Mar:<not> ±jMar:CRV ±kMar:StateV +/−n^2Mar: EmptyV +mNuc:ActIndicMnV

Where MoV = modal verb, CRV = current relevance verb (Perf), StateV = Prog, EmptyV = empty (the source of *do*), ActIndicMnV = active indicative main verb, Nuc = nucleus, Mar = margin, and i, j, n, m are indices that are referred to as cohesion in Pike and Pike (1982).

Whenever *be* or *have* is the first verb in the sentence and negation is also present, then Neg is moved to a position to the right as required. Details of this change will not be discussed here.

In the later version, *Grammatical Analysis* (1982:204–7), a different account is pursued. The first syntagmeme for the Decl(arative)Act(ive)NonEmphaticVP has the form as in (77).

(77) DeclActIndNonEmphatic

VP = ±

Mar	MoV
Mode	Mod>

±

Mar	NegW
—	Not-Do>

±

Mar	CRV
CR	{-N}>

±

Mar	State
State	-ing>

+/−

Mar	<doV>
Empty	>Not-Do

\+

Nuc	ActvV
Pred	Ts>

The syntagmemes which occur in this structure are in (78).

(78)

a. ModalV = +

Nuc	ModalRt
Mode	

+/−

Mar	TsSuf
Tm	>Ts

b. CRV = +

Nuc	CRCVRt
CR	—

+/−

Mar	TsSuf
Tm	>Ts
	>Mod

c. StateV = +

Nuc	StateVRt	+/−	Mar	<-N> TsSuf
State	—		Tm/	>Ts
			Asp	>Mod
				>{-N}

d. ActvV = +

Nuc	VRt	+/−	Mar	<-ing> <-N> TsSuf
Pred	(>BT		Tm/	>Ts
	>T		Asp	>Mod
	>BI			>{-N}
	>I			>-ing
	>BEq			
	>Eq)			

e. doV = +

Nuc	doVRt	+/−	Mar	TsSuf
Empty	—		Tm	>Ts

The nucleus verb root possesses cohesion features reflecting the verb type, e.g., bi-transitive, transitive, bi-intransitive, intransitive, etc.

The key to this analysis is the cohesion component of the generated tagmemes. One also needs to know the conventions. The symbol ± means 'optional element'; +/− means 'obligatory if something else is present and obligatorily absent otherwise'. In terms of cohesion, the presence of Mod suppresses the margin of the next verbal tagmeme of VP. The presence of Not-Do indicates that *not* follows the first verbal margin of VP or, if there is no verbal margin, then *do* precedes *not*. {-N} is required in the margin of the first verbal tagmeme following the Current Relevance Verb. The *-ing* occurs as margin of the first verbal tagmeme following the State Verb. Tense (TsSuf) occurs in the margin of the first verbal tagmeme of the VP. The constituent tree representing the VP in the sentence *Little Miss Muffet must have sat on the tuffet* would then be as seen in (79).

(79)

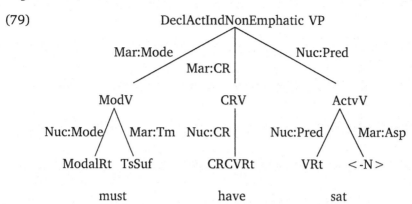

Two things are immediately noticeable from this treatment. The syntagmemes for the main verb root will have a margin that can be the target for cohesion with EVERY POSSIBLE element that could occur to its left, i.e., modal, CR, State, or tense. For English, only four such things can show up there. In other languages, this number could be very, very large, cf. (89) and the repetition in the Mar slot. Whenever each occurrence of a grammatical phenomenon is LISTED separately, as in this case, one can suspect that a generalization is not being captured. Here, since there are no movement rules in *Grammatical Analysis*, each possibility must be prepared for in advance. This is a serious complication.

The second difficulty is the treatment of negation. In Pike and Pike (1974), the generalization regarding the position of negation in English is captured by a PLACEMENT RULE which moves *not* to the appropriate position. But in *Grammatical Analysis*, one finds each different position of Neg treated as a separate ALLOCONSTRUCTION. These alloconstructions are alternatives, one for each position of Neg, after *have*, after *be*, after a modal verb, or after *do*, if no other auxiliary is present. The Pikes point out that this account results in a certain degree of complexity.

> The occurrence of *do* can be treated as an insertion occurrence cohesion feature; it is required if the negative occurs and no verbal margin occurs.

> The varying distribution of the negative tagmeme is treated as leading to variants or alloconstructions of the verb phrase, and is best treated by *an appended rule*. [Our emphasis] (1982:207)

3.6 New developments

Before leaving this discussion of tagmemics, we need to cover two further topics: Pikes' notion of the referential hierarchy, and some further details of Longacre's specific version of tagmemics, especially as they are related to discourse.

3.6.1 Pikes' referential hierarchy. The notion of the referential hierarchy is a development carried out jointly by Ken Pike and Evelyn Pike, found most clearly presented in Pike and Pike (1982:321–58), Pike and Pike (1983:35–73), and Pike (1982:97–105). We present here only a very brief summary of this proposal.

We have described the basic orientation of the tagmemic approach, pointing out the emphasis within the theory on HIERARCHY, and in particular the hierarchical structure of grammar. To describe the grammatical structure of a text does not exhaust its nonphonological structure, however. Texts typically are presented within a cultural framework of presuppositions, including such matters as: types of purposive behavior and their specific manifestations, cause-and-effect relations among events, the nature of the world and its inhabitants, moral values and prohibitions, etc. Further, each individual in the culture has what is possibly a unique specific version of such cultural norms, colored by individual experience; because texts are commonly composed by individuals, it is expected that the specific cultural framework being referenced is that of the individual story-teller, which may depart from more widely held cultural norms in significant ways.

It is to deal with matters such as these, and to provide a context within which the pragmatics of the speech event can be described, that the referential hierarchy has been proposed. In a real sense, it is an attempt to find correspondence between the text and the real world as interpreted by the culture. Given the simple fact that events in the real world may be simultaneous, while the linguistic recounting of events is necessarily sequential because of the nature of language, it is clear that there is not a one-to-one mapping between the grammatical and referential hierarchies, and thus both are needed.

Events which take place in the real world involve both actions of various sorts, and individuals who perform those actions. These actions and individuals, then, form the primary points of contact in referential structure. Further, events rarely take place singly in isolation; most typically they occur as part of a series of events intended to carry out a purpose. Such a purposive series of events is defined in the theory as a VECTOR, and it is the configuration of vectors which makes up the events portrayed in referential structure. Many (possibly all) of these vectors are universal in the sense that they characterize human behavior; they deal with such matters as fulfilling basic needs and establishing and maintaining relationships (see the COYOTE FOOD-GETTING VECTOR and the DECEIT VECTOR, respectively, discussed below). On the other hand, however, the details of a vector as actualized in a particular culture (and indeed, in a particular instantiation of the cultural vector in a given text) can be expected to show a great deal of variation.

Similarly, the individuals who participate in the events have all the characteristics of human beings (and other creatures, in the case of folktales) everywhere. But they have also culturally defined social roles, they have a philosophical orientation as participants in the culture represented in the text, and they have expectations regarding their own actions and those of other participants, also culturally defined. A text deals commonly with specific individuals, who become interesting because of the way they depart from or, conversely, fulfill powerfully cultural stereotypes. The discussion of the participants in the text below provides illustration.

To illustrate this notion of the referential hierarchy, we present an outline of a text discussed in Pike and Pike (1982). This text is from the Mixtec language (the Mixtec data is omitted here), for which the following translation is provided, with each sentence numbered for ease of reference in the discussion.

(80)   (1) A story about a rabbit and a coyote and the moon. (2) A rabbit was standing at the edge of the water. (3) Just then a coyote arrived. (4) "What are you doing, Rabbit?" said the animal. (5) "I'm one who is just here, Uncle," said the rabbit to the coyote. (6) "Here I am stooping over looking into the water. (7) I am looking at a cheese. (8) Don't you want to go get that cheese which is in the water here? (9) Do us a favor, go in and get the cheese from there." (10) And the coyote said, "I'll go, in that case." (11) The coyote jumped vigorously. (12) The animal entered the water that he might go get the cheese. (13) And what did the coyote know of the fact that it was the moon itself! (14) And the rabbit saw at once that the animal entered the water. (15) ('Plop' is the way the water went.) (16) And the rabbit hit (the trail), hurrying as he went. (17) Thereupon the coyote came up (to the surface). (18) The animal saw that the rabbit no longer stood there (since the rabbit had gone off running). (19) The coyote wanted revenge on the rabbit who had tricked him. (20)

However, had the rabbit stood there longer, the coyote would have eaten him. (21) The story of the animals has ended. (1982:326–33)

This text can be understood in its referential structure in relation to five vectors. Although such vectors are perhaps universal in their nature, they have a characteristic Mixtec interpretation and, in this particular text, a specific manifestation. In the following discussion we abbreviate the details of analysis of Pike and Pike and add a few comments of our own.

Reference to the COYOTE FOOD-GETTING VECTOR is found scattered throughout the text: he arrives at the scene with food in mind (3); the greeting ritual is carried out in accordance with Mixtec expectations, but in addition it is an attempt to put the rabbit off guard (4–6); the rabbit appeals to the coyote's search for food by suggesting an alternate target (7–9); the coyote jumps after the reflection of the moon in an attempt to get food (11–12, 14–15, 17); as a result the rabbit gets away (17–18, 20). This particular vector is the main focus of the text and gives it coherence and intelligibility by providing an explanation for why the particular events are listed and presented as they are.

The second major vector is the DECEIT VECTOR. The rabbit notices that the water reflects the moon (6–7); the rabbit responds to the coyote's greeting politely, in an attempt to set him at ease (5–9); the rabbit diverts the coyote from himself as a food source to the cheese—actually, the reflected moon (7–9); the coyote allows himself to be deceived (10); the coyote realizes he has been deceived, but too late to still seize the rabbit (18–19). This vector provides interest to the story which it would not have if it were simply recounted that the coyote ate the rabbit. While deceit is undoubtedly a fact of life in every culture, it takes on a characteristically Mixtec flavor in this account by highlighting the cultural themes of the wiliness of the rabbit and the relatively low mental capability of the coyote and his constant search for food (we return to these themes below).

There is a COMPLAINT VECTOR in the text as well. The coyote surfaces after diving into the water (17), and he finds that the rabbit is no longer there (18). This constitutes the cause for his wanting to get even with the rabbit as presented in (19).

Finally, there is a PHYSICAL VECTOR (the coyote surfaces because of the need for air (17)), and an unspecified vector to explain the presence of the rabbit at the water (3). It is suggested that he was either out looking for food himself (which would make it an instance of the RABBIT

FOOD-GETTING VECTOR), or out just for exercise (which would make it the
RABBIT EXERCISE VECTOR).

This set of vectors, then, provides the information:

(a) a rationale for the presence of the specific events in the text
(b) a rationale for the actions of the participants in the text
(c) a matrix of coherence to unify the text into a single whole

Further, this referential information, by focusing on the relation of
the events to one another, provides an accounting of the events and
their interrelationships which is not possible through the grammatical
hierarchy alone. The fact that the vectors are not presented linearly in
grammatical sequence (see details of their manifestation in the text as
summarized above) provides additional evidence that the two hierarchies are both needed.

Note further that the rabbit and the coyote are not arbitrarily chosen
as characters for this particular story. It is a fact of Mixtec folklore that
the rabbit is considered to be a wily individual, able to survive in spite
of his small size through the use of his wits. The coyote, by contrast, is
an animal much to be feared for fierceness and enormous appetite, but,
characteristically, the coyote is seen to be rather slow-witted, making
him an easy mark for the rabbit.

The storyteller undoubtedly had a purpose in recounting this tale,
and such a purpose provides us with an extratextual vector which helps
also in interpreting the text correctly. Unfortunately, the purpose of the
narrator in this particular case is not given to us, so our comments here
are subject to modification. Most likely the intent is simply entertain-
ment, but highlighting the rabbit's cleverness as an example to be emu-
lated, especially in contrast to the mere large physical size of the coyote
(such physical size being essentially innate and therefore not a characteristic a particular individual can do much to emulate), would not be
unexpected. Thus, the referential structure comes into play in yet another way to aid in understanding the text.

It will be noted that none of these bits of information is strictly semantic nor strictly syntactic. It would be expected that a different text
would use different vectors or provide different details of manifestation
even if the same vectors were used. Further, it would be expected that a
text in a language of a different culture would provide details which reflect the purposive behavior of that culture rather than Mixtec culture.

3.6.2 Longacre's approach. In recent years Robert Longacre (Longacre 1976, 1983, 1985, 1987, 1989, and 1996) has developed a version of tagmemics that is sufficiently distinct from that of Pike to warrant special discussion. In the brief summary that follows, we present only the major areas of his contribution, making no attempt to be exhaustive.

As a summary statement, we point out that Longacre's major contribution is in the area of textlinguistics. First, he has proposed a taxonomy of text types, using four binary features. AGENT ORIENTATION distinguishes between texts which are oriented in relation to specific agents (as in narrative or hortatory discourse types) and those which are not (as in procedural or expository types). CONTINGENT TEMPORAL SUCCESSION distinguishes between those texts in which a chronological succession of events is important (as in narrative and procedural text types) and those in which such chronological succession is not important (as in hortatory and expository types). PROJECTED TIME has to do with whether the events portrayed in the text have or have not taken place at the time of the telling; [−Projected Time] texts include common narratives and procedural accounts, while [+Projected Time] texts include prophecy and instructions on accomplishing a task. Finally, the feature TENSION is proposed to distinguish texts which manifest conflict as a major theme from those which do not, thus serving to distinguish subtypes among the various major text types defined by the three major features. Note the following chart:

(81)

	+Ag-Orientation	−Ag-Orientation	
	NARRATIVE	PROCEDURAL	
+contingent succession	Prophecy	How-to-do-it	+projected time
	Story	How-it-was-done	−projected time
	BEHAVIORAL	EXPOSITORY	
−contingent succession	Hortatory	Budget Proposal	+projected time
	promissory	Futuristic Essay	
	Eulogy	Scientific Paper	−projected time

Such a typology provides not only a framework within which text structure can be investigated, but also information as to how the investigation might best proceed, because different text types manifest different structural patterns in a given language.

For example, a second major theme of Longacre's work in textlinguistics (though not unique to his work) is the contrast in narrative discourse between events and nonevents in narrative discourse, and the establishment of the notion of an EVENT LINE (e.g., 1983:14ff). A significant modification advanced by Longacre, however, is that languages have more than just the event and nonevent distinction; in fact there is a hierarchy of events definable in terms of the degree that they are essential to the text. In Longacre 1987, he suggests a universal hierarchy as follows:

1 Storyline itself ("the sequence of sequential, punctiliar, and (at least partially) causally connected actions and events which are represented in the narrative" 1987:51)

 2 Backgrounded actions and events (preparatory or resulting from storyline)

  3 Backgrounded activities (contrasting with storyline events by being overlapping rather than sequential, durative rather than punctiliar)

   4 Setting (temporal and locative, introduction of participants)

    5 Irrealis (modals, conditionals, negatives—all describe a world other than that portrayed on the storyline)

     6 Author intrusions (performatives, evaluation, morals)

      7 Cohesive clauses (adverbial, referring back to previous parts of the storyline)

These different 'bands' of events thus provide a framework (a SPECTRUM OF DYNAMISM) for characterizing the degree to which a given event has a role in moving the story along. If an event is crucial to the story, it is on the storyline; otherwise, it can be characterized as representing noncrucial, nonevent-line information as portrayed in bands 2–7. A listing of the events on the storyline provide an abstract which corresponds to the MACROSTRUCTURE of the text (the term is from van Dijk).

Of particular interest in Longacre's work is his proposal that different languages utilize different syntactic devices to identify the classification of events along one of the bands proposed above. Such facts as the distribution of specific tenses and aspects, the occurrence of particles and conjunctions of specific types, verb classes, even word order—all of these can be used by language for providing such information.

For example, Longacre provides the following analysis of a Mark Twain text in English:

> In a minute a third slave was struggling in the air. It was dreadful, I turned away my head for a moment, and when I turned back I missed the king! They were blindfolding him! I was paralyzed; I couldn't move, I was choking, my tongue was petrified. They finished blindfolding him, they led him under the rope. I couldn't shake off that clinging impotence. But when I saw them put the noose around his neck, then everything let go in me and I made a spring to the rescue—and as I made it I shot one more glance abroad—by George! here they came, a-tilting!—five hundred mailed and belted knights on bicycles! (1981:338)

In this text the following sorts of patterns occur:

> past tense forms in independent clauses—'I turned away my head for a moment'

> past tense forms in dependent clause—'when I turned back'

> past progressive forms—'In a minute a third slave was struggling in the air'

> past tense forms in verbs whose adverbial qualifiers indicate that they are depictive rather than dynamic—'here they came, a-tilting'

> statives with or without modals—'I was paralyzed'

Of these, only the first marks events actually on the eventline, with the others on different, less essential bands. To produce or interpret a text properly involves an understanding of the way such distinctions are used to communicate various levels of information within a text.

Or note the spectrum proposed for Biblical Hebrew in (82).

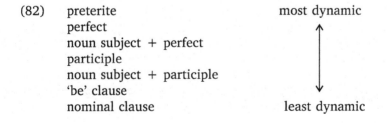

(82)   preterite   most dynamic
        perfect
        noun subject + perfect
        participle
        noun subject + participle
        'be' clause
        nominal clause   least dynamic

Note that in Biblical Hebrew the occurrence of a noun with a given aspect is not as salient as the occurrence of the same aspect without the noun, the former construction indicating that the action being described is limited to that participant alone, a restriction not valid for the latter construction.

Longacre (1989) demonstrates that data from Halbi (an Indo-European language of India), Northern Totonac (a language from Mexico), Aguacatec (a Mayan language of Guatemala), Kickapoo (an Algonquian language), and Gujarati (an Indo-Iranian language of India) all show similar patterns. Thus, knowledge that a given text is of a narrative type provides clues as to the sorts of structures to anticipate in its analysis.

Moreover, languages typically have means of PROMOTING or DEMOTING events from one band to another along the hierarchy. For example, commonly in English adverbial *when*-clauses are preposed and in Band 7; but when postposed they appear to be promoted to Band 1 (and thus on the main eventline). Compare the two sentences: *when he saw the wolf coming, the little pig was up in the tree* versus *the little pig was up in the tree when he saw the wolf coming.* In the former case, the adverbial clause recapitulates an event (the wolf's coming) stated earlier; in the latter case the adverbial clause encodes a situation in which the same event is on the eventline, even though it is in a subordinate clause (and thus has been promoted to Band 1). Similarly, relative clauses, though containing predications, are demoted off the rank scheme entirely, serving simply as NP modification. Clearly such patterns of expression have to do with the encoding of the series of events and concomitant information and thus are sensitive to the textual structure as a whole.

As a final point of illustration in Longacre's work in textlinguistics, we draw attention to the notion of PROFILE. It is clear that most texts do not have uniform structure, even when only events on the event-line are considered. Rather, there are differences in terms of the speed with which events are recounted, the amount of background information which is included with regard to such events, the degree of tension involved, and other matters of development. The notion of peak provides a reference point for describing the development profile which results.

Note two further crucial terms: the CLIMAX of a narrative is defined as the point of maximum tension, and the DENOUEMENT as the crucial event which makes resolution possible (we discuss these two terms further below) either climax or denouement or both may manifest the formal properties highlighting characteristics at surface peak. Then it can be demonstrated that commonly in narrative there are two peaks: the ACTION PEAK corresponds to the climax or denouement; the DIDACTIC PEAK corresponds to that point in the text where the purpose of its recounting is portrayed. In the Biblical flood narrative, for example, the action peak is the point in the text in which the flood waters crest, while the didactic peak is that point at which God makes a covenant with Noah and the others never to send another flood (Longacre 1985). The profile of a text, then, is a description of the degree of tension portrayed within it. The peak is the point of highest tension, with mounting tension toward the peak and loosening tension away from it.

The notion of PEAK is a very important one, not only from the point of view of the creator of the text, but from the point of view of the analyst as well. We mentioned several devices by means of which mainline events are commonly distinguished from other levels of information in a narrative text. What is of major interest regarding peak is the fact that at this point in the narrative the rules which were found to hold elsewhere in the text now are seen to be suspended. Among the patterns found at peak are the following: the TENSE AND ASPECT pattern characteristic of mainline events elsewhere now is no longer found; PARTICLES which served to mark mainline events are missing; patterns of PARTICIPANT REFERENCE may be violated; there are MORE PARTICIPANTS present on the scene than elsewhere in the text; PARAGRAPH AND SENTENCE LENGTH may be longer or shorter than usual; DIALOGUE may suddenly become more or less frequent. In a word, patterns which are characteristic of mainline structure elsewhere in the text are commonly radically disrupted at peak. Such rhetorical devices serve to identify formally the point of climax which is indicated also semantically in the text, with the differences from nonpeak text marking the peak as (in Longacre's words) "a zone of turbulence" (1983:25).

A major contribution of Longacre which is not limited to textlinguistics is his departure from classical tagmemics in his proposal of a distinction between surface structure and deep structure (also termed notional structure). A SURFACE STRUCTURE description is one in which the hierarchical organization of formal syntactic structures is emphasized; there is little difference between Longacre and Pike on this point. Thus there are levels of syntactic structure such as morpheme, stem, word, phrase, clause, sentence, paragraph, discourse. Longacre proposes a THEORY OF EXPONENCE (1983.279ff) in which the theoretically possible relations holding between various levels of the hierarchy are accounted for (see also §3.3). In particular focus is the typical hierarchical structure of units at one level being composed of units of the next lower level, but with various patterns of recursion and various degrees of embedding and level-skipping (the occurrence of units from more than one level lower in the hierarchy) explicitly accounted for. The result is a taxonomy of hierarchical relationships. The form-meaning composite definitional of the tagmeme is prominent throughout the surface structure hierarchy.

More important as a theoretical innovation is Longacre's proposal of NOTIONAL STRUCTURE as a second level of structure (1983:305ff). Like surface structure, notional structure also is hierarchically organized. At the lowest level is DERIVATION, which commonly corresponds with the stem surface structure level (new members of a class are derived from members of the same or another class, commonly by affixation). Corresponding to notional INFLECTION is surface structure word, and corresponding to notional structure CONCRETION is surface structure phrase.

It is the higher hierarchical levels which are most illuminating as to the usefulness of this proposal. Notional structure PREDICATION is a composite of a PREDICATE and the ARGUMENTS involved in it (Longacre provides a formalism of predicate calculus to capture generalizations here); it is commonly mapped onto a surface structure clause. Combinations of notional PROPOSITIONS (representable in statement calculus) are commonly expressed as surface structure sentence. The surface structure paragraph level is the common means of encoding notional structure REPARTEE, and notional PLOT is commonly encoded in a discourse (we return to this topic below).

Although these mappings are typical, others are possible, and it is this very departure from the more routine sort of mappings which is most communicatively effective (e.g., the encoding of a predication as a phrase through a process of nominalization to downplay its significance in the text as a whole).

Longacre is careful to point out that this distinction between notional structure and surface structure is not a distinction clearly between form and meaning, agreeing with the major tenet of tagmemics that every unit is a form-meaning composite. Indeed, while surface structure is primarily concerned with form, form itself has meaning (as seen in the differing patterns of focus in the two encodings of the same notional predications in *Seymour sliced the salami with a knife* and *Seymour used a knife to slice the salami*). Similarly, although notional structure is primarily concerned with meaning, it is not without its formal patterns (as when a pattern such as repeated but negated predicates as in *John went home, he didn't stay at the party* can be proposed as characterizing notional possibilities which can be formalized through the use of logical operators).

It is in its application to text structure that the distinction between notional structure and surface structure would appear perhaps to have its most usefulness. For the most part, surface structure deals with such matters as sentence and paragraph structure and how they are used to communicate such information as setting and episodes (which may be crucially classified as major and minor). Sentences can be seen as either dominant or ancillary (related to their rank according to Bands, as described above), and the relations among sentences within one paragraph can be defined along a finite number of parameters, e.g., reason-result, cause-effect, thesis-antithesis, and other such posited relations, as well as notions of sequentiality and simultaneity. Often such relations are marked syntactically in a specific way, but not always. Except for the notion of peak as the crucial point of the text, this material is fairly well known and will not be elaborated on further in this summary.

Notional structure, on the other hand, warrants some detailed discussion. Essentially, at the highest hierarchical level it corresponds to what is more commonly referred to as PLOT. It has as common characteristics the categories of EXPOSITION, which is commonly manifested in surface structure as information relevant to spatial and temporal setting, and introduction of participants. The INCITING MOMENT is that point in the narrative in which the conflict of the plot is introduced and begins to be developed, usually manifested in surface structure as a series of episodes (commonly paragraphs or larger units). The CLIMAX is the crucial point in the plot which draws everything to its highest point of tension. The term DENOUEMENT is used to refer to postclimax events which serve to resolve the tension and begin to effect a resolution. As mentioned above, either climax or denouement or both may be marked as surface peak. There may also be a FINAL SUSPENSE rhetorical section in which the author wraps up details which are relevant to the text but not crucial to the climax itself, commonly appearing in surface structure as a further sequence of episodes. Finally, the CONCLUSION wraps up final details, portraying in surface structure whatever information is still needed for final resolution, possibly with an explicit moral associated with it. The entire text may be sandwiched between an APERTURE (e.g., *Once upon a time...*) and a FINIS (e.g., *And so they lived happily ever after...*), but these are formulaic patterns and contribute little or nothing to the interpretation of the text and thus are considered to be surface structure strings which have no correlates in notional structure.

It can be seen that discourse study as practiced by Longacre shows considerable similarity to more well-known literary studies. What is of particular interest here, however, is the attempt to provide a systematic theory of analyzing such structures from a linguistic point of view, proposed as applicable universally to language. Let us, in conclusion, try to gather the thread of discussion in this chapter into a table of characteristics of the tagmemic model.

3.7 Tagmemic theorizing

In summary, we can say that the tagmemic research tradition is oriented on the particular facts of a particular language rather than language universals, on language descriptions not on grammars, and on the use of language by real speakers and hearers. For purposes of comparison, we now list some further properties of the *Grammatical Analysis* model.

Summary of the Tagmemic Model (*Grammatical Analysis* 1982)

1. Levels: there are multiple levels that correspond to the size of the structural piece, e.g., discourse, paragraph, sentence, morpheme, etc. Because no underlying structure is posited, the word 'level' is used in a manner unlike that in the *Aspects* model.
2. Primitive symbols: There is a much richer inventory of symbols in the tagmemic approach. In the nonterminal vocabulary, there would be perhaps three times as many as in the *Aspects* model, because for each class symbol there would be symbols for the corresponding role and slot fillers. The actual number of these, however, may be less; many are simply nucleus and margin. Another enriching factor is the large number of subcategories for class, e.g., Active Indicative NonEmphatic Positive VP.
3. Rules produce a constituent order, a constituent structure, a constituent distribution, and categories (class).
4. Rules make direct reference to grammatical relations such as subject, direct object, and many other less easily described relational categories. There are also explicit symbols for function within each tagmeme, i.e., which is central (nucleus), which periphery (margin).
5. Context sensitivity is provided by the cohesion features of each tagmeme. Although the claim is that everything must be evaluated in context, many items are listed without any symbol written in this space. Thus, the grammar model is basically context-free.
6. Multiple generative components are present. This is true of the three hierarchies and perhaps also of different levels in a single hierarchy.
7. Sentences are grammatically unrelated. Since there is nothing like a transformation present, one must rely on

the semantics to establish similarities. Therefore, there is no real place for capturing STRUCTURAL similarities between statements and their corresponding questions, for example. It may also be difficult to use the semantics to guarantee that just the related sentences are so marked. For example, the sentence *someone broke the window* should be related by the passive to the sentence *the window was broken* and should not be related by the passive to *the window broke*. But, perhaps the role for *the window* in the last sentence is scope and not undergoer.

8. Components are separated (grammatical, phonological, and referential) but there is no sequencing in a derivation.

4

Stratificational Linguistics

4.1 Introduction

The theory of stratificational linguistics is most closely associated
with the name of Sydney Lamb. Therefore, the presentation in this chapter comes mostly from sources that he has authored. We have also considered works by John Algeo, Ilah Fleming, David Lockwood, Peter
Reich, and William Sullivan.

4.2 General ontology, methodology, and world view

The most prominent feature of stratificational linguistics, which
Lamb has recently renamed COGNITIVE LINGUISTICS, is its reliance on
STRATA. Linguistic structure is conceived of as being organized into a
number of layers. Each stratal layer has its own rules of syntax called its
TACTICS and each layer is related to others through relationships known
as REALIZATIONS. Since there are different layers or subparts, the
stratificational model is not made up of only one kind of unit combined
in manifold ways to yield a complex.

The emphasis on relationships reflects another central notion of
stratificational analysis; a language is a system relating meaning and
sound. Much of the general ontology of the proposals made by linguists
in this tradition rests on emphasizing this RELATIONSHIP idea at the expense of PROPERTIES of things. For example, Lamb writes:

> A language may be regarded as a system of relationships. As
> such, it is not directly observable. The linguist can only ob-
> serve the manifestations of linguistic structure, i.e., samples

of speech and/or writing, and the situations in which they occur. Yet, SG strives to generate a specific text in a specific situation. (1966:3)

Therefore, we cannot observe something like subject or noun phrase directly any more than we can point to the meaning of *and*. It signifies a relationship between people, places, things, etc., and nothing in the world itself.

An important feature is that there are a number of different kinds of "organization structures which form a connected network when woven together to encode a communication act" (Fleming 1988:2).

Another striking thing about stratificational linguistic theorizing is the mention at the most general level of the neurology and cognition of language. As Sullivan says:

The immediate aim of SG is to account for the production and deciphering of spoken or written texts of arbitrary length. This includes what is produced, how it may be produced, what is understood, and how it may be understood, including pragmatic and sociocultural purposes of the discourse. If possible, the model used should also give insight into language acquisition and language change. In any case, the model used must be internally consistent in a logical sense and must not contradict anything we know about the structure and operation of the brain. Note that this is a requirement, not a claim that SG is a neurological theory of language.

The long-term aim of SG is to account for language and language use as a portion of general cognitive-neurological functions. This includes logical and nonlogical thought, slips of the tongue, troublesome ellipses of all kinds, communicative grunts, etc. This suggests to me that linguistics will ultimately have to develop a neurological theory of language. (1980:301–02)

4.2.1 The world view. For Lamb, a language is a system of relationships and as such represents a second-order entity; "It is not directly observable" (1966:3). In this statement alone, one can see a rejection of the positivistic attitude that knowledge must be directly observable. Lamb, moreover, sees the goal of linguistic description to be the characterization of these relationships that underlie the linguistic data. In words such as 'underlie' one finds a reliance on principles not overt in the data. Analysis itself is nothing more than simplification and generalization.

(83)   abc + abd + abe + abf + abg
          is equal to
       ab(c + d + e + f + g)

Lamb states (1966:3) that in the algebraic expression in (83) the latter expression is simpler and contains a generalization, because *ab* occurs only once in the latter expression but five times in the former. In writing *cranberry* and *blueberry* the linguist is doing nothing more.

(84)   blue
               } berry
        cran

Stratificationalists make it quite clear that they are not interested in describing some platonic ideal, the essence of reality only imperfectly realized in the real world. Yet, on the other hand, they also wish to describe something free of extralinguistic disturbances (though deciding what is extralinguistic may be difficult). Lockwood (1972:10) speaks of IDEAL PERFORMANCE, which is to contain competence "...plus conventions for its activation." Thus, they would strive to study not only the knowledge of a speaker but also all linguistically significant factors involved in putting this knowledge to use. There should be a direct relationship between competence and performance. And, moreover, as Lamb recently described it, the position of SG is to describe a TYPICAL SPEAKER-HEARER in a diverse speech community.

Another point that receives much emphasis is the bidirectionality of linguistic processes, which are described as ENCODING and DECODING. As Lockwood describes it:

> Communication through the medium of spoken language is concerned with the conveying of concepts by means of vocal noises. Let us attempt to outline a simple view of what goes on when two individuals communicate using language. One participant in the communication process, let us label him A, goes from concepts inside his brain to muscle movements leading to the articulation of vocal sounds. A second participant, B, receives these vocal noises as they have been transmitted through the air. He perceives them by means of his auditory mechanism, which ultimately leads to a stimulation of his conceptual apparatus. (1972:1)

In this view, language is a kind of code, and communicating is the process of encoding concepts and its inverse decoding. The notion is quite familiar and so intuitive that the question may be asked whether there is any conceivable alternative to it. We note that two processes do seem to be involved in that learners of a new language will at some stage be able to comprehend better than they are able to produce the new language.

As appealing as the idea 'language is a code' may be, it is not the only model conceivable. Indeed, the dominant paradigm of speech perception, the motor theory of speech, rests on quite different assumptions. Vastly oversimplifying, the motor theory claims that speech perception involves some kind of matching of internal signal and the incoming signal. Humans do not obviously comprehend or analyze by analysis. In fact, we may use analysis by synthesis. In light of the motor theory, the need for bidirectionality in one's linguistic paradigm becomes less acute.

Perhaps the item receiving the most stress in stratificational theorizing is the need for description of cognitive processes in real time. In fact, Lamb (1989), Sullivan (1980), Lockwood (1972, 1973), and especially Reich (1973a) employ the research strategy of REDUCTIONISM. In its crudest form, the reductionist philosophy states that "mind equals brain," that behavior, no matter how complex, is reducible to the biology of brain states. Therefore, linguistic models should resemble the models of neural circuitry. Thus, Reich says:

> Property (1) The brain consists of a network of interconnected neurons which communicate with each other by means of discrete impulses. Therefore,

> Requirement (1) Linguistic behavior shall be modeled by building networks out of a few types of formally defined elements.

> Requirement (2) These elements shall communicate with each other by means of a few different types of signals...

> Requirement (3) Permanent information is not stored within the logical elements themselves, but only indirectly through their connectivity... (1973a:87)

He goes on to plead for PARALLEL PROCESSING, simultaneous processing of more than one signal, for ASYNCHRONOUS PROCESSING, stating things do not need to be in step, that there be limits on the longest sequence of logical operations performable (set at 200 logical operations per syllable). He also advances the idea (something perhaps analogous to the Katz-Postal hypothesis) that language behavior below the semantic level is only network activation and not network modification (e.g., change of information).

4.2.2 Ontological primitives. As has in part already been stated, stratificational linguists assume that the language system consists of a number of different strata. The number of strata used by any one investigator has varied over the course of development of the theory from three to six. Algeo (1973:6) says of this variation, that the major investigators all use at least three: the SEMOLOGICAL, the GRAMMATICAL, and the PHONOLOGICAL. Moreover, on each stratum there will be a syntax, the so-called TACTICS, and between strata, connections called REALIZATIONS. These will be described in greater detail below. Since language is basically a system of relations, the connections (relationships) make up one of the most important primitives. According to Lamb (1966:8–9), three aspects of connections in the network of language need to be distinguished. Within the network connections there are LINES and NODES. These nodes can be thought of as the MANNER of connection between endpoints and not as entities themselves. For this reason, Lamb can claim that there are no first-order units, only second-order relations. Irrespective of their ontological status, the nodes occur with dichotomies in three dimensions: (a) ORDERING (ordered or unordered); (b) DIRECTION (up or down); (c) LOGIC (possessing OR or AND logic). We now discuss these primitives and their status in a formal grammar of the type defined in chapter one.

The nodes used in Lamb's version of stratificational linguistics have properties of components of electrical circuits, in particular those of switches or gates. Moreover, it is often useful to imagine derivations or proofs in the sense of chapter one as the flow of current in such systems of ordered and unordered, upward and downward, and AND and OR gates. To illustrate the traits of AND and OR gates, we will consider the accompanying diagrams, known in elementary logic as truth tables.

(85)   Truth tables for AND and OR

    a. Truth table for & (AND)

	q	
p & q	T	F
T	T	F
p		
F	F	F

    b. Truth table for V (OR)

	q	
p V q	T	F
T	T	T
p		
F	T	F

(Where T stands for 'true' and F for 'false'.)

These tables show that the value of p & q is true if and only if both p is true and q is true. Or, as a switch, current will flow from an AND gate only if both incoming legs have current simultaneously as in (86).

(86)   AND switch

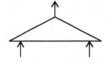

In the case of the symbol V (OR), p V q is true if and only if either p is true or q is true or both. As a switch, current will flow only if there is current in one of the incoming legs, or both:

(87) OR switch

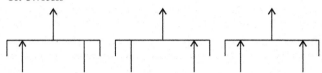

In order to indicate whether the gate is upward or downward, the following convention is used:

(88) a.   Upward AND

      b.   Downward AND

      c.   Upward OR

      d.   Downward OR

The gates can be thought of as either merging or separating a signal. If an upward AND has current flow from the top in both wires, then the current flow will flow through to the other side; if from the bottom, then current will flow out both wires at the top.

(89) Upward AND

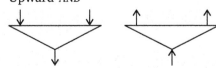

If a downward OR has current flow from the top, then there will be current flow in either one (but not both) of the downward wires; if from one of the wires from the bottom, then current will flow out the top.

Ordering is indicated schematically by separating the wires at a node and unordering by joining the wires at the node. All the above examples are ordered. The ordering of an AND gate is a sequential relationship, while ordering of an OR gate means that there is a logical relationship of priority.

(90)   Ordered OR

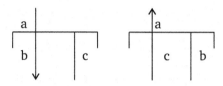

For example, an unordered downward AND will produce an impulse in both wires on the downside simultaneously, an ordered downward AND produces an impulse in the left wire before it produces an impulse in the right wire. The downward ordered OR has the interpretation seen in the left-hand diagram in (90): take c if possible, if not, then b is the default.

Although the relationships are thus thought to be small in number, they still can be combined in a large number of ways to produce a complex network. There are apparently a limited number of patterns in combinations: SIGN PATTERNS, TACTIC PATTERNS, ALTERNATION PATTERNS, and KNOT PATTERNS. In the first of these, the sign pattern, AND nodes are over OR nodes. Of these, the ANDs may be ordered or unordered depending upon whether one is on the lexicological, morphological, or phonological stratum. On the lexicological stratum, for example, *understand* and *undergo* will be realized through ordered ANDs, which sequence the *under* temporally before the *stand* and before the *go*; these are then gathered into upward ORs, which realize the parts. The diagrams in (91) and (92) are from Lamb 1966:13.

(91)

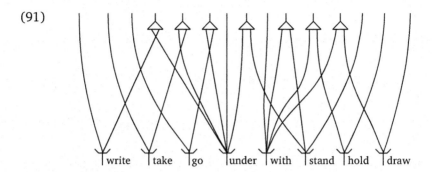

write   take   go   under   with   stand   hold   draw

On the morphological stratum, *den, Ed, Ned, end,* etc. are ordered sequences under AND, which are gathered together as /d/, /e/, and /n/ with upward ORs.

(92)

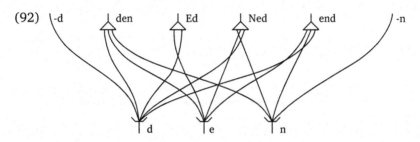

On the phonological stratum, phonemes are realized as nonsequential combinations of features under unordered ANDs, which are gathered by ORs.

(93)   Patterns of a stratum from Lamb (1966:16)

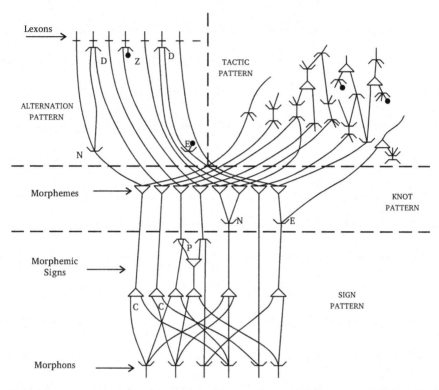

The tactic pattern of a language is typically made up of downward
ANDs and upward unordered ORs. The upward ORs correspond to situations in which units have two or more alternative functions, the
syntagmatic and paradigmatic functions of a sign. For example, a tactic
pattern would presumably restrict English [h] to syllable initial positions and [ŋ] to syllable final positions. The tactic pattern would also
appear in connection with the various patterns in the English verb
phrase, portraying the strict subcategorization.

The alternation pattern is that pattern that connects stratal levels.
Typically, it is bounded by downward ORs above and upward ORs on the
bottom. Also, the alternation pattern has many connections without
nodes in cases where no alternation occurs.

The knot pattern links (thus the name) the sign pattern with the alternation pattern via the tactic pattern. Formally, it is a set of upward
ANDs with occasional upward ORs below them.

An entire stratal level may thus be divided into these four pattern types. Just as the name entails, the tactics of the stratum is seen in the tactic pattern, whereas the realization of the stratum is manifested in the sign, alternation, and knot patterns. Thus, there is a division into types of connections that dovetail with special subfunctions of a stratum (Lamb 1966:12–18).

It is sometimes advantageous to use an algebraic formalism instead of the network formalism. Lamb (1966:9) employs the notation given in (94).

(94) a. unordered downward AND   a / b·c

b. unordered downward OR   d / e,f

c. unordered upward AND   g·h / i

d. unordered upward OR   j,k / l

e. ordered downward AND   m / n o

f. ordered downward OR   p / q+r

g. ordered upward AND   s t / u

h. ordered upward OR   v + w / x

Ilah Fleming (1988) uses slightly different viewpoint and notational devices in her version of stratificational analysis. She combines features of tagmemics into the account by specifically using symbols with FUNCTION and FILLER as well as CONSTRUCTION and STRATUM.

Some other significant differences between Lamb and Fleming include the use of string constituents, a division into constituents that allows multiple constituents at the same level. In other words, a sentence *John hit Bill on the head* would not have a structural analysis as in IC analysis (or an *Aspects*-like form with S → NP Aux VP) as in (95), but would rather have a constituent analysis as in (96).

(95)

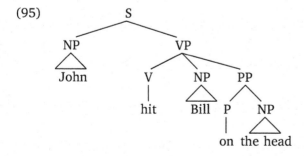

(96)

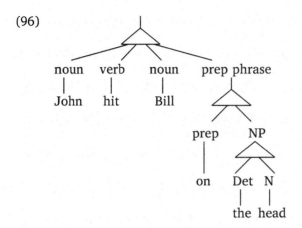

Some of her notational conventions are:

(97)   Relation   Notation   Example

   a.   Construction   Initial letter cap   Event

   b.   Function or position   All caps   AGENT,
                                                                           PRECEDING

   c.   filler   All lowercase   thing

   d.   stratum   Superscript caps ^{S}Event

   e.   relative position   numerals   1.up 2.set

                                                                            or

                            relative sequential PRECEDING:noun
                            position   CENTRAL:verb

   f.   is realized by   /

   g.   realizes   \

   h.   in the environment of   ‖

   i.   is composed of   =

   j.   is filled by   :

   k.   optional   ( )

   l.   or   { }

   m.   and   [ ]

   n.   includes

   o.   a member of   ⊂

   p.   is not   −

To illustrate this usage, consider the semantic to morphological realization relations in (98).

(98) ^{S}TENSE / ^{M}VP.C1

The tense function of the semantic stratum is realized as a VP on the morphological level, and in fact the central or nuclear constituent on that level (designated as C).

For the general class of verbs, past is realized in several alternate ways. One is by the phonological unit -D, suffixed to the verb root (as shown by F ("following"), represented in (99)).

(99) ^{S}past /   {-D ⊂ suffix ‖ verb root -1
              {vowel replacement ⊂ simulfix ‖ verb root -2

Another that the past sememe of the semantic stratum is realized at the morphological stratum, in the marked case, by vowel change in the environment of verb root class 2, e.g., *rang* from *ring*.

Fleming also posits three strata in the language system but relates the top stratum (i.e., the semantic stratum) to the extralinguistic communication situation. The bottom linguistic stratum (or strata, which are the phonemic, graphemic, gestemic or kinesic, depending upon the medium) are related to the extralinguistic physical phenomena (e.g., phonetic, graphs, etc.).

4.2.3 Methodology. There is little in the literature we have consulted on the methods of stratificationalists. It seems they generally proceed from lower to higher levels, and the sentence or clause is not considered the highest level. Instead, they would attempt to encompass texts. Since it is claimed by stratificationalists that there should be some structural similarity between the relational network of language and "brain circuitry," matters cognitive are of paramount importance. Despite these claims, stratificational work is better known for its theorizing than for its experimental work employed in psycho- or neurolinguistics. It has been used, however, for some studies of aphasia and also in contrastive analysis (Fleming 1967 and Gleason 1973). In some cases, data from these sources may be used to argue for certain stances. Introspection, observation, elicitation, and experimentation are all deemed valid sources of data. There has been little interest in language universals in this tradition. Theories are evaluated in this paradigm according to Hjelmslev's empirical principles: INTERNAL

CONSISTENCY, RELATIVE COMPLETENESS, and RELATIVE SIMPLICITY (Sullivan 1980:324). Sullivan goes on to claim that SG, and not the standard *Aspects* model or its successors, has been able to achieve workable simplicity because of the homogeneity of SG vis-à-vis other approaches; it consists of a very small set of axioms and primitives, each of which is comparable to the other. In transformational grammar, he says (p. 325), different kinds of transformations cannot be compared, nor can lexicon, rule ordering conventions, etc. We note that, like many generative accounts, stratificational analyses often remain fragments and do not claim to have dealt with a language exhaustively. Nevertheless, since all aspects of language are to be encompassed and all levels as well, much is still only suggestive and programmatic. But, here, SG does not stand alone.

Lamb's most important pronouncement on methods concerns his concept of effective information. The highest goal of a theory is that it convey maximum effective information from minimum surface information. In defining effective information, Lamb (1966:41) says that two descriptions convey the same effective information if they account for (or predict) the same data. It is only comparison of analyses conveying the same effective information that is a valid exercise for the SIMPLICITY METRIC. We return to this topic in the next section.

4.3 The specific assumptions of Lamb's *Outline* model (1966)

Just as Chomsky's *Aspects* model formed the basis of discussion of much of the work in GTG in the following years, so also does Lamb's *Outline of Stratificational Grammar* (1966) establish a set of reference points upon which subsequent refinements occurred and against which we can highlight other approaches.

4.3.1 Strata. We have already described the various kinds of patterns and the properties of nodes within the general stratificational approach. We now turn to the specifics of the strata according to Lamb's (1966) presentation.

The strata of a language are defined by an assembly of patterns. A stratal system consists of a knot pattern, the alternation pattern and tactic pattern above it, and the sign pattern below it (except for the phonetic). Most languages require six such stratal systems (Lamb 1966:18): (a) phonetic; (b) phonemic; (c) morphemic; (d) lexemic; (e) sememic; and (f) semantic. For each stratum the knot, alternation, and sign pattern is known as the REALIZATION SYSTEM, and the tactic pattern as the TACTIC SYSTEM. For clarity, the stratal name is often attached to the words tactic and realization, e.g., morphotactic, phonotactic, etc. The phonetic and phonemic strata together are the phonology of a language, the lexemic and morphemic strata together are the grammar of a language, and the sememic and semantic strata are together the semology of a language. Moreover, each upward AND in an Xemic pattern is an Xeme, where X stands for phon(e), morph, lex, sem(e) or (for the phonetic) hypophoneme, and (for the semantic) hypersememe. The individual strata possess unique features in each case. Both the elements of a stratum and the connections differ from stratum to stratum. The upward ANDs of a knot pattern are unique for each stratum, since the morphemes are different from the phonemes, etc. Every node in the realization pattern represents a separation of strata; every AND in a sign pattern involves a difference in size of units of neighboring strata; every upward OR represents a neutralization of units distinct on a higher stratum. There are also important ordering differences among strata. Morphemes are ordered (in many languages) while sememes need not be. In the stratal distinctions, Lamb sees a similarity to Chomsky's deep and surface structure.

> The latest formulation of Chomsky's variety of transformational grammar (1965) approaches a stratal distinction in regarding "deep structure" and "surface structure" as different levels; but these levels are only partly separated since they share many features with each other, including phonological features...The process way of thinking is similar to that indulged in by many people who believe that man is descended from the ape. The more advanced view is of course that man and the ape are descended from a common ancestor which was not the same as either. (1966:34–35)

One of the most valuable portions of Lamb (1966:41–59) is that section of the *Outline of Stratificational Grammar* that deals with the evaluation of competing proposals. This section is especially important because of the possibility of competing and alternative analyses. While the details of Lamb's proposal are too technical to discuss in any depth, we will give a synopsis of the core ideas.

The two key concepts in choosing a linguistic description are: (a) the EFFECTIVE INFORMATION of a graph, and (b) the SURFACE INFORMATION. The grammar network to be preferred is the one that maximizes effective information with a minimum of surface information. Such a network will capture the most generalization. In defining effective information, consider graphs that are alternative, i.e., those that have the same top and bottom lines (the points at which a line does not lead upward or downward to another stratum). Two alternatives, however, may not have the same effective nor the same surface information. In example (111) (Lamb 1966:43), the two graphs are alternatives. Moreover, the two graphs have the same effective information iff (if and only if), for any combination of downward impulses along the top line(s) of each, the downward set of impulses of one is the same as the other and, for any combination of upward impulses along the bottom line(s) of each, the upward set of impulses of one is the same as the other.

(100) a.

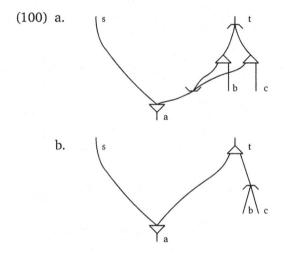

   b.

For example, the downward set of (100a) contains *ab,* and *ac,* because a downward impulse can start from *s* or *t* or both. The upward set is just *st.* In (100b), we find that the downward set is *ab* and *ac* just as in (100a), while the upward set is *st.* Therefore, the two graphs are not only alternatives they also have the same effective information. Yet, the two graphs have unequal surface information; (100b) is simpler and thus valued more highly in grammatical description. Surface information is computed by considering the number of nodes, lines, and some other factors of configuration too complex to discuss here (Lamb 1966:48–52). Nevertheless, Lamb's attempts to deal with the question of grammar evaluation is an important one, since it is exactly such considerations that dominate in any comparison.

4.3.2 Networks versus rules. While SG normally employs the network or its equivalent algebraic formalism to describe language, nearly all of it can be seen to be equivalent to the rewrite rule formalism that we are using to compare different approaches to linguistic theorizing.

Peter Reich has especially pursued these kinds of questions (1973b). As Reich points out, one can conceive of a sequence of context-free rules as network as well. For example, (101) is equivalently expressed as (102).

(101) A → B C

(102) A / B C

An unordered AND node would correspond to a rewrite rule with no linear arrangement of elements on the right hand side of the arrow as in (103).

(103) A → {B C}

The OR nodes correspond to the rules in (104).

(104)

$$A \rightarrow \left\{ \begin{array}{c} B \\ C \\ \\ D \\ E \end{array} \right.$$

These cases all seem simple enough. There is, however, an unexpected turn when dealing with upward nodes. What, for example, is the rewrite rule equivalent of (105)?

(105) A B / C

In Chomsky's original definition of productions there is no possibility for rules of the type in (106).

(106) A B → C

In fact, upward OR or AND nodes have the effect of coupling two individual rules together, i.e., rule 6 or rule 7 will apply or rule 6 and rule 7 will apply. Such rules of rule combination—some call them

METARULES—prove to be a very useful device, since more controls can be put on rules while at the same time not increasing the size of the language produced. If we are to allow metarules (restrictions or orderings over the set of rules or productions), then the definition of a formal grammar will have to be revised to include this feature.

(107) Definition of a grammar with metarules

$$G = (V_T, V_{NT}, \{S\}, P, M(P)).$$

V$_T$ and V$_{NT}$ are together the vocabulary of TERMINAL and NONTERMINAL STRINGS respectively. V$_T$ and V$_{NT}$ must be disjoint (i.e., not overlap in membership). S is the START SYMBOL(s). P is the set of RULES or PRODUCTIONS, which must be finite in number and conform to the scheme
$$\pi x \delta \rightarrow \pi y \delta,$$
where x and y are from the vocabulary, i.e., V$_T$ or V$_{NT}$, and the symbols π and δ come from the free monoid (V$_T$ U V$_{NT}$)*, cf. §1.4. M is a set of metarules defined over one or more productions P.

In this same essay, Reich mentions another idea that will prove to be useful in a proposal made much later. He says:

If we allow parenthesis notation in our algebraic formulas, by applying substitution to the seven rules of Figure 3, we see that we can express the same grammar using only two rules, as shown in Figure 6. (1973:97)

The grammar Reich is describing is shown in (108).

(108) a.   S → SUBJ ((hit, kissed) OBJ)
      b.   SUBJ, OBJ → ((a, the)(boy, girl))

Notice that Reich is suggesting the need for rules of the type A → ((B C) D), with a phrase marker like (109).

(109)

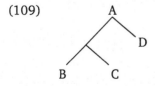

If he had only provided for the node above B and C with a rule as in (110) this would yield the phrase marker in (111).

(110) A → [[$_E$B C$_E$] D]

(111)

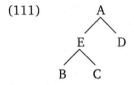

This kind of rule is also disallowed by Chomsky's original definition because only symbols to the left or right of a symbol can be considered in writing rules and only one level is written at a time. Yet, as Reich has correctly intuited, more than one level is often needed in rule writing. Only in the work of Gerald Gazdar does this important discovery, as well as the need for metarules, receive its proper statement (see chapter six).

While Reich can be credited post hoc for discovering the metarule and rules producing multiple-level strings, he goes on to doubt the usefulness of the rule concept at all.

There is another significantly different viewpoint of this approach and the GTG approach in regard to globality. The classical GTG model introduced in chapter two conceives of grammar as a serial device, i.e., rules apply in local sequence, though some may be cyclically ordered. There is no access to rules long ago applied or rules not yet applied; only the output of the last rule may be examined in a decision about whether and how to apply the next rule. By contrast, SG eschews this kind of constraint on the power of grammars. "All outputs on every stratum remain present and can be referred to for conditioning environments as many times as desired" (Fleming 1986:3). Such globality must surely magnify the power of the grammar system, and appropriate constraints should be imposed to reduce the potency. There are some indications that human language processing time increases with the length of a string less rapidly than would be the case if human languages were based on the most powerful of grammar types (see chapter one). Therefore, there seem to be cognitive arguments in favor of grammars of circumscribed capacity and complexity.

Some researchers in stratificational linguistics are attempting to provide just such constraints in the hope of reducing strength. Fleming (1986:6) suggests, for example, four constraints:

1. Realization relationships are more highly valued than tac-
    tic relationships. This proposal can perhaps be related to
    transformationalist attempts to divide a grammar into a
    more powerful and a less powerful component. Tactics
    might be, for example, treatable in a context free manner
    with the realizations context sensitive.
2. Word orders should be directly generated if possible.
3. Constituent analysis should be purely tactic if possible;
    mixing tactic and realization relationships leads to greater
    power.
4. Parsimony of information applies. An account that gives
    information once is to be preferred. The constraints on
    what should be generated are stated in terms of the upper
    stratum only, not in both.

4.4 Fleming's *Communcation Analysis* (1988 and 1990)

Ilah Fleming also employs a version of stratificational linguistics she
calls "communication analysis," as is illustrated in her two volumes
(Fleming 1988 and 1990). She assumes that grammars are for encoding
and decoding communication. Therefore, there are five areas of concern: (1) communication situation—culture, language, social setting, social relationship; (2) semantic; (3) morphosyntax; (4) expression
level—graphemic, phonemic, prosodic, and kinesic; and (5) physical
phenomena—hand movements, auditory perception, articulatory movements, visual, tactile perception. These three aspects are organized as in
(112).

(112) Communication model

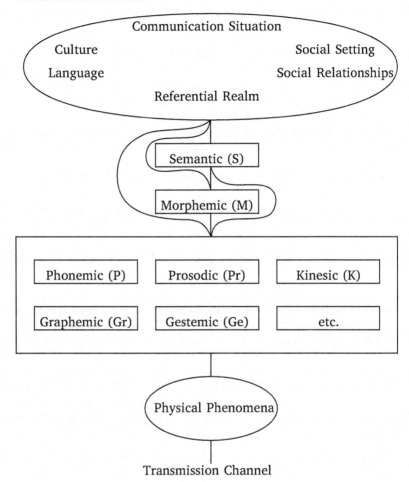

This approach also has the function of language as a concern in addition to form (Fleming 1990:19). It provides a way to get at many different kinds of data systematically and in small chunks. It will bring into focus analytical investigations that still need to be made when more than one way is found to do something. The question that needs to be answered is *why* one way is to be selected over another.

4.5 The problem-solving capacity of stratificational grammar

The problem that we have followed in the three previous approaches is that of the English auxiliary constellation. This will again be our procedure here. We note that several proposals for the auxiliary construction in English have been made (cf. Lamb 1964 and Fleming p.c.). We have chosen to examine the suggestion made in Lockwood (1972: 153–5), since this analysis addresses not only this particular problem but the issue of discontinuous dependency in general.

The most important formal component is the DIAMOND NODE, which we have not yet introduced. It has the characteristics shown in (113).

(113) to higher   to upper

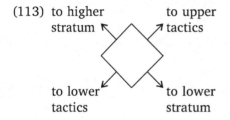

The diamond node is used by stratificationalists as a bridge between the tactics and realization modes at a particular level. Typically, only three of the connections on the diamond are active in constructions, one upward to the tactics of the construction (upper right connection), one downward to lower tactic or to lower realization (the lower left or right connection, respectively), and one lateral to its function in the tactics of its stratum, which is usually at a different level (upper left connection). Let us first consider one account of the passive in the statificationalist framework. The following discussion is taken from Lockwood (1972:150–5).

(114)

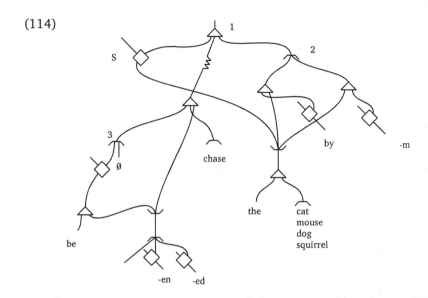

In (114) the first downward ordered AND (labeled as 1 on the chart) will have a left connection to an NP subject. The middle line from the AND will be realized as the verbal structure. This might be *be + chase + en/ed* if passive, or it might be just the verb if active (whether it is active or passive is determined by the downward ordered OR labeled 3; the left branch will be attempted first and will result in the passive form if the diamond node below it is activated by selection in the sememic stratum; otherwise the active will result because the right-hand branch from 3 will have to be taken, leading to a null realization of *be + en/ed*). The third line down from the AND will lead to an NP preceded by ^{L}/by/ (for the sentence *The cat was chased by the dog*) or a noun phrase followed by ^{L}/m/ marking causative case (as in *The dog chased the cat*). Then note the downward OR (labeled as 2), which will also lead to a downward AND that has a right branch with the lexeme ^{L}/m/; whatever its source, ^{L}/m/ is realized as a Ø on nouns and as a suffix on pronominal forms such as *him, them, whom*. Note the presence of the diamond nodes that must be activated by higher levels to ensure that the subject NP, the *by*, the *-en/-ed*, or the *-m* become active. This diamond node is in this sense triggering functional information from higher levels in all realizations as follows:

(115) ^{L}/by/   realizes   \ ^{S}/Ag/
       ^{L}/m/   \ ^{S}/Gl/
       ^{L}/ed/   \ ^{S}/Past/
       ^{L}/be/ ... ^{L}/ben/   \ ^{S}/Gl/ . ^{S}/Fc/
       S (Subject)   \ ^{S}/Ag/, (^{S}/Gl/ . ^{S}/Fc/)

whereby Ag = agent, Gl = goal, Fc = focus.

Thus, ^{L}/by/ is realized whenever its diamond node receives activation from ^{S}/Ag/ (agent at the sememic stratum).

The agent focus is the unmarked case but goal focus is realized portmanteau when that option is chosen. For instance, for goal focus the subject realization is accompanied simultaneously with a realization of ^{L}/be/ as well as with a verbal suffix ^{L}/en/. If the focus does not accompany the goal, then the goal is realized by ^{L}/m/, since the clause is active. There is thus a strong tie between the active verb form and the presence of pronominal objects in active clauses. Similarly, the agent can either be realized as subject or as *by* + NP depending upon which receives activation through its diamond node. Thus, the diamond nodes in (114) represent the interfaces between information structure of agent or goal focus (functional information) and active-passive (formal information).

Turning now to the English auxiliary, we have seen in the previous chapters that discontinuous realization is the heart of the problem. The *Aspects* solution to the overlapping discontinuity of stems and affixes was to resolve it by generating the stem and affix of the auxiliary elements together, e.g., *have* + Prt, and then to separate the two by transformation and thus to exploit the context-sensitivity of transformations. In the stratificational network account the lexemic analysis (lexical realization) connects to the sememic sources (semantic forms, ^{SS}/Past/ = sememic past tense, ^{SS}/Pf/ = sememic perfect, ^{SS}/Pg/ = sememic progressive, ^{SS}/Ps/ = sememic passive). Elements of the sememic stratum are not ordered left-to-right, whereas elements on the morphemic stratum are. The exploitation of that key feature is seen in the following in which the commas express the lack of left-to-right order of the -emes:

(116) unordered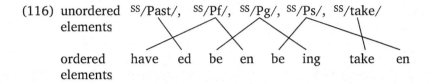
      elements

      ordered
      elements

had been being taken

This account makes use of the feature that the sememic stratal level is not ordered left-to-right and, therefore, the unordered sememes can have two discontinuously ordered morpheme realizates; the branches cross at a point where left-to-right ordering is not yet in play. We can expand this idea to a more explicit account of the lexotactics of the auxiliary in (117).

(117)

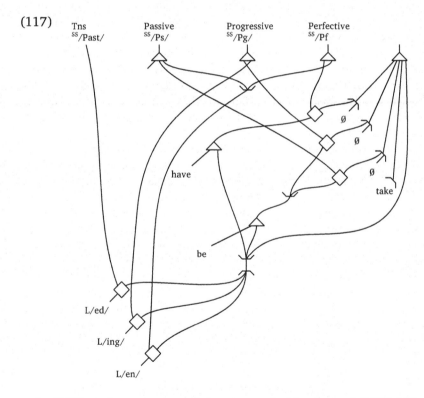

In (117) we have protrayed the proposal of Lockwood (1972:153–5). He does not discuss the modal auxiliaries of English, but we believe it would be relatively easy to extend this proposal to include them. The major features of the analysis are a downwards AND in the upper right hand corner of the diagram. It shows the tactics of the auxiliaries, their left to right order. Each of them can, of course, be realized as Ø under the upward ORs, which is the same as saying that they are optional elements. Diamonds below the ORs play their seminal role in bringing down from the sememic stratum the sememe realizates to activate the tactics of the auxiliary construction of *have* + some suffix or *be* + some suffix. The suffixes themselves are connected to the lexemes /ed/, /ing/, and /en/ by the now familiar diamond node, which is activated by the sememic level and tactic level above. Note that the homophony of Passive and Progress auxiliary stem *be* and the Passive and Perfect suffixes *-en* is captured by the upward ORs under the sememic level.

The discontinuous dependency of the passive construction is the same as above in that ordered interstitial structure is an ordered realizate of unordered sememic forms on high. The first finite verb takes the tense suffix and the suffixation of the additional verb is determined by the order in which the suffixes are made available. As Lockwood (154) discusses, there must be some way to interpret the downward ordered ANDs in some way that they don't make available their connections simultaneously. There is no special provision made for this circumstance. He speculates that perhaps they are made available one at a time in arbitrary sequences and the lexotactics will complete each part before another begins.

To relate this solution to previous ones, we note that the meaning structure is realized in two parts, as can be seen from the two connections between the sememic level and the diamond enablers. There is a definite left-to-right order in the verbal complex as is determined by the downward AND at the top of the tactics. The auxiliaries are all treated at the same level under AND. The passive and the progressive both lead to an upward OR that gathers the lines, since both require the auxiliary form *be,* even though the suffixes are different.

The discontinuity poses no insuperable problem here because at the sememic level units do not need to be ordered left-to-right and so there is no restriction on crossing branches. The required lexical forms are produced in place and linked with crossing lines to the higher sememic levels.

4.6 Stratificational theorizing

In summary, we can say that the stratificational research tradition is oriented to language relationships not language units. It emphasizes that language consists of interrelated levels each with its own tactics. It captures generalization by gathering common items and categories in one place and links them to distant locations. The focus is on idealized performance not actual performance or competence. For the purposes of comparison we now list some further properties of the stratificational model.

Summary of the Stratificational Model—*Outline of Stratificational Grammar* (1966)

1. Levels: there are at least three levels that correspond to the various subdisciplines of linguistics, i.e., morphology and syntax, phonology, and semantics. There is no level in terms of derivation.
2. Primitive symbols: There is only a small number of symbols. In fact, the emphasis is on relations among these and not on the symbols themselves.
3. Rules produce a constituent order, a constituent structure, and a constituent distribution by means of the tactic patterns.
4. Each tactic pattern is in itself a kind of microgrammar, which is independently generative and which is connected to other minigrammars by means of realization rules, i.e. knot patterns, sign patterns, and alternation patterns; this idea is perhaps expressible as rules over rules. Such higher order rules are not found in the original definition of a formal grammar in chapter one and are tantamount to metarules, rules of connection over grammars or connections over rule sets.
5. Context-sensitivity can be controlled by means of AND nodes, which require two things simultaneously for the passage of an impulse. Still, an AND so constructed is unlike a context-sensitive rule in that there is no difference between the changing element and the environment needed for it to change.
6. There are multiple generative components. A particular construction can begin at any stratal level without having connectivity to other strata, higher or lower.
7. There are long distance cross-stratal and intra-stratal connections. Sentences, phrases, words, texts, paragraphs, phonemes, basically, any two or more units can be related in principle by means of connections across any distance.

In this sense this approach is potentially powerful and therefore, is in need of restriction if the theory is intended to describe all and only human languages.

8. There is separation of components into strata with sequencing in the majority of cases, though alternation patterns may jump a stratum.

9. Each stratum has four subcomponents according to rule type (cf. (93)).

10. The model is bidirectional and interested in ideal performance, not competence out of real time.

5

The Great GTG Schism

5.1 Introduction

In chapters two, three and four, we have sketched the classical model of generative transformational grammar (GTG), tagmemics in contemporary versions, and stratificational linguistics (SG) of the *Outline* and later vintages. All of these arose before 1965. Indeed, Pike (p.c.) has informed us that the basic ideas for tagmemics were being discussed as early as 1949. SG also can date its heritage from the 1950s; Lamb states that he discovered some of the important parts of this approach as a graduate student at the University of California at Berkeley during this period.

While SG and tagmemics have undergone numerous continuous changes since the mid 1960s, there has been no change so radical that current work is totally unreadable to someone schooled in the previous period. The same cannot, however, be said of the GTG paradigm. Since 1965 this approach has passed through periods of dramatic recasting and reemphasis. So much so, in fact, that linguists familiar only with the *Aspects* model would be lost in the current literature. Despite these radical changes, Chomsky and his followers regard themselves as participants in a continuous tradition, calling their proposals: (a) EXTENDED STANDARD THEORY (EST); and then (b) REVISED EXTENDED STANDARD THEORY (REST); and, after 1980, (c) GOVERNMENT AND BINDING (labeled more recently PRINCIPLES AND PARAMETERS THEORY (P&P)).

Some of the major impetus to alter the *Aspects* model came from linguists working within the research tradition of GTG. In particular, the linguists George Lakoff, James McCawley, Paul Postal, and John 'Haj' Ross proposed a version of GTG in the time immediately succeeding 1965 that broke with some of the assumptions of *Aspects*. This "Great

Schism" from within yielded the movements known as EST, proposed by Chomsky and followers, and Generative Semantics, proposed by Lakoff, McCawley, Postal, Ross, and others. As will be presently discussed, these latter named linguists were more interested in a direct role for the interpretation of sentences, i.e., semantics, in the development of syntactic analysis. The former named linguists, by contrast, continued to assert that a theory of the syntax of a language could and should be developed independently of the interpretation assigned to it, a position known as AUTONOMOUS SYNTAX.

In the last year of the 60s, another change occurred that, in the eyes of some, counts as the second revolution in linguistics in the sense intended by Kuhn—the first proposal with a totally explicit semantics. The logician Richard Montague in an essay entitled "Proper treatment of quantification in ordinary English" (PTQ) offered an apparatus that could do for semantics what Chomsky's *Aspects* could do for a fragment of English syntax. Chomsky's *Aspects* could produce strings of symbols (sentences) from their constituent parts via the PS rules and lexicon as well as the transformations. Montague set forth a proposal to derive the interpretations of complex expressions from the meaning of their parts and information about how the parts were put together syntactically. The influence of Montague grammar, as this proposal came to be known, was immediate but not universal. For one thing, Montague grammar required nonelementary knowledge of set theory, intensional logic, and model theory, all disciplines with formidable formalism. A number of the followers of generative semantics became converts to the notion of an operational, though highly formal brand of semantics, able to solve a highly important subclass of semantic problems in English. Chomsky and his followers persisted, however, in a form of syntax that remained independent of semantics. It is to these latter kinds of developments that we now turn (Montague Grammar is discussed in some detail in chapter six).

5.2 General ontology, methodology, and world view (EST, REST, P&P)

Since the basic orientation of EST, REST, and P&P are nearly the same as for the *Aspects* model—though the emphasis may be different—we will concentrate on the aspects of dissimilarity.

Chomsky's later work makes the point that native speakers of a language have intuitions both about well-formedness and about structure (this second aspect is not stressed as much in earlier work). Linguistic theory must account for the fact that a competent speaker knows, for example, not only that *very fat* is a well-formed sequence of structure and that *fat very* is not, but also that *very* modifies *fat* and not the reverse.

The notion of ILL-FORMED also comes in for some differentiation. In his "Presupposition and relative well-formedness," Lakoff (1971) argues that well-formedness is a gradable concept. For example, the following sentences from Radford (1981:7) seem to get progressively less natural.

(118) a. My uncle realizes that I'm a lousy cook.
      b. My cat realizes that I'm a lousy cook.
      c. My goldfish realizes that I'm a lousy cook.
      d. My pet amoeba realizes that I'm a lousy cook.
      e. ?My frying pan realizes that I'm a lousy cook.
      f. ??My sincerity realizes that I'm a lousy cook.
      g. *?My birth realizes that I'm a lousy cook.

Such examples illustrate that the question of the acceptability of sentences is a complex of at least three factors. Is a sentence *syntactically* ill-formed—does it fail to abide by the grammar of English? Or, is it *semantically* ill-formed—is it, for example, uninterpretable or meaningless? Or, is it *pragmatically* ill-formed—does it violate the proper use put to sentences? In the *Aspects* model, violations of strict subcategorization and selectional restrictions such as those exhibited in (118) were regarded as errors of syntax. By contrast, later work viewed selectional restriction incompatibilities as a semantic error (Jackendoff 1972). Further, sentences such as (119) are pragmatically peculiar because the use of conjunction between two such unrelated sentences is strained (though perhaps allowed in quite peculiar circumstances).

(119) The square root of two is an irrational number and Dole was considered the leader in the primaries.

In the developments after 1965, one also sees a strong tendency to rely more and more on UNIVERSAL GRAMMAR and, consequently, to spend less effort on formulating language-specific rules. The rules of a particular language are conceived of as wildly overgenerating structures by means of very general, highly unspecified rules; the universal principles may then serve as filters, removing all but those few allowed structures. This emphasis on universal grammar is the result of the goal of attempting to account for child language acquisition. The more that can be attributed to universal grammar, the less there is for the language-specific grammar to account for. And if universal grammar can be considered to be innate, which is the approach taken in the theory, there is less for the language acquirer to learn. Thus language acquisition becomes a more manageable task.

5.3 General ontology, methodology, and world view of generative semantics

Generative semantics differed from EST and its successors by placing the role of semantics and pragmatics more into the foreground than did Chomsky's work. While there are few who would today continue to argue for the specific claims of generative semantics, the contribution of this other branch off the *Aspects* stem lies in its richness of interesting examples and ground-breaking proposals for the semantics of the 1970s. In his "Pragmatics in natural logic," George Lakoff (1975) argues for devising a natural logic for natural language based on PERFORMATIVES, variables in the syntax, use of pragmatic categories such as SINCERITY, POLITENESS, etc., and FUZZY, GLOBAL, TRANSDERIVATIONAL CORRESPONDENCE GRAMMARS. The details of this proposal will not be presented here; the curious reader is referred to Lakoff (1975) for further discussion.

Generative semantics also has less to say about the acquisitional aspects of language, emphasizing instead the universality of a small number of categories such as PREDICATE, which can be realized as verbs, nouns, quantifiers, adjectives, etc. The difference between generative semantics and the *Aspects* account of syntax can be illustrated with the phrase marker of the sentence *every philosopher contradicts every philosopher*. In the classical *Aspects* approach there is a subject NP *every philosopher* and a VP *contradicts every philosopher*. Moreover, there is an object NP *every philosopher* inside the VP in the usual manner.

(120)

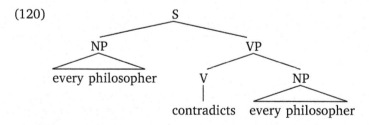

In the generative semantics account of the underlying form of this sentence, however, the familiar structure is deviated from to a significant degree. There is, for example, a great deal more structure and there is the assumption that *every, philosopher,* as well as *contradicts* are all predications. Note also that NP may dominate variables such as x and y, which have no surface realization. These are present to keep track of the scope of relationships.[6]

(121)

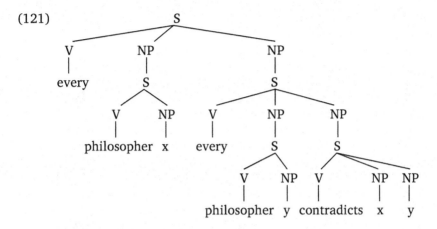

In this deep structure the syntax of English is made to look much like the rendering of this meaning in symbolic logic (predicate calculus), i.e., $\forall x(\text{philosopher}(x)$ & $\forall y(\text{philosopher}(y) \rightarrow \text{contradicts}(x,y)))$.[7] The changes needed to account for the surface categories and the changes needed to yield the surface structure syntax of English are performed by transformations. In generative semantics, these were often not stated explicitly and many were assumed to be quite powerful in nature, since the starting point, i.e., the logical representation, could be quite distant from the surface structure of English. It was for reasons of this type that Chomsky rejected the most powerful generative semantics approaches. We note, however, that generative semantics arose, in part, to capture

---

[6]Scope is one of the most important features of modern syntactic treatments. The notion comes from symbolic logic. An operator has a certain domain or scope of expressions over which it can act. Things outside this scope are, as a result, not influenced by it (McCawley 1972:511). In the sentence *every man loves some woman* most speakers prefer the interpretation in which *every man* has *some woman* in its scope, i.e., the interpretation that for each of the every men there is some woman that he loves. For some speakers of English there is a second interpretation in which *some woman* lies outside the scope of *every man.* The reading produced in this case is that in which some particular, specific woman is universally loved by all men.

[7]The predicate calculus makes use of the quantifier symbol $\forall$, which roughly corresponds to the English quantifiers *all, every,* and perhaps others. Thus this sentence of the predicate calculus could be paraphrased roughly as: For every philosopher x and for every philosopher y, then x contradicts y.

the generalization that many languages could have the same or similar deep structures, since the meanings were the same or similar in many languages (thus presupposing the universality of meaning), whereas the manifest differences across languages could be accounted for in terms of different transformations. This claim that languages share a common core has its own characteristic manifestation in Government and Binding theory, as we shall see.

Generative semantics also espoused the notion of LEXICAL DECOMPOSITION. This trend again was an attempt to capture generalizations at the underlying level that were not apparent in specific languages because of the differing surface structures. In English, for example, we say *John remembered Mary* whereas in many other languages *remembered* may be rendered as *to remind oneself*. In English we use *kill;* other languages may have sequences of verbs. In fact, the adverb *almost* seems to be able to modify *kill* in a manner that argues for its decomposition into a combination of abstract PRELEXICAL FORMS that appear combined into the surface verb *kill. John almost killed the grass* can be interpreted to mean that *he almost caused it to die,* or that *he caused it to almost be not alive,* etc. Thus the sentence would have an underlying structure as in (122).

(122)

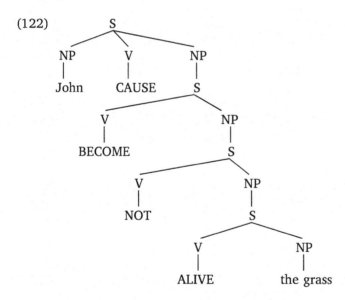

The verbs (predicates) are written in capitals because these are regarded as abstract nonlexical forms that, after syntactic combination by means of a rule of RAISING, are realized lexically in English as *kill*. This is diagrammed in (123).

(123)

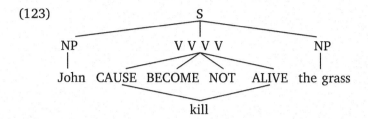

As we have already stated, generally the specifics of generative semantics revealed themselves to be only transitory, however, and were largely supplanted in the 1970s spiritually, though by different investigators, by those employing Montague Grammar and other models with explicit semantics.

5.4 Specific developments in EST, REST, and P&P after 1970

As was discussed in chapter two, the *Aspects* model consisted of a set of phrase structure rules (the categorial part of the grammar), a lexicon, a transformational component, and the nonsyntactic components of grammar—the semantic and phonological components. In the post-1965 period, the phonological component developed more or less independently; the semantic component remained—with a few exceptions—largely unchanged; the remainder of the grammar, however, was recast radically with major revisions in the phrase structure rules, lexicon, and the transformational component. In this section, we consider these proposals.

Crucial to developments in the theory is an increasing reliance upon the notion of MODULARITY in grammar; there are independent components of grammar that work, each autonomously but in grand concert, to account for the grammatical strings of a given language. Among the modules commonly proposed are those in (124).

(124) X-Bar Syntax module
       Theta Theory module
       Case Theory module
       Binding Theory module
       Bounding Theory module
       Control Theory module

Each module is governed by its own set of PRINCIPLES, considered as universally valid for all languages alike and thus defining the nature of possible grammars of human languages. Languages may differ, however, in that limited choices may be made as to how specific PARAMETERS of a module are realized in a given language. Thus, for example, the linear ordering between a *head* of a constituent and its *complement* as defined in X-bar syntax (see below) must be stated for any given language to specify whether it is typologically *head first* or *head last*. Nevertheless, the number of parameters and the choices available in each one is quite limited, with the result that the principles of universal grammar account for the generalizations seen across languages.

In addition to this modular approach, there are other characteristics of this approach which deserve special attention. First, it is proposed that there is a universal principle of GOVERNMENT which functions to constrain the way in which the principles of the individual modules are applied. There is active in natural language a kind of grammatical glue that ties some items to others along the constituent lines that connect them according to certain configurational principles. Specific examples are included in the discussion to follow; suffice it to say here that government is a principle of syntactic configuration, a formal principle that requires that constituents to which government applies must be associated in the appropriate manner within a phrase-structure tree or the sentence in question is ungrammatical.

Second, within this approach the notion of EMPTY CATEGORIES is highly important. These are constituents which have themselves syntactic significance but no phonological manifestation. Their presence must be posited for syntactic reasons (in some cases with phonological effects); thus they are phonologically null, but syntactically active. This is not an innovation of the theory (the roots of it can be seen in the x and y variables used in Generative Semantics in the preceding discussion, as well as in the deltas of Jackendoff's interpretative approach of the early 1970's and even in Chomsky's *Aspects* (1965), cf. §2.5). Generative theory has always taken the position that there is more to language than meets the ear. Still, empty categories in P&P take on an importance that could scarcely have been hinted at in these earlier approaches. It will turn out that there are at least three specific empty categories that are necessary in the framework of Universal Grammar, all necessarily phonologically null, but with different syntactic characteristics (details are found in the discussion to follow). These are the following:

t	the trace of movement; there is a distinction drawn between traces of movement of NPs and traces of movement of all other constituents, but the same formal specification is used for the traces themselves
PRO	the "missing" subject of infinitival and gerundial complement sentences found widely in languages of the world
pro	the "missing" subject occurring in languages which allow that NP subjects need not be overt (used also to represent implicit objects)

In addition, the empty category *e* is often used in examples and discussion in a generic manner, to indicate that an empty category is present, but with no specific claim being made as to its specific characteristics.

We turn now to a consideration of the various modules and their characteristics (in this summary of P&P we rely heavily on Haegeman 1994).

5.4.1 Theta Theory. Theta Theory has to do with the relationship between predicates and their arguments, including matters of subcategorization, redefined as the THETA GRID for the lexical items in question. Crucial is the THETA CRITERION: Each argument is assigned one and only one theta role; each theta role is assigned to one and only one argument. The Theta Criterion is one portion of the PROJECTION PRINCIPLE, the others being that heads determine phrase type (see §5.4.2 dealing with X-Bar Theory) and the EXTENDED PROJECTION PRINCIPLE, which states that every sentence must have a subject, whether represented in the theta grid or not. Theta roles are those "case"-type notions which are made use of in many linguistic theories, including such roles as AGENT, THEME (or PATIENT), EXPERIENCER, BENEFICIARY, GOAL, SOURCE, and LOCATION. To provide a complete theta grid for a lexical item, then, is to specify how many arguments it takes, what sorts of arguments are possible (e.g., NP vs. IP (Inflectional Phrase = S) vs. CP (Complementizer Phrase = S', S introduced with a complementizer)), and the thematic relation holding between each argument and the lexical item in question. Constituents which make up the theta grid for a lexical entry are those which are obligatory and are generally considered to constitute the COMPLEMENTS of the lexical item (optional elements by contrast are considered to be ADJUNCTS); arguments of substitution and movement can often be adduced to provide evidence for analysis in this regard. For example (some details here may need revision, this summary being primarily for purposes of illustration):

(125)

kill:	verb	NP	NP
		AGENT	THEME

speak:	verb	NP
		AGENT

give:	verb	NP	NP	PP
		AGENT	THEME	BENE

believe:	verb	NP	NP/IP
		AGENT	THEME

A distinction is drawn between INTERNAL ARGUMENTS (those within VP, i.e., THEME and BENE in the examples above) and EXTERNAL ARGUMENTS (those occurring in the subject position and thus outside of VP, typically underlined in the theta grid). The actual theta role filled by an external argument is in part a function of the combined VP itself, so that its precise role in the lexical entry must be somewhat flexible (cf. *John broke the vase,* with *John* as AGENT (assuming a volitional action), with *John broke a leg,* with *John* as EXPERIENCER). There are numerous questions involved here, and in fact the precise theta roles are often omitted in such entries, with only the number and types of arguments stated.

Note that the Extended Projection Principle (EPP) requires that a subject be present in every sentence, even if the theta grid of the predicate does not call for one (in which case the subject position has no theta role). For example, expletives (in English, *it* and existential *there*) manifest no theta role, so that all of the following are grammatical:

(126) a.   A boy was standing on the bridge.
      b.   There was a boy standing on the bridge.
      c.   That John is tall seems to be true.
      d.   It seems to be true that John is tall.

The point is that the fact that the (a) and (b) sentences, and the (c) and (d) sentences are all grammatical requires explanation because the (b) and (d) sentences both contain an expletive that is missing from the (a) and (c) sentences. If such expletives manifested a theta role, sentences containing them would be a violation of the Theta Criterion, because the theta grid of the predicates in question does not vary whether the expletive is present or not. It must be the case, therefore, that expletives do not manifest a theta role and that they are present only as fillers of the otherwise empty subject position.

Furthermore, auxiliaries manifest no theta role, so that all the following (and other auxiliary patterns) are grammatical: *John ran, John will run, John will be running, John was running, John had run, John had been running, John could have been running.* Again, the point is that if the auxiliaries added theta roles, there would be a violation of the Theta Criterion because each of the above manifests but a single argument *John.*

Of particular interest perhaps is the status of passive and UNACCUSATIVE constructions in this theory. Passives may be considered to be derived by a lexical rule from verbs which are inherently transitive; a rule like the following may be considered as a possible candidate:

(127)
$$
\text{V:}\quad
\begin{array}{|c|c|}
\hline
\underline{\text{NP}} & \text{NP} \\
\hline
\text{X} & \text{THM} \\
\hline
\end{array}
\; + \; \text{Pass} \;\rightarrow\; \text{V}_{\text{pass}}\text{:}
\begin{array}{|c|c|}
\hline
\text{NP} & (by + \text{NP}) \\
\hline
\text{THM} & \text{AGENT} \\
\hline
\end{array}
$$

That is, a verb which is subcategorized as taking an internal THEME argument and an external (subject) argument of any type may be suffixed by the Pass(ive) morpheme, with the result that the theta role for the external argument is lost, and an AGENT argument may optionally occur manifested by $by + \text{NP}$. It is proposed that a further result of passivization is that the verb loses its ability to assign abstract case to its internal argument, see the discussion of Case Theory in §5.4.3. The result is that the EPP still requires an external argument to appear, but that argument manifests no theta role as far as the verb is concerned and is generated empty. So the active sentence will have a representation like

(128) [John will watch Mary]$_{\text{IP}}$

while the corresponding passive sentence will have a representation like

(129) [e will be watched Mary by John]$_{\text{IP}}$

in which *be watched* is the V_{pass} form of the verb *watch,* and *e* represents an empty category, a place holder with no lexical or phonological content (present in this case only because of the EPP); in both sentences, *Mary* is the NP manifesting the role of THEME (the 'target' of the watching). Because the passive *be watched* cannot assign abstract case to its internal argument *Mary,* the sentence in this form is ungrammatical; NP Movement (see the discussion of Movement in §5.4.6) moves *Mary* from its present position where it cannot be assigned case (but is assigned its appropriate theta role) to subject position (replacing the *e*), where it can be assigned abstract Nominative case by the verbal construction (actually, by the inflection associated with the verb, INFL, the head of IP($=$S)), leaving a coindexed trace behind marking its source:

(130) [Mary$_i$ will be watched t$_i$ by John]$_{IP}$

This representation, then, carries information both about its surface or S-Structure, and about its notional or D-Structure. Note that expletives can occur with some passives as well, likewise supporting the notion that passive subjects are assigned no theta roles:

(131) a. e were arrested five people by the police.
      b. Five people were arrested by the police.
      c. There were five people arrested by the police.

A syntactic pattern related to the passive is that known as 'unaccusative'. The proposal is that there are two types of one-argument verbs, the difference between them at times is marked morphologically (though not convincingly in English).

The two different types of one-argument verbs may be contrasted as to whether they have only an external argument (typical 'intransitive' verbs) or only an internal argument (typical 'unaccusative' verbs). (See the discussion of Relational Grammar in chapter eight for examples and analysis within that framework.)

Consider Italian. Italian shows examples of movement of nominal structures from within VP to a position preceding the auxiliary, provided the head of the NP is the clitic *ne* 'of them'; in such a case only the head is obligatorily moved, and in particular any Spec (determiner or equivalent) of NP is left behind:

(132) a. *Giacomo ha insultato due studenti.*
        'Giacomo has insulted two students.'
      b. *Giacomo ne ha insultato due.*
        'Giacomo has insulted two of them.'

The second sentence here may be considered to have as its D-Structure something like the following:

(133) *Giacomo ha insultato due ne.*

A similar pattern is found also in passives in some instances; note first that the movement of the NP filling the internal theta role of the passive predicate may remain within VP, so that both of the following are grammatical with the same meaning:

(134) 'Many students were arrested'

   a. *Furono arrestati molti studenti.*
   b. *Molti studenti furono arrestati.*

If the pronominal *ne* 'of them' occurs as head of NP, however, the same pattern as that seen in the sentences above results:

(135) ***Ne** furono arrestati molti.*   'Many of them were arrested'

   from: *Furono arrestati molti ne.*

This is taken as confirmatory of the claim that at D-Structure the NP in question is in fact part of VP, so that the sentences in (132)–(133) and the passives in (134)–(135) share that commonality of structure. Turning now to the main point, it is significant that one-argument verbs in Italian show differing patterns in regard to the surface distribution of *ne:*

(136) a. *Molti studenti telefonano.*   'Many students telephone.'
      b. *Molti studenti arrivano.*   'Many students arrive.'
      c. *Molti **ne** telefonano.*   'Many of them telephone.'
      d. **Ne** telefonano molti.*
      e. ***Ne** arrivano molti.*   'Many of them arrive.'

In order to account for this difference, it is suggested that although both 'telephone' and 'arrive' are one-argument verbs, they differ in terms of their theta grids. In particular, to capture the similarity between 'arrive' and the passive examples in (134)–(135) and the patterns regarding NPs internal to VP in (132)–(133), it is suggested that 'arrive' in fact has its one argument as an internal argument within VP (such verbs are termed 'unaccusatives'), while one-argument verbs like 'telephone' have no internal argument, but only an external argument. Thus:

(137)

		NP
telephonare:	V	AGT

		NP
arrivare:	V	AGT

In this regard, then, it is particularly interesting also that the two types of one-argument verbs manifest a second difference otherwise lacking explanation, viz. that they take different auxiliaries for perfect tense; 'unaccusatives' take *essere,* and 'intransitives' take *avere:*

(138) a.   *Giacomo **ha** telefonato.*   'Giacomo has telephoned.'
     b.   *Giacomo **è** arrivato.*   'Giacomo has arrived.'

Consider English for a moment. It may be the case that *arrive* and *sleep,* while both taking a single argument, differ in their theta grids, and in exactly this same way. Specifically, it has been suggested that *sleep* has only an external theta role, with no internal theta role, whereas *arrive* has only an internal theta role, with no external theta role:

(139)
      sleep: V

NP
EXP

    arrive: V

NP
AGT

Although *arrive* has no external theta role, the EPP does require that it have a subject. Thus, strings like the following are found in D-Structure:

(140)   three men slept
       e arrived three men

For the latter (apparently because *arrive* cannot assign abstract Accusative case), *three men* must be moved into a position where it can get Nominative case from INFL at S-Structure:

(141)   three men$_i$ arrived t$_i$

This difference in structure between *arrive* and *sleep* in English is reflected in the possibility of occurrence of the expletive *there;* because such expletives do not manifest theta roles, it follows that they can occur only in a position where there is no theta role assigned, i.e., as subject with *arrive* but not *sleep:*

(142)   *there slept three men
       there arrived three men

As with Italian *ne*-cliticization patterns and auxiliary selection, the possibility of *there*-insertion in English is a fact of the language that must be accounted for in any case; within this theory the assumption is that the difference in theta grids is the significant factor.

5.4.2 X-Bar Theory. X-Bar Theory has to do with constituent structure (phrase structure). The claim is that for all phrasal structures in all languages there are universal constraints on relationships within a construction (so that all languages are essentially alike as regards phrase structure).

There are four significant types of constituents which are involved in X-Bar structures: head, specifier, complement, and adjunct. The HEAD is the "core" of the phrase, the only required element; it is the lexical constituent of which the phrasal structure itself is the MAXIMAL PROJECTION (see below). COMPLEMENT and ADJUNCT provide some 'modulation' of the head constituent; while it is not always easy to distinguish between them, it is usually the case that complements are more closely related to the head than adjuncts (and linearly adjacent to the head). Moreover, subcategorization in Theta Theory (see discussion in §5.4.1) typically takes the complements into account and ignores the adjuncts (which commonly can occur freely with constituents of varying subcategorization characteristics). The notion of SPECIFIER (commonly abbreviated as Spec) is set forth to account for the parallelism holding, for example, between clauses and NPs in constructions like the following:

(143) a.   John proved the theorem
      b.   John's proof of the theorem (< John proof the theorem)

The idea is that the specifier serves to delimit in some sense the range of possible referents for the head. Thus it is proposed that in (143) the NP *John* stands in the same relationship to *prove* and to *proof,* as does the NP *the theorem.*

It is typical within the theory that three levels of structure are recognized: X'' (XP, the maximal projection of X), X' (which may be recursive), and X (this last being the lexical head itself). Specifiers are dominated by the maximal projection, with adjuncts and complements dominated by the X' level. Further, S is defined in this approach as IP (Inflectional Phrase) and thus also analyzable in terms of head, specifier, complement, and adjunct in a manner parallel to other phrase types. For (143) (assuming *of* and *'s* are inserted by rule as required):

(144) a.

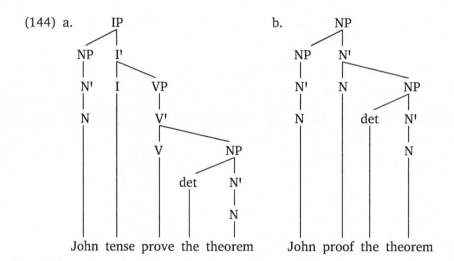

John tense prove the theorem   John proof the theorem

Based upon such a characterization, the specifier position in both is NP (*John*) (it could also be determiner in NP); the head of IP is *Inflection* (INFL abbreviated here as *I* and corresponding to tense, and also agreement, it will turn out), the head of NP is N (*proof*); the complement of IP is VP; the complement of VP is NP (*the theorem*), the complement of NP is NP (*the theorem*). The parallelism in the structural relationships holding among *John, prove/proof,* and *the theorem* is evident and intentional. It is precisely in capturing such parallelisms that X-Bar Theory finds its application.

For categories other than NP and IP, the identification of Spec is not always as transparent. For AP it is common for adverbs to be considered Spec; so (assuming *of* is inserted by rule as required):

(145)

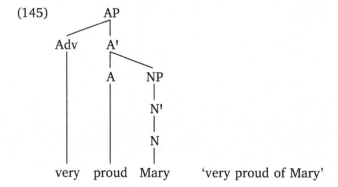

very proud Mary   'very proud of Mary'

For PP it is suggested that adverbs of a restricted type may serve as Spec; so:

(146)

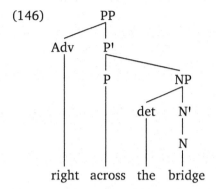

For VP the Spec designation is even more tenuous, with *all* (after movement) the primary candidate; so for the VP of *the men all saw Mary* (see discussion below):

(147)

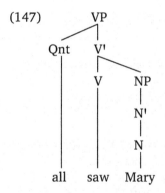

It is necessary, of course, for arguments to be set forth to support suggested analyses, although there is often room for debate in specific cases. Among the arguments typically proposed are those which are primarily semantic. Typically, complements manifest information related to grammatical function. So in the PP example, the NP *the bridge* is the constituent (commonly referred to as the object of the preposition) marking the scope of the preposition; similarly, VP, AP, and NP are commonly treated in a parallel manner, with an NP occurring within the construction functioning as in some sense an 'object' of the head of the phrase (note the IP *John proved the theorem* and the NP *John's proof of the theorem* above, as well as the AP *very proud of Mary,* where the NP

Mary is the 'target' for the pride being referred to). As mentioned above, it is expected that complements make up part of the Theta Grid (see §5.4.1) of the head in each construction, while adjuncts do not.

There are syntactic arguments which can be set forth as well. First, the theory predicts that complements occur closer to the head of the phrase than adjuncts do, and the latter are usually optional. There are also syntactic arguments based on patterns of substitution. In English, *one* can be substituted for an entire NP:

(148) a.   Mary has a beautiful cup and John has a beautiful cup too.
      b.   Mary has a beautiful cup and John has one too.

or for the head of NP (leaving adjuncts unaffected):

(149) a.   Mary has a beautiful cup and John has an ugly cup.
      b.   Mary has a beautiful cup and John has an ugly one.
      c.   The student from UT was wiser than the student from A&M.
      d.   The student from UT was wiser than the one from A&M.

It appears that *one* cannot substitute for a head of NP alone, leaving complements unaffected:

(150) a.   The student of linguistics was wiser than the student of physics.
      b.   *The student of linguistics was wiser than the one of physics.

Such a pattern of substitution may help to determine in a given example whether a constituent is a complement or an adjunct to the head of NP.

Similarly, the construction *do so* can replace only contiguous sequences within VP (in italics in the following examples):

(151) a.   John will *study linguistics in the library tonight* and Mary will do so too.
      b.   John will *study linguistics in the library* tonight and Mary will do so tomorrow.
      c.   John will *study linguistics* in the library tonight and Mary will do so at home tomorrow.
      d.   ?John will *study linguistics* in the library *tonight* and Mary will do so at home.
      e.   *John will *study* linguistics in the library tonight and Mary will do so physics at home.

The sentence in (151d) is marginal, and the one in (151e) is clearly un-grammatical. Again, such patterns may be helpful in determining structural relationships, *do so* substituting only for VP or V' containing complements (and optionally adjuncts adjacent to complements), never for V alone.

It is this sort of argument which is used in support of the proposal that words like *all* are in Spec of VP. For example, the following are related by movement of *all:*

(152) All the boys are watching the boats. →
       The boys are all watching the boats.

Further, English manifests a pattern of VP deletion:

(153) a.   John has seen Mary and Bill has seen Mary too. →
           John has *seen Mary* and Bill has too.
      b.   John will take Mary to the movies and Bill will take Mary
           to the movies too. →
           John will *take Mary to the movies* and Bill will too.

This pattern of VP deletion provides some evidence that when *all* is moved, it must become part of VP (and since Spec is typically the position preceding the head in English, likely filling Spec of VP):

(154) The boys are all watching the boats and the girls are all
           watching the boats, too. →
       The boys are *all watching the boats* and the girls are too.

For a given language, X-Bar Syntax predicts that the ordering patterns of the head of the construction and its phrasal specifier, and of the head of the construction and its modifiers, will be the same for all phrase types. Thus it is expected that in every type of structure the specifier will either precede or follow the head, and likewise for the complements and adjuncts. Because X-Bar Syntax is assumed to be consistently binary, the result is that the phrase-structure rules often can be collapsed into a single format. In English, for example, at the sentence level the subject NP (filling the specifier position of IP) precedes the head, and the VP (the complement of IP) follows; thus:

(155) IP → NP I'   I' → I VP

Similarly, within the VP, constituents like *all* (arbitrarily represented here as Qnt) precede the head, and NP and PP complements follow, as in *The men all believed the truth.* Thus:

(156) VP → Qnt V'   V' → V NP

Further, within the NP, determiners (functioning as specifiers in this structure) precede the head, and the NP and PP complements follow, as in *the book about linguistics.* Thus:

(157) NP → det N'   N' → N PP

Finally, within the PP, constituents like *right* (arbitrarily represented here as Adv) precede the head, and the NP complement follows, as in *right across the bridge.* Thus:

(158) PP → Adv P'   P' → P NP

The parallelism among these structures is striking and can be summarized in a single abstract format:

(159) XP → Spec X'   X' → X YP

(Adjuncts can be incorporated in a parallel manner.) Not every language is as consistent as this, of course, in which case the precise ordering of constituents for each phrase type must be stated explicitly. Furthermore, languages with VSO or OSV ordering, in which a verb and its object are separated by the subject, are a complication in this theory.

In addition to capturing the structural parallelism between structures like *John proved the theorem* and *John's proof of the theorem* above, there are some other highly important results of X-Bar configurations which should be pointed out. First, the head of the maximal projection governs the whole through a structural relationship known as M-COMMAND. It is usually the case, therefore, that the head assigns abstract case to NP complements (see §5.4.3). So, in the above examples, P assigns Accusative case to NP, as does V.

Furthermore, the Spec-Head relationship is commonly the relationship where agreement is manifested. So, within NP, there may be agreement between the determiner and the head:

(160) a banana/some bananas/*a bananas/*some banana (in the
       sense intended)

Though subject-verb agreement is limited in its overt manifestation in English, the Spec-Head relationship in IP is where it occurs, as expected under the assumptions of the theory (here INFL manifests both tense and agreement notions):

(161) a.   John is running.
       b.   The boys are running.
       c.   John has run.
       d.   The boys have run.

5.4.3 Case Theory. Case Theory accounts for the S-Structure distribution of NPs. Crucial is the CASE FILTER: Every overt NP must be assigned abstract case.[8] It is very important in this discussion to keep distinct the notions of ABSTRACT CASE and morphological case; while morphological case distinctions are often used as evidence for case assignment, the lack of such surface distinctions does not count as negative evidence against abstract case assignment. Thus while in English some pronominal forms show a full set of case distinctions (cf. *I, me, my; he, him, his; we, us, our; they, them, their*), nonpronominal NPs do not (*John* is realized as *John,* whether Nominative or Accusative, though there is a distinction for Genitive, *John's*).

In testing for application of the Case Filter in a given language, two sorts of information must be included. First, the case assigners for the language in question must be identified; for English (and likely for all other languages as well) these include P and V (which assign abstract Accusative case (Acc)), finite INFL (which assigns abstract Nominative case (Nom)), and (in some analyses) A and N (which assign abstract Genitive case (Gen)). Therefore, heads of phrases (i.e., lexical categories and finite INFL) always assign case; these are the X-level constituents as represented in X-Bar Theory. Second, the configurational relationship of the case assigners and the NPs to which they assign case is crucial, constrained by the notion of GOVERNMENT:

---

[8]The modifier *overt* (having lexical content) here is important because a specific empty category PRO, though an NP, occurs precisely where case cannot be assigned. See the discussion of Control Theory in §5.4.6.

(162) A governs B iff   (i) A is a governor;
                         (ii) A m-commands B;
                         (iii) minimality is respected.
        Governors are the lexical categories and tensed INFL.

In most contexts, m-command can be interpreted as equivalent to the traditional notion of c-command (see chapter two); rather than making
reference to 'the first branching node' of c-command, however,
m-command makes reference to 'the first maximal projection' (XP). The
fact that minimality is respected simply means that if two governors (for
Case Theory, the case assigners) compete for the same NP, the one structurally closer takes precedence; thus, in a sentence like *John put the book on the
shelf*, both *put* and *on* are in an m-command relationship *to the shelf*, but *on*
is structurally closer and therefore takes precedence (with the result that in
a language in which the actual surface case is different when assigned by
put as opposed to being assigned by *on*, this could be overtly verified).[9] It is
commonly required also that no constituents intervene between the governor and the NP (the notion of adjacency); finite INFL appears in many
languages not to be subject to this constraint.

A major result of the Case Filter is that in some sentences NPs must
occur in D-Structure to satisfy the Projection Principle, but they are not
in a configuration in which they can be assigned abstract case and thus
must be moved into a position where they can be assigned abstract case.
For example, as mentioned above, in English the case-assigners are
specified as V, P, and finite (inflected) INFL (and by some analysts N
and A as well); of particular relevance in this summary, nonfinite INFL
and passive verbs are not case-assigners. Given these assumptions, the
derivation of passive sentences follows (here the *t* in S-Structure is the
trace identifying the point of origin of the moved constituent with
which it is co-indexed):

(163) D-Structure   e was given the book to Bill
       S-Structure   the book$_i$ was given t$_i$ to Bill

To satisfy the Theta Criterion, the passive verb *was given* requires only two
arguments, the direct object argument, and the indirect object (shown by
the prepositional phrase), with the external argument for subject (here
empty) present because of EPP (no external theta role is assigned by the

---

[9]Thus, PP serves as a barrier to government. The fact that it is a maximal projection is
not accidental in this regard, and the notion of barrierhood is often employed in current
theory as a means of simplifying the array of constraints otherwise necessary.

passive verb in English). The passive verb *was given,* however, is not among the case-assigners for English, so that the NP *the book* cannot receive abstract case in its D-Structure position; the result is that *the book* must be moved into a position where it can receive abstract case, which it can do if the subject position (which will be assigned abstract Nominative by finite INFL) is empty as in this example. If it cannot be moved (because the subject position is filled) the result is an ungrammatical sentence, whose ungrammaticality is attributed to the fact that the NP *the book* violates the Case Filter (the Theta Criterion is violated also in this example because *John* is assigned no theta role):

(164) *John was given the book to Bill.

Typically, maximal projections (i.e., XP structures) constitute BARRIERS to government (see footnote 10), with one important exception allowed by the theory; some specific verbs (termed 'EXCEPTIONAL CASE MARKING (ECM) Verbs' because of their unique behavior) can govern into IP structures in their complements and assign case to NP subjects of nonfinite verbs, e.g.:

(165) John expects [Mary to call him].

Here *John* gets Nom from inflected INFL with *expect,* *him* gets Acc from *call,* but *Mary* cannot get Nom from the INFL with *to call* because it is nonfinite and thus not a case assigner in English. But *expect* is an ECM verb and thus assigns Acc to *Mary* allowing the sentence to be recognized as grammatical. Cf. *John expects [her to call him]* where the Acc case shows up as surface accusative case also. Not all verbs are ECM verbs, however, requiring that the INFL of the clause embedded as their complement be finite and thus also a governor for the NP subject:

(166) a.   *John hopes [Mary to call him].
      b.   John hopes [Mary will call him].

In addition, for the verb *hope,* the embedded complement may be either IP (as above), or CP (Complementizer Phrase) with *that,* information included within its theta grid:

(167) John hopes [that Mary will call him].

For some sentences which would otherwise be ungrammatical, English requires that some verbs occur with a CP structure with *for* as C to assign

case (the identity of the complementizer *for* with the preposition *for* is perhaps not accidental):

(168) a.   John prefers [for Mary to call him].
      b.   *John prefers [Mary to call him].

Finally, there is a distinction to be made between STRUCTURAL CASE (as
summarized above) and INHERENT CASE; the latter is a lexical specification whose usefulness is found in providing an account for instances in
which the governed NP carries a surface case different from that typical
of other NPs in the same configuration, and possibly also in so-called
'double object' constructions. An example is that of German verbs which
'take dative direct objects'. The verb *helfen* 'to help' is an example; while
typical transitive verbs take direct objects with a surface Accusative
case, *helfen* assigns to its direct objects Dative case:

(169) a.   *Ich sehe den Mann.*   'I see the man.' (Acc)
      b.   *Ich helfe dem Mann.*   'I help the man.' (Dat)
      c.   **Ich helfe den Mann.*

The two verbs have identical theta grids as concerns the number of arguments, but *helfen* has its internal argument specified lexically as
carrying inherent Dative case (represented here as a third line in the
theta grid):

(170)

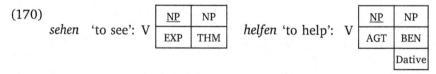

sehen 'to see': V	NP	NP		*helfen* 'to help': V	NP	NP
	EXP	THM			AGT	BEN
						Dative

Such a lexical specification, as always with lexical information, over-
rides the structural case assignment rule which would otherwise apply;
the fact that more lexical information is required serves also to capture
the fact that such verbs are exceptional to the more general rule. Evidence in support of this analysis for German is that when the NP object
is moved to subject position by Passive, the NP which is assigned Acc
structurally in the active counterpart is now assigned Nom, while the inherent case of the NP assigned inherent Dat by *helfen* shows no change:

(171) a.   *Er wird gesehen.*   'He is seen.' (Nom)
      b.   *Ihm wird geholfen.*   'He is helped.' (Dat)
      c.   **Er wurde geholfen.*

One example of double-object verbs will suffice. English shows a relationship with some verbs as follows:

(172) a.   Mary gave flowers to John.
      b.   Mary gave John flowers.

Thus the verb *give* occurs with either an NP direct object and a PP with *to,* or with two NPs. There is a problem, however, in that in the sentence with two NPs there is no ready mechanism to assign case to the second NP (both should apparently be abstract Accusative, and the second NP (*flowers*) is separated from the verb that must assign it case by the first (*John*), thus violating adjacency). The proposed account is one in which the relationship between the two sentences is captured lexically (in this instance, unlike the more general passive relationship, restricted to a small class of verbs), with the case of the second NP in the double-object sentence assigned inherently. Perhaps:

(173)

V	NP	NP	PP
	AGT	THM	BEN

$\rightarrow$

V	NP	NP	NP
	AGT	BEN	THM
			Acc

That is, the notional theta roles remain the same, but the ordering of constituents differs. This is, of course, an optional rule, limited to this specific subclass of verbs.

5.4.4 Binding Theory. Binding Theory seeks to explain the interpretation of nominal elements. There are three clauses of the Binding Theory, in terms of which ANAPHOR, PRONOUN, and R-EXPRESSION (referring expression) are technical terms which must be defined for each language:

> Principle A: An ANAPHOR must be bound in its governing category.
> Principle B: A PRONOUN must be free in its governing category.
> Principle C: An R-EXPRESSION must be free everywhere.

While the notion 'governing category' is for a few cases somewhat problematic to define, it can in the vast majority of instances be considered to be the minimal structure in which can be found: (1) the element to be interpreted, (2) its governor, and (3) a subject. For English, the ANAPHORS include reflexives and reciprocals, which must find their antecedent within the same clause:

(174) a. John$_i$ saw himself$_i$ (himself = John)
    b. [John and Bill]$_i$ saw themselves$_i$ (themselves = John and Bill)
    c. [John and Bill]$_i$ saw [each other]$_i$ (each other = John and Bill)

For English, PRONOUNS include the traditional nonreflexive pronouns, which must find their antecedent outside the clause in which they occur:

(175) a. John$_i$ saw him$_j$ (*him = John)
    b. John$_i$ gave the book to him$_j$ (*him = John)

(Such pronouns must, of course, find their antecedent in a larger context, whether linguistic or nonlinguistic. This area of textlinguistics is virtually untapped within the theory; its investigation falls in the area of language use in pragmatics, not strictly syntax.) For English, R-EXPRESSIONS include all NPs having lexical content; they derive their unique interpretation from the universe of discourse rather than being contingent upon the linguistic context, so that they 'refer' by their very nature. By saying they must be free everywhere, it is the case that they have no antecedent that governs them (see the definition of Government in (162)):

(176) a. John saw Bill. (*Bill = John)
    b. John gave the book to Bill. (*Bill = John)

When text structure is examined, it is apparent that the distribution of NPs, like that of pronouns, is typically heavily constrained; the specific details of the distribution of NPs versus pronouns in text in a given language is a further matter of pragmatics to which attention may fruitfully be directed.

It is proposed that traces of movement (see the discussion of Movement, §5.4.6) are subject to the Binding Theory as well, so that the module has application more widely than simply the interpretation of such nominals as those mentioned above. In particular, it is claimed that traces of NP Movement are like anaphors and subject to Principle A (they must be bound within their governing category), while traces of WH Movement are like R-expressions and subject to Principle C (they must be free everywhere, never c-commanded by a constituent in an argument position). Such a claim involves the Binding Theory module more thoroughly as a constraint, and as a result simplifies the statements of movement, as desired. We return to this topic in §5.4.6.

5.4.5 Control Theory. Control Theory concerns the interpretation of the specific empty category defined as PRO. Crucial is the PRO THEOREM: PRO must be ungoverned. What this means is that among the empty categories for NPs (traces of movement are the other major examples) is one of a specific type, which always and only occurs in a position where case cannot be assigned to it; this empty category is labeled PRO, which now serves as a technical term to refer to just that constituent. The only place PRO shows up is where a [Spec,IP] position is required by the EPP, but no case is assigned because the INFL is nonfinite and no ECM is necessary.

Control Theory, then, assigns an index to PRO to represent its interpretation (parallel to the assignment of indices to anaphors and pronouns by Binding Theory). Typically, nonfinite clauses are embedded within finite clauses, and the verbs in the finite clauses are either 'subject-control' or 'object-control' verbs, so that PRO has different interpretations in the two types of contexts. Consider some examples:

(177) a. John hoped to bathe.
      b. John told Mary to bathe.
      c. John promised Mary to bathe.

In (177a) *hope* is associated with a finite INFL which assigns Nom to *John;* the second verb, *bathe,* appears in its infinitival form (nonfinite INFL) which cannot assign Nom, although the EPP predicts that a subject NP should be present in the [Spec,IP] position. *Hope* is not, however, an ECM verb (**John hoped Mary to bathe*). Thus, the following is proposed as approximating the D-Structure:

(177) a'. John hoped [PRO to bathe]

Here PRO satisfies the EPP, but it cannot be assigned case either by INFL of *bathe* (nonfinite) or by *hope* (non-ECM); this is precisely the position in which PRO is expected to occur. Control Theory must determine the referent for PRO; in this particular example there is only one NP available (*John*), and coindexing with that NP accords with the interpretation:

(177) a''. John$_i$ hoped [PRO$_i$ to bathe]

This interpretation receives some support from the distribution of anaphors in the embedded clause:

(178) a. John$_i$ hoped [PRO$_i$ to bathe himself$_i$]
     b. *John$_i$ hoped [PRO$_i$ to bathe him$_i$]

In both (178a) and (178b) the governing category is the embedded clause, containing the pronominal form itself, its governor (*bathe*), and a subject (PRO); coindexation must take place with the anaphor in (178a), it must not take place with the pronoun in (178b), and the necessary indexation between *John* and PRO ties in properly with the resulting interpretation. The pronoun in (178b) of course refers to someone other than John, cf.

(179) John$_i$ hoped [PRO$_i$ to bathe him$_j$]

The verbs *tell* and *promise* show similar characteristics:

(180) a. John$_i$ told Mary$_j$ [PRO$_j$ to bathe]
     b. *John$_i$ told (Mary$_j$) [PRO$_i$ to bathe]
     c. John$_i$ promised Mary$_j$ [PRO$_i$ to bathe]
     d. *John$_i$ promised Mary$_j$ [PRO$_j$ to bathe]

Verbs like *tell* are classified as OBJECT-CONTROL VERBS, those like *promise* as SUBJECT-CONTROL VERBS. It is this classification which functions in cooperation with Control Theory to result in the correct interpretation. Note the patterns of anaphor distribution in such sentences:

(181) a. John$_i$ told Mary$_j$ [PRO$_j$ to bathe *himself$_i$/herself$_j$]
     b. John$_i$ promised Mary$_j$ [PRO$_i$ to bathe himself$_i$/*herself$_j$]

Such distinctions are commonly assumed to have universal validity (the notion of object- versus subject-control is widely used).

Note, however, that there is an additional interpretation of PRO which is sometimes available, treated within the theory as ARBITRARY PRO (PRO$_{arb}$). Consider sentences like the following:

(182) a. To bathe is heavenly.
     b. Studying P&P is thrilling.
     c. To eat chocolate ice cream is to fall in love.

Here the "subject" of the nonfinite INFL is unspecified, and it is apparently not controlled by any NP elsewhere within the string. Further, the interpretation given to such sentences is that the identity of the subject is irrelevant—whoever carries out the activity is expected to have the same experience. Thus:

(182) a'. [PRO$_{arb}$ to bathe] is heavenly
      b'. [PRO$_{arb}$ studying P&P] is thrilling
      c'. [PRO$_{arb}$ to eat chocolate ice cream] is [PRO$_{arb}$ to fall in love]

There is some confirmation available in that if a reflexive anaphor occurs in such sentences, it must be *oneself*:

(183) To bathe oneself/*himself is heavenly.

Similar to (182c):

(184) To eat chocolate ice cream is to find oneself/*himself falling in love.

The following are interesting in this regard as well:

(185) a. John mastered P&P without applying himself/*oneself.
      b. To master P&P without applying *himself/oneself is an amazing feat.

The fact that *oneself* is grammatical and other anaphors are not indicates that it is PRO$_{arb}$ that is involved here as the governor of the anaphor.

5.4.6 Movement. While not a module as such, patterns of movement are very interesting and important when viewed in cooperation with the principles of the modules summarized above; there is a module referred to as BOUNDING THEORY which is involved here, which we return to under the discussion of Subjacency.

Within P&P, movement within the core grammar (that central portion of the syntax governed by Universal Grammar) is not characterized as a series of ordered transformations as in earlier versions of transformational grammar, although language-specific movement rules may be necessary to deal with peripheral matters beyond the scope of the constraints of UG. Rather, within P&P core grammar, movement is governed by a single rule: MOVE α (move something somewhere). As it stands, of course, such a rule is disastrously overly general and produces an infinite number of ungrammatical sentences. Thus constraints are needed. In particular, the following questions must be answered: (1) What sorts of constituents can be moved? (2) What are the landing sites the constituents can move to? (3) How far can the constituents be moved? When such questions are answered, the rule of Move α becomes much more constrained.

The sorts of constituents (the targets for movement) which can be moved by move α are of two types: they are either heads of constructions (i.e., X-level constituents, e.g., N, V, A, P, I) or maximal projections (X''-level constituents, e.g., NP, VP, AP, PP, IP); no other constituent qualifies as a suitable candidate for movement under the constraints of Universal Grammar.

The landing sites for movement of constituents include unoccupied positions (e.g., [Spec,CP], [Spec,IP], [C,CP], all only if present but unoccupied) and positions where adjunction is possible. Crucial is the PRINCIPLE OF STRUCTURE PRESERVATION, which requires that no constituent be obliterated by movement (hence movement only to positions which are unoccupied) and that any novel structural configurations resulting from movement *respect the principles of phrase structure,* so that the result is comparable to that produced by X-Bar Syntax (hence adjunction); it is also required that the labels on constituents not be changed, which is a further constraint on landing site in that the moved constituent must be compatible with the label on that site (which makes [Spec,CP] ideal for WH Movement, given that the wh-constituent can be NP, PP, AP, etc.). Also crucial is the notion that all movement leaves behind a trace of the moved constituent in the position from which it was moved; in every instance of movement, it must be the case that the moved constituent m-commands its trace (traces of NP movement are thus comparable to anaphors in terms of Binding Theory).

The distance a constituent can be moved is subject to the constraint of SUBJACENCY, defined in terms of bounding nodes, as follows:

(186) Movement cannot cross more than one bounding node, where bounding nodes are IP and NP.

There is, however, a parameter involved here in that languages may differ as to what they recognize as bounding nodes. For English the bounding nodes are IP and NP as stated above. For Italian, however, the bounding nodes are NP and CP (we do not go into the relevant arguments in this summary).

Finally, of all the types of movement which are possible, three specific types attract major attention: NP Movement, WH Movement, and

Head-to-Head Movement. In summary (details considered below), NP Movement moves only NP constituents, and it is the case that such constituents are moved always and only from a position in which they cannot receive abstract case, to a position where they can receive abstract case; thus NP Movement is closely tied with the Case Filter. WH Movement, on the other hand, is a label used to characterize movement of constituents without reference to the Case Filter; while the label WH Movement is used, it is not only wh-constituents which are affected by it. It is true that question words and relative pronouns are moved by the rule (which in English are mostly wh-words, hence the name), but NPs and other constituents may also be moved by WH Movement (of course, some wh-constituents are in fact NPs as well). Head-to-Head Movement is quite restricted in its application, manifested in English only in movement of INFL in questions from [I,IP] to [C,CP] and Verb Raising moving verbs from [V,VP] to [I,IP] to receive inflection.[10] Any other types of movement are considered to be language-specific peripheral matters.

NP MOVEMENT has been discussed in §5.4.3 in terms of Case Theory. Essentially, NP Movement is always *from* a position in which a theta role is assigned (by the theta grids of the constituents involved) but no abstract case, *to* a position in which abstract case is assigned but no theta role. Recall the case of passive above:

(187) D-Structure   e was given the book to Bill
      S-Structure   the book$_i$ was given t$_i$ to Bill

As mentioned above, passive verbs (here *was given*) lose their ability (by what we consider a lexical operation) both to assign abstract case to their internal arguments and to assign a theta role to their external arguments. Thus the NP *the book* in its D-Structure position above cannot receive Accusative case, and there is no external theta role to be assigned (though a (covert) subject must occur because of the Extended Projection Principle). The movement of *the book* to subject position allows it to get Nominative case from the finite INFL, but no additional theta role; its theta role remains that of THEME, transmitted through the trace left behind by the movement (the coindexing of *the book* and the trace results in the chain <*the book$_i$*, t$_i$>). The second major way in which NP Movement applies is for what is known as 'raising' constructions. In English, *seem* is a verb which takes a clause as its internal

---

[10]Due to the exigencies of space, we will not include discussion of Head-to-Head Movement in this summary.

argument and has no external argument (though it still has a subject position because of the Extended Projection Principle). If the clause serving as argument has a nonfinite verb, however, the NP subject of the clause will not be assigned abstract case; typically, then, the NP moves to subject position of *seem:*

(188) D-Structure   e seems [Bill to be happy]
      S-Structure   Bill$_i$ seems [t$_i$ to be happy]

If the embedded clause has a finite verb, of course, no movement is necessary (the NP will get Nominative case from the finite verb); in that case the subject position is filled by an expletive, which does not require a theta role (recall the discussion of Theta Theory above):

(189) D-Structure   e seems [that Bill is happy]
      S-Structure   it seems [that Bill is happy]

The third sort of construction in which NP Movement is manifested is one-place predicates which have only an internal argument and lack an external argument (although the subject still occurs syntactically because of the Extended Projection Principle). The data for such constructions (termed unaccusatives, see §5.4.1, Theta Theory) in English is not uncontroversial, but it may be the case that a verb like *appear* is an example (it is commonly assumed that the theta role manifested is in some sense a THEME, if only because the verb is one of movement or change of state, with little or no volition involved). Under that assumption, the following is found:

(190) D-Structure   e arrived three men
      S-Structure   three men$_i$ arrived t$_i$

This is in contrast to other 'intransitive' verbs which do have external theta roles:

(191) D-Structure   three men slept
      S-Structure   three men slept

It is NP Movement which with *arrive* moves *three men* from its position within VP to [Spec,IP].

WH MOVEMENT always moves a constituent into a position where no theta role is assigned. The easiest cases to examine are those involving question words:

(192) D-Structure   John will see whom
      S-Structure   whom$_i$ will John see t$_i$

It is assumed that such question words at S-Structure are under Spec of CP (of which C(omplementizer) is head and CP the maximal projection and IP the X-Bar complement), which has no inherent phrasal label and thus can allow any sort of constituent to be dominated by it without violating the Principle of Structural Preservation. A similar construction is that of relative clauses:

(193) D-Structure   Bill knows the man [John will see whom]
      S-Structure   Bill knows the man [whom$_i$ John will see t$_i$]

Two other examples suggested for English WH Movement are PP Extraction and Heavy NP Shift. The following illustrates PP Extraction:

(194) D-Structure   The heat in Dallas is overpowering
      S-Structure   The heat t$_i$ is overpowering [in Dallas]$_i$

Here the PP *in Dallas,* generated as modifying *the heat* at D-Structure, is postposed (and adjoined) by WH Movement (it does not end up in a theta-marked position). The following illustrates Heavy NP Shift:

(195) D-Structure John told the story of his operation to his friends
      S-Structure John told t$_i$ to his friends [the story of his operation]$_i$

While "heavy" is difficult to define, the complexity of the NP object in this example is clear, especially when contrasted to the following:

(196) D-Structure   John told the story with great enthusiasm
      S-Structure   *John told t$_i$ with great enthusiasm [the story]$_i$

Two facts are especially noteworthy in discussion relative to movement. First, in each case above the 'antecedent' which is moved m-commands its trace. Further, there is a restriction on how far a constituent can be moved, defined in terms of BOUNDING THEORY. The theory insists that the concept of subjacency (see above) must be adhered to. All the examples above adhere to subjacency, but now note the following:

(197) D-Structure The claim that the heat in Dallas is overpowering is
true

S-Structure *The claim that the heat t_i is overpowering is true
[in Dallas]$_i$

What fails in this second sentence (with the intended interpretation) is
not the constituent which is moved (PP is a maximal projection), nor
the landing site (it is properly adjoined as in the grammatical examples); rather, its ungrammaticality is due to the fact that three bounding
nodes are crossed in the proposed derivation. The D-Structures for the
sentences in question are the following (the bounding nodes are indicated by numerals):

(198) a. [[the claim [that [[the heat [in Dallas]$_{pp}$]$_{np}$ is
1

overpowering]$_{ip}$]$_{cp}$]$_{np}$ is true]$_{ip}$
2   3

b. [[the heat [in Dallas]$_{pp}$]$_{np}$ is overpowering]$_{ip}$
1

To extrapose the PP *in Dallas* in the second sentence is to cross one
bounding node (NP); for the first sentence, however, the extraposition
must cross three bounding nodes. It is this violation of subjacency
which is suggested to account for the ungrammatical nature of the first
sentence.

In this regard, note that for some instances of movement involving
embedded clauses a cyclic approach is utilized, moving the constituent
more than a single time but each time in accordance with the syntactic
structure and principles alluded to already. For example:

(199) D-Structure   John had said Bill thought Jane saw who
S-Structure   who$_i$ had John said Bill thought Jane saw t_i

The following is its full bracketed structure, including e in Spec of CP:

(200) [e [John had said [e [Bill thought [e [Jane saw who]$_{ip}$]$_{cp}$]$_{ip}$]$_{cp}$]$_{ip}$]$_{cp}$
1   2   3

Here *who* appears to cross three bounding nodes (all IP). Under a cyclic
analysis, however, it is assumed that *who* in fact moves three times,

each movement being in accordance with subjacency (movement of the auxiliary *have* is ignored here):

(201) [e [John had said [e [Bill thought [e
       [Jane saw who]$_{ip}$]$_{cp}$]$_{ip}$]$_{cp}$]$_{ip}$]$_{cp}$
              1

       [e [John had said [e [Bill thought [who$_i$
       [Jane saw t$_i$]$_{ip}$]$_{cp}$]$_{ip}$]$_{cp}$]$_{ip}$]$_{cp}$
              1

       [e [John had said [who$_i$ [Bill thought [t'$_i$
       [Jane saw t$_i$]$_{ip}$]$_{cp}$]$_{ip}$]$_{cp}$]$_{ip}$]$_{cp}$
              1

       [who$_i$ [had John said [t'$_i$ [Bill thought [t'$_i$
       [Jane saw t$_i$]$_{ip}$]$_{cp}$]$_{ip}$]$_{cp}$]$_{ip}$]$_{cp}$

This cyclic analysis finds some support in the fact that if one of the [Spec,CP] positions is filled, the sentence is ungrammatical; this is a result of the fact that since that position is filled, the question word cannot move to that position cyclically and thus must move farther than subjacency will allow. Such a state of affairs can result if an attempt is made to move two or more question words in the same derivation (such structures in the real world are found in English only in pragmatically-conditioned questions, where the hearer is asking the speaker to repeat a previous statement). For example, consider a basic D-Structure like the following:

(202) [e [John said [e [Bill thought [e [Jane saw Tom
       yesterday]$_{ip}$]$_{cp}$]$_{ip}$]$_{cp}$]$_{ip}$]$_{cp}$

Keeping that particular relation among constituents in mind (it is crucial in considering the following discussion to keep the scope of the question words the same), consider a parallel D-Structure containing question words:

(203) [e [John said [e [Bill thought [e [Jane saw who
       when]$_{ip}$]$_{cp}$]$_{ip}$]$_{cp}$]$_{ip}$]$_{cp}$

The facts of English are such that only one question word can move:

(204) a. Who did John say Bill thought Jane saw when?
      b. When did John say Bill thought Jane saw who?

In particular, strings like the following in which both question words move are ungrammatical:

(205) a. *Who did John say Bill thought when did Jane see?
      b. *When did John say Bill thought who did Jane see?

This state of affairs has its account in Subjacency. In the following D-Structure for the sentence in question the bounding nodes are numbered:

(206) [e[John said [e [Bill thought [e [Jane saw who
      when]$_{ip}$]$_{cp}$]$_{ip}$]$_{cp}$]$_{ip}$]$_{cp}$
          1   2   3

If the movement of question words is cyclical, the following derivation ensues (here using *who* and ignoring subject-auxiliary inversion):

(207) [e [John said [e [Bill thought [who$_i$ [Jane saw t$_i$
      when]$_{ip}$]$_{cp}$]$_{ip}$]$_{cp}$]$_{ip}$]$_{cp}$
          1

      [e [John said [who$_i$ [Bill thought [t'$_i$ [Jane saw t$_i$
      when]$_{ip}$]$_{cp}$]$_{ip}$]$_{cp}$]$_{ip}$]$_{cp}$
          1

      [who$_i$ [John said [t'$_i$ [Bill thought [t'$_i$ [Jane saw t$_i$
      when]$_{ip}$]$_{cp}$]$_{ip}$]$_{cp}$]$_{ip}$]$_{cp}$
          1

There is no violation of Subjacency, and the sentence is grammatical. If the second question word (here, *when*) is to be moved, however, there are only two ways this is possible. If it were to move at some intermediate point in the derivation above, so that its landing site corresponds to one of the traces of the previously moved *who,* the result is ungrammatical (see examples above), even though Subjacency itself is not violated. The reason proposed for the ungrammaticality in such a case is that such a movement violates the basic principle of CYCLICITY, *viz.* that operations relevant to a given level of structure must apply at that level, not on a higher level (it is also important that such movement would obliterate the trace of the previously moved question word, thus making interpretation of the D-Structure source for that word impossible without violating Subjacency. Thus, once the most deeply embedded sentence has been affected by rules, and the derivation moves on to the next 'higher' sentence, there can be no return to the most deeply embedded sentence and thus any subsequent movement of *when* is disqualified. The only alternative would be to move both question words at the same time, but here again Subjacency comes clearly into play. Consider the D-Structure again:

(208) [e [John said [e [Bill thought [e [Jane saw who
           when]$_{ip}$]$_{cp}$]$_{ip}$]$_{cp}$]$_{ip}$]$_{cp}$

Suppose *when* is moved first by WH Movement:

(209) [e [John said [e [Bill thought [when$_i$ [Jane saw who
           t$_i$]$_{ip}$]$_{cp}$]$_{ip}$]$_{cp}$]$_{ip}$]$_{cp}$
           1   2   3

There is now no place *who* can move to without violating Subjacency; the only intermediate landing site is filled by *when*. Thus, *when* could continue to be moved into higher sentences, but *who* cannot move at all. As a result, for English, no sentence moves more than one question word, and it is the principle of Subjacency wich provides an account for this state of affairs.

5.4.7 Subject-in-VP Hypothesis. Chomsky and Lasnik (1991) propose that D-Structure (the result of the applications of X-Bar rules, consistent with the theta grids of the constituents involved) is approximately the same for all languages. What is in focus in such a claim is the relationships holding among the constituents (specifiers, heads, complements, adjuncts), not the specific orderings (which follow from details of application of parameters of X-Bar Theory in a given language). They further propose that the level of representation referred to as Logical Form will be the same for all languages, the function of LF being, at least in part, that of providing a sort of "universal logic" for interpretation of relationships among constituents as part of the semantic representation. Given this two-part proposal, it follows that syntactic differences of ordering among languages lie largely at the level of S-Structure, essentially that level reached after application of rules that have come to be characterized as transformational.

The proposed structural configuration for English, building on the model proposed in their paper, is as follows for the sentence *John met Bill* (the phrase-structure tree here is simplified, ignoring the internal structure of INFL and leaving our several layers of structure and labels):

(210)

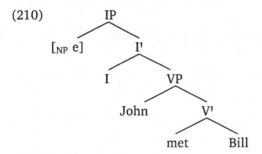

This is, of course, quite different from the sort of structure presented earlier, with all NPs present under VP, and an empty category NP alone in subject position under [Spec,IP]. One of the motivations proposed for this sort of configuration is that [Spec,IP] is "anomalous" (their term) because it is the only position to which a theta role may or may not be assigned, depending upon the verb (e.g., there is no theta-role assigned for passive verbs and unaccusative verbs). In addition, although the theta role for the NP in [Spec,IP] is assigned by the verb, the position itself is unexpectedly not under the maximal projection of the verb, VP. Both of these problems are solved if the proposal is made that both subject NP (here, *John,* in Spec of VP) and object NP (here, *Bill,* as complement of V) are under VP.[11] This configuration might also provide a more ready account for the 'compositional' nature of the assignment of the theta role of the subject NP by the sequence V + NP: given the two sentences *John broke a vase* vs. *John broke a leg* the thematic role of *John* cannot be determined until the verb and its complement are accounted for. In the proposed configuration the node V' provides the appropriate association of V and NP, and the whole is c-commanded by the subject NP *John.*

Assuming such a tree structure, Chomsky and Lasnik propose two specific rules which are needed in the derivation to provide the surface form:

---

[11]Apparently they assume that the position held in the example by *John* will be empty for passives and unaccusatives, but not required by EPP either, not being a subject position.

1. a rule of NP Raising raises the subject NP from initial position in VP to initial position in IP ([Spec,VP]→[Spec,IP])
2. Verb-Raising raises the verb from under V' to consolidate with INFL so that its morphology can be attached or checked.

It is pointed out explicitly in the paper that SVO and VSO languages can be distinguished by the specific derivational position at which these two rules apply In particular:

(211) SVO languages apply the rule NP Raising and the rule of Verb-Raising both at S-Structure, yielding

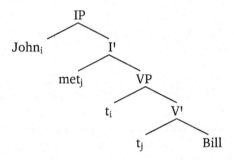

Neither of these two rules then is left to apply at LF.

(212) VSO languages, by contrast, apply Verb-Raising at S-Structure, leaving NP Raising to apply at LF only

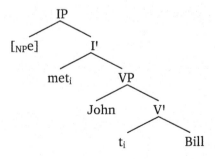

The two languages then have the same D-Structure (presented above) and the same LF (comparable to the English SVO example); they differ only at S-Structure.

Chomsky and Lasnik suggest in addition (following up on a proposal by Pollock) that the AGREEMENT component of INFL can be further broken up (the Split-INFL Hypothesis) into AGRs (Subject Agreement) and AGRo (Object Agreement). Then the raising processes for NP can be separated into subject and object types, depending upon the case-marking or agreement characteristics of the language in question (e.g., if case-assignment is not possible for the NP in its D-Structure position, it must move). It is only a slight oversimplification to say that under this proposal VSO languages result from applying Verb-Raising at S-Structure and both Subject-Raising and Object-Raising at LF only; SVO languages result from applying both Verb-Raising and Subject-Raising at S-Structure, with Object-Raising applying at LF only; OSV languages result from applying Object-Raising at S-Structure and Verb-Raising and Subject Raising at LF only; SOV languages result from applying both Subject-Raising and Object-Raising at S-Structure, and Verb-Raising at LF only. Space restrictions prevent a more thorough account of this proposal here.

All too briefly we have sketched the major points of the continuation of the *Aspects* tradition after 1970. We close this section with a table showing the much more complex apparatus of this new approach as a comparison to the 1965 model (based upon Haegeman 1994:501):

(213)

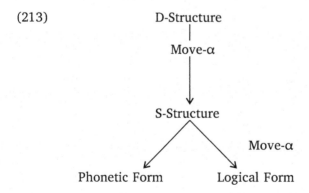

Summary of the P&P model

1. In opposition to the *Aspects* model, the P&P model stresses the modularity of the parts of a grammar.
2. Transformational rules in P&P are much less specific, i.e., weaker than in the *Aspects* model, e.g., MOVE α. There is

more use of filters and constraints to remove the non-well-formed structures produced by overgeneration.

3. There is a greater use made of principles and less of rules, e.g., SUBJACENCY, STRUCTURE PRESERVATION, the CASE FILTER, the THETA CRITERION, etc.

4. The phrase structure of a language is generated by an X-Bar type syntax that stresses cross-categorial generalization and that does justice to the natural head-complement structure of language.

5. There is more use made of empty categories. In the P&P approach, at least three kinds are discussed. These phonologically null but syntactically active elements turn out to be in complementary distribution with one another.

6

Lexical-Functional Grammar

6.1 Introduction

Lexical-Functional Grammar (LFG) began in the mid-1970s (e.g., Bresnan 1978) when its proponents, dissatisfied with the results produced by the classical GTG paradigm, turned to developing a model to take syntactic function more directly into account. There are a number of characteristics which place LFG well within the same general research tradition, however, among them (1) the emphasis on universal constraints on human language, (2) the adoption of the explanation of child language acquisition as a primary task of a linguistic theory, (3) the modular approach to linguistics (allowing language to be studied free from its communicative context), (4) a distinction between competence and performance (at least at this stage of theory development), and (5) the general research paradigm requiring explicit proposals which must be tested against language data within a framework of argumentation. Nevertheless, LFG differs radically from classical GTG models in that there is an emphasis on syntactic function in addition to form, and it is a declarative system rather than a dynamic one (i.e., there are no transformational rules and so nothing "moves" in the theory). In addition, as will be demonstrated below, there is a strong emphasis on the nature of the lexicon and lexical entries, and it is this emphasis, together with proposals regarding universal characteristics of language, that allows generalizations to be captured. Although there are suggestions that discourse factors play a role in some of the constructions to be accounted for, all indications are that LFG is a sentence-grammar theory. The research carried out within this point of view is extensive; for this

We are very grateful to Mary Dalrymple for reading an earlier version of this chapter and making valuable suggestions. All errors are, of course, our own.

163

summary we have focused our attention primarily on Bresnan 1978 and Bresnan 1982 (especially Kaplan and Bresnan 1982), Bresnan and Kanerva 1989, Bresnan 1990, and Bresnan and Moshi 1990; we omit numerous details of this well-developed theory in this overview, focusing our attention on matters of conceptualization crucially relevant to its comparison with other points of view. One of the goals of the theory is to provide a linguistically realistic account of language structure that is at the same time amenable to computational application; we focus here only on the linguistic proposals.

6.2 General ontology, methodology, and worldview of LFG

A crucial claim of LFG is that two distinct levels of syntactic structure must be distinguished. A CONSTITUENT STRUCTURE (or C-STRUCTURE) of a sentence is a conventional phrase-structure tree consisting of a labeled bracketing indicating the superficial arrangement of words and phrases in the sentence, including information regarding syntactic categories, terminal strings, and their dominance (that is, constituency) and linear precedence relations; it is the input to the phonological component. A FUNCTIONAL STRUCTURE (or F-STRUCTURE) is a representation of the surface grammatical functions of constituents of a sentence (its source is discussed below), including information such as grammatical function names, semantic forms, and symbols for syntactic features; it is commonly assumed that f-structure is the sole input to the semantic component, although this is a matter of current debate within the theory. The f-structure conveys the conventional information regarding subject and object, and predication; it represents such information in terms of a set of ordered pairs associating an attribute (e.g., subject) and a value of that attribute for a specific sentence (e.g., the specific NP occurring with that function in a given sentence, see the following examples). It is important to note that SEMANTIC REPRESENTATIONS are different from both c-structures and f-structures, leading to three levels of representation distinct from the phonological. Because these two levels of syntactic structure are recognized and each is generated directly, no transformational rules are needed.

By way of example, consider (214):

(214) A girl handed a toy to the baby.

This string is produced by the following context-free c-structure rules:

(215) S → NP VP
      NP → DET N
      VP → V NP PP

These rules produce the following c-structure tree:

(216)

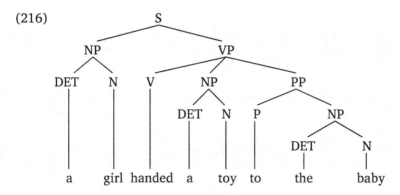

By way of contrast, note that the corresponding f-structure for (214) is as follows:

(217)
$$\begin{bmatrix} \text{SUBJ} & \begin{bmatrix} \text{SPEC} & \text{A} \\ \text{NUM} & \text{SG} \\ \text{PRED} & \text{'GIRL'} \end{bmatrix} \\ \text{TENSE} & \text{PAST} \\ \text{PRED} & \text{'HAND} \langle (\uparrow\text{SUBJ})(\uparrow\text{OBJ})(\uparrow\text{TO OBJ}) \rangle \text{'} \\ \text{OBJ} & \begin{bmatrix} \text{SPEC} & \text{A} \\ \text{NUM} & \text{SG} \\ \text{PRED} & \text{'TOY'} \end{bmatrix} \\ \text{TO} & \begin{bmatrix} \text{PCASE} & \text{TO} \\ \text{OBJ} & \begin{bmatrix} \text{SPEC} & \text{THE} \\ \text{NUM} & \text{SG} \\ \text{PRED} & \text{'BABY'} \end{bmatrix} \end{bmatrix} \end{bmatrix}$$

There is, of course, much that requires explanation here. Note first that there is a pairing of ATTRIBUTES (i.e., grammatical functions or features) and VALUES. Thus, for example, the TENSE attribute in the sentence (214) has the value PAST. Further, the three NPs (and all other structures as well) have their own constituents and values associated with them, so that *a girl* has the pairings of SPEC and A, NUM and SG, and PRED and 'GIRL' indicated in the first box in (217). Heads of NPs are considered to be (semantic) predicates in the same way as verbs are, as indicated by the labeling in (217).

F-structures are universal, the input to the semantic component for semantic interpretation. It is the lexical entry for the predicate *hand* here that does most of the work in developing the appropriate f-structure. Representations such as (↑SUBJ) indicate the mapping holding between the thematic arguments of the predicate (discussed immediately below) and the appropriate structure in the phrase-structure tree. For English, SUBJ is defined by a language-specific rule as the NP that is a daughter of S and precedes VP (see (236) below). In the tree in (216) this is the NP *a girl*. Thus, it is the f-structure for *a girl* that is mapped to the first argument for the verb *hand* in this sentence for its interpretation.

It is the case, then, that in developing such an f-structure, the theory depends heavily on the lexicon and proposals regarding the nature of Universal Grammar. In this very brief introduction we present only the barest outline of these claims, referring the reader to the literature for detailed discussion.

Consider first universals pertaining to argument structure. The proposal is made that there is a *universal hierarchy of thematic roles,* as follows:

(218) agent > beneficiary > goal > instrumental > patient/theme
        > locative

The fact that this hierarchy captures is that a specific verb may make use of essentially any subset of the roles included here, but it is crucial that they are always arrayed for any verb in this particular order in the lexical entry. As we will see, the ordering is important because it determines the sort of mappings that may hold between the thematic roles and syntactic functions.

A second universal notion has to do with the *classification of syntactic functions. Typically, two features are used to distinguish among syntactic functions: [+r] means that a given argument is thematically restricted (and thus may encode only certain choices from the hierarchy in (218)); [−r] means it is not thematically restricted (and thus can be individuated by an argument with any thematic role); [+o] means that an argument is objective; [−o] means it is not. Given this orientation, the following classification of syntactic functions results:*

(219)
$$\begin{bmatrix} -r \\ -o \end{bmatrix} \text{SUBJ} \qquad \begin{bmatrix} +r \\ -o \end{bmatrix} \text{OBL}\theta$$

$$\begin{bmatrix} -r \\ +o \end{bmatrix} \text{OBJ} \qquad \begin{bmatrix} +r \\ +o \end{bmatrix} \text{OBJ}\theta$$

Here θ abbreviates multiple functions, so that OBLθ refers to a family of arguments, each of which has an oblique function, one for each thematic role (goal, instrument, etc.). OBJθ by contrast refers to the class of secondary, restricted objects, those with fixed semantic roles, that are individuated in some languages. I.e., not all objects are equal: some objects have greater access to properties like passivization, distribution adjacent to the verb, manifestation of agreement on the verb, the ability to undergo unspecified object deletion, etc.; the other objects are OBJθ. What (219) represents is that virtually any thematic role may be encoded as SUBJ, but only certain restricted thematic roles may be encoded as an oblique function. Note that this use of features results in the following natural classes of syntactic functions:

(220) SUBJ, OBJ $[-r]$
      OBJθ, OBLθ $[+r]$
      SUBJ, OBLθ $[-o]$
      OBJ, OBJθ $[+o]$

That is, only subjects and objects are $[-r]$; only obliques and restricted objects are $[+r]$; only subjects and obliques are $[-o]$; only objects are $[+o]$. The significance of these natural classes will become evident in the discussion to follow.

The third highly important notion to illustrate here is that of lexical mapping principles, which are of three types. Consider first the following INTRINSIC RULE CLASSIFICATIONS (we include these as a sample of such principles, which include more than these few):

(221) Agent encoding principle: ag
                                  |
                               $[-o]$

I.e., the thematic role agent cannot be encoded as object (and thus may occur only as subject or oblique).

(222) Theme encoding principle: th/pt
                                  |
                               $[-r]$

I.e., the thematic role theme is unrestricted in function (and thus may occur as either subject or object).

(223) Location encoding principle: loc
                                         |
                                        $[-o]$

I.e., the thematic role location is encoded as a nonobjective function.

(224) Applied and theme encoding principle: θ   θ
                                                 | or |
                                               $[-r]$ $[+o]$

I.e., in addition to theme and patient being classified as $[-r]$ (stated in (218)), applied arguments (those introduced as object arguments within VP as a result of valency-increasing morphology in some languages) also may be $[-r]$ (and thus may emerge as passivizable or unaccusative objects); alternatively, they may be classified as $[+o]$ (in which case they emerge as restricted objects and thus unpassivizable). There is a restriction on application of this latter $[+o]$ classification, however:

(225) Applied benefactive and recipient encoding principle: *θ
                                                                  |
                                                                $[+o]$

I.e., "indirect objects" universally lack the $[+o]$ classification otherwise available to nonsubject arguments by (224); they are more likely to appear as SUBJ than other applied arguments.

The second type of lexical mapping is referred to as MORPHOLOGICAL OPERATIONS. Consider the following as an example of such a rule for English passive:

(226) Passive: θ̂
                    |
                    ∅

What this rule states is that the highest thematic role in an argument structure (based upon the universal hierarchy in (218)) is to be suppressed (it can optionally be expressed as an adjunct).

The third type of lexical mapping is that of DEFAULT RULE CLASSIFICATIONS. The following are two examples:

(227)   θ̂
                         |
                       [−r]

I.e., the highest thematic role will be unrestricted (and thus will be eligible to be subject). If agent is present it is by the hierarchy in (218) the highest thematic role; note, however, that if (226) Passive applies, agent is suppressed, so that it is the next highest thematic role emerges as subject in such constructions, as required.

(228)   θ
                         |
                       [+r]

I.e., lower roles than the highest will be restricted (and thus will be nonsubjects). Of course, (228) applies only to arguments that are not already specified for [r].

The result of application of such rules is referred to as the ARGUMENT-STRUCTURE (A-STRUCTURE) of a lexical item (see details to follow immediately), which must be associated with syntactic functions and consequently with the c-structure tree. Governing the whole operation of mapping between thematic roles and syntactic functions is a WELL-FORMEDNESS CONDITION (WFC), which consists of two parts:

(229) The Subject Condition: Every lexical form must have a subject.

(230) Function-Argument Biuniqueness: In every lexical form, every expressed lexical role must have a unique syntactic function, and every syntactic function must have a unique lexical role.

Consider, then, the following derivation illustrating how the thematic roles become associated with syntactic functions in the sentence under discussion *A girl handed a toy to the baby.* The verb *hand* in English has a three-place argument structure, with the arguments necessarily arrayed in the order required by the universal hierarchy of thematic roles (218):

(231)   hand ⟨ agent   goal   theme ⟩

Assignment of syntactic functions based upon intrinsic rule classifications results in the following:

(232)   hand < agent   goal   theme >
       intrinsic   [−o]   [−r]

The default rule classifications then apply to yield the following:

(233)   hand < agent   goal   theme >
       intrinsic   [−o]   [−r]
       default   [−r]   [+r]

This configuration can now be associated with the classification of syntactic functions based upon the array of syntactic features shown in (219) and (220), as follows:

(234)   hand < agent   goal   theme >
       intrinsic   [−o]   [−r]
       default   [−r]   [+r]
       _____
                         SUBJ OBJ_{goal}/OBL_{goal} SUBJ/OBJ

The Function-Argument Biuniqueness provision of the WFC then forces a choice regarding the mapping of goal and theme to syntactic functions. Because SUBJECT is already assigned (to agent, the highest thematic role in the argument structure), only OBJ is available for the theme argument (and of course theme could not manifest both ultimately because of the same condition); further, English (unlike some other languages) allows only themes to be thematically restricted objects (OBJ_{goal}), so that goal cannot be associated with OBJ_{goal} and must therefore be OBL_{goal}:

(235)   hand < agent   goal   theme >
       intrinsic   [−o]   [−r]
       default   [−r]   [+r]
       _____
                         SUBJ OBJ_{goal}/OBL_{goal} SUBJ/OBJ
       WFC   SUBJ OBL_{goal} OBJ

It remains to associate such a representation with the c-structure tree in (216) as produced by the c-structure rules. Important in this regard is the fact that although the surface encoding of SUBJ, OBL_{goal}, and OBJ varies among languages, in each language for the comparable proposition the same relationships among constituents results from the argument structure of the lexical entries involved. To carry out the mapping from syntactic function to c-structure configuration, the c-structure rules are supplemented by language-specific F-DESCRIPTION SCHEMATA. English, of course, is a configurational language and thus assigns grammatical functions to specific c-structure configurations. Appropriate mapping rules for English are as follows (again, for ease of presentation we over-simplify here and refer the reader to the literature for full details):

(236) S→   NP   VP
              ($\uparrow$ SUBJ) = $\downarrow$ $\uparrow = \downarrow$

      VP→V (NP)   (TO NP)
              ($\uparrow$ OBJ) = $\downarrow$ ($\uparrow$ OBL$_{\text{goal}}$) = $\downarrow$

What these rules indicate is that the SUBJECT function in English is that NP immediately dominated by S and preceding VP, and the OBJECT function is that NP immediately following V and dominated by VP. The OBL$_{\text{goal}}$ argument is encoded as an oblique construction, manifested (in this instance) as a to + NP prepositional phrase. The pairing of upward and downward arrows is a formal representation of the fact that the f-structure of the appropriate argument (indicated by the upward arrow) must be unified with the f-structure of the constituent with which the mapping is associated. Thus, ($\uparrow$SUBJ) = $\downarrow$ indicates that the f-structure of the SUBJ argument must be unified with the f-structure of the appropriate NP, in this case that dominated by S and preceding VP, as required; the formalism $\uparrow = \downarrow$ with VP indicates that the f-structure for VP and the f-structure of V that is its head must be unified. We return to this topic below, where we will also observe that lexical entries themselves have associated f-description schemata.

Consider now a related sentence:

(237) A girl handed the baby a toy.

Note that the VP rule of the c-structure rules must be modified slightly to allow for sentences of this type, as follows:

(238) VP → V (NP) (NP) PP*

Here the optionality of the NPs allows for the generation of both transitive and intransitive verbs (including those with two objects as in (237)); the asterisk with PP indicates that there may be more than one PP, or none.

Consider a comparison of (237) to (214), repeated here for ease of reference:

(239) (214) A girl handed a toy to the baby.
       (237) A girl handed the baby a toy.

Obviously, the sentences are very similar and the relationship between them can be precisely stated: instead of the TO NP ("indirect object") syntactic function encoding the goal argument of *hand* in (214), an OBJ function is found in (237) and positioned immediately following the verb, with the OBJ function encoding theme in (214) now final in the VP in a "second object" position.

The number of verbs in English that manifest such comparable structures is very large, though the pattern is not available for all three-argument verbs:

(240) John gave the flowers to Mary.
       John gave Mary the flowers.

       John mailed the package to Mary.
       John mailed Mary the package.

       John sent the book to Mary.
       John sent Mary the book.

but:

(241) John communicated the news to Mary.
       *John communicated Mary the news.

       John reported the events to Mary.
       *John reported Mary the events.

Nevertheless, for those verbs that allow it, there is a generalization to be captured here; that is, for each pairing there is but a single lexical item involved, but with two syntactic configurations in which it may occur. It is a major strength of LFG that it captures such generalizations without using transformational rules.

In deriving (237) we begin with the same lexical entry for *hand,* with the same intrinsic rule classifications applying; here the [+o] alternative for theme arguments represented in (224) is taken rather than the [−r] alternative, and the goal argument is considered "applied" and takes the [−r] alternative:

(242)	hand ⟨ agent	goal	theme ⟩
intrinsic	[−o]	[−r]	[+o]

The default rule classifications then apply, yielding the following:

(243)	hand ⟨ agent	goal	theme ⟩
intrinsic	[−o]	[−r]	[+o]
default	[−r]		[+r]

This configuration can now be associated with the classification of syntactic functions, as follows:

(244)	hand ⟨ agent	goal	theme ⟩
intrinsic	[−o]	[−r]	[+o]
default	[−r]		[+r]
	SUBJ	SUBJ/OBJ	OBJ$_{theme}$

Again, The Function-Argument Biuniqueness provision of the WFC has its role to play, forcing a selection once again for the goal argument. While the SUBJ role and the thematically restricted OBJ$_{theme}$ are allocated, the nonthematically restricted OBJ is available:

(245)	hand ⟨ agent	goal	theme ⟩
intrinsic	[−o]	[−r]	[+o]
default	[−r]		[+r]
	SUBJ	SUBJ/OBJ	OBJ$_{theme}$
WFC	SUBJ	OBJ	OBJ$_{theme}$

Again a linear sequencing of arguments is possible, assuming a revision of the VP mapping conventions as follows (here OBJ2 represents OBJ$_{theme}$):

(246) VP → V   (NP)   (NP)

(↑ OBJ) = ↓   (↑ OBJ2) = ↓

What this rule says is that a lexical entry encoding OBJ and OBJ2 as internal arguments maps OBJ onto the leftmost NP within VP and OBJ2 to the following NP. The f-structure of OBJ and OBJ2 must be unified with the f-structure of the associated NPs, as indicated.

Note that lexical entries also have schemata to convey f-structure information; it is this information that is unified with the f-structure of the syntactic function to which it is mapped by rules such as those in (246). The following are the appropriate entries for the vocabulary in (237):

(247) a: DET, (↑ SPEC) = A
                    (↑ NUM) = SG

girl: N, (↑ NUM) = SG
                 (↑ PRED) = 'GIRL'

handed: V, (↑ TENSE) = PAST
                 (↑ PRED) = 'HAND ⟨ (↑ SUBJ) (↑ OBJ) (↑ OBJ2) ⟩ '

the: DET, (↑ SPEC) = THE

baby: N, (↑ NUM) = SG
                 (↑ PRED) = 'BABY'

toy: N, (↑ NUM) = SG
                 (↑ PRED) = 'TOY'

In the generation of an actual sentence (termed 'instantiation'), the schemata are attached appropriately to the c-structure tree. For (237) the result is as in (248).

As a second step in instantiation a new (actual) variable is introduced for the root node of the tree and every node for which the schema indicates the presence of the ↓ metavariable (indicating that one component of the sentence's f-structure corresponds to that subconstituent). The result for (237) is as in (249).

(248)

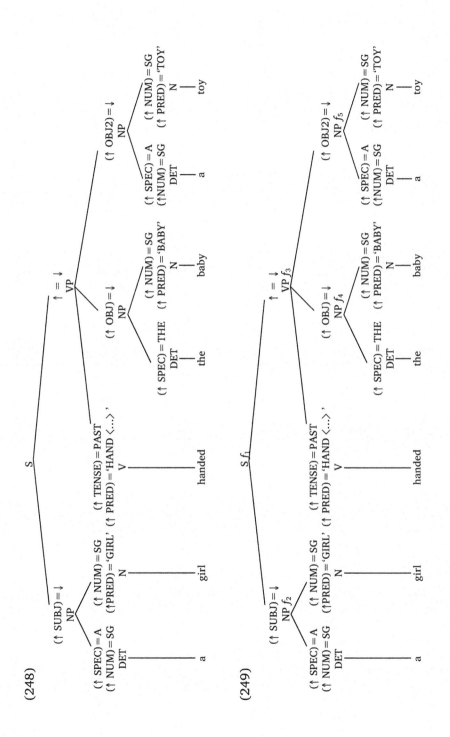

(249)

The functional description (f-description) of a sentence is thus derived from both the c-structure tree and the lexical entries. For (249) the total f-description is as follows (in such formal representations each f represents a distinct function):

(250) (f_1 SUBJ) = f_2 from the sentence's
     f_1 = f_3 f-description
     (f_3 OBJ) = f_4
     (f_3 OBJ2) = f_5

     (f_2 SPEC) = A   from *a*
     (f_2 NUM) = SG

     (f_2 NUM) = SG   from *girl*
     (f_2 PRED) = 'GIRL'

     (f_3 TENSE) = PAST   from *handed*
     (f_3 PRED) = 'HAND ⟨ (↑ SUBJ) (↑ OBJ) (↑ OBJ2) ⟩ '

     (f_4 SPEC) = THE   from *the*

     (f_4 NUM) = SG   from *baby*
     (f_4 PRED) = 'BABY'

     (f_5 SPEC) = A   from *a*
     (f_5 NUM) = SG

     (f_5 NUM) = SG   from *toy*
     (f_5 PRED) = 'TOY'

Here the first four lines represent application of the rules of (236) and (247) as follows: given a specification like (f_1 SUBJ) = f_2, find the equivalent node in the tree where the characterization (↑ SUBJ) = ↓ is found; this rule states that the arrow pointing upward points to the constituent to be identified as f_1, the arrow pointing downward points to the constituent to be identified as f_2. The remaining specifications in (250) result from the values of the various lexical items involved in this particular sentence, applied in the same way. When all relevant rules have been applied, the result is (249).

By algorithm, then, the grammaticality of any string can be evaluated; a sentence is deemed grammatical if there is no mismatch of relevant features for any constituent and thus those features can be unified; the sentence is deemed ungrammatical if there is such a mismatch because unification fails. The offending sentence is judged as syntactically ill-formed, even though it has a valid c-structure, thus allowing for a fine-grained characterization of grammaticality. Note, for example, a sentence like (251):

(251) *A girl handed the baby a toys.

The sentence in (251) will be judged ungrammatical because the OBJ2 NP will carry the following incompatible f-descriptions resulting from two schemata associated with the same node:

(252) a. $(f_5$ NUM) = PL   from *toys*
      b. $(f_5$ NUM) = SG   from *a*

Other violations of agreement are handled in the theory in a similar manner.

Consider now two additional sentences that are related to the above: *A toy was handed to the baby by a girl,* and *The baby was handed a toy by a girl.* These are both instances of a passive construction, but they both involve the same verb *hand* found also in (214) and (237). Crucial in an LFG analysis is that the sentences are related to one another not by a syntactic transformation, but by a lexical relationship. For reasons of space we limit our discussion here to one of these two sentences: *A toy was handed to the baby by a girl.*

It is, of course, the same verb *hand* that is involved here, so we begin with the same lexical entry:

(253)   hand < agent   goal   theme >
      intrinsic   [−o]   [−r]

As mentioned with regard to (226) above, passivization is considered to be a morpholexical rule in English, and it has the effect of invoking passive morphology on the verbal element and suppressing the highest thematic role in the argument structure (in this case the agent):[12]

---

[12]The lexical entry for passive *be* in English requires that it have as its complement a past participle. As shown in the derivation that follows, that past participle has its own argument structure, which is comparable to that of the associated finite verb except that its SUBJ argument is suppressed.

(254)   hand < agent   goal   theme >
        intrinsic   [−o]   [−r]
        PASSIVE   Ø

The default rule classifications then apply, yielding the following:

(255)   hand < agent   goal   theme >
        intrinsic   [−o]   [−r]
        PASSIVE   Ø
        default   [+r]

This configuration can now be associated with the classification of syntactic functions, as follows:

(256)   hand < agent   goal   theme >
        intrinsic   [−o]   [−r]
        PASSIVE   Ø
        default   [+r]
                                    OBL_{goal}   SUB/OBJ

Here the Subject Condition provision of the WFC has its role to play, forcing a selection once again for theme, although on the grounds of the requirement that there be a subject rather than selecting from among competing syntactic functions as in the example above:

(257)   hand < agent   goal   theme >
        intrinsic   [−o]   [−r]
        PASSIVE   Ø
        default   [+r]
                                    OBL_{goal}   SUBJ/OBJ
        WFC   OBL_{goal}   SUBJ

In this configuration the agent cannot be manifested as a syntactic argument in its own right and appears as an oblique argument, a prepositional phrase with *by*.

Crucial in all these examples is the following generalization: in all these sentences the same verb *hand* occurs, and with the same argument structure; differences among the sentences lie in the specific mappings holding between the argument structure and the syntactic functions and consequently the associations to constituents of the c-structure tree.

6.3 The problem-solving capacity of LFG

Having sketched all too briefly the basic orientation of LFG, we turn now to the problem we are considering throughout this text, that of accounting for the forms of the auxiliary in English. Because LFG allows for no transformational rules, any use of a rule like AFFIX-HOPPING is not available; thus some other means must be found to capture the cross-level dependencies which characterize the English auxiliary.

In LFG auxiliaries are treated as main verbs which take embedded complements, and it is the (in)compatibility of f-descriptions from the different constituents, following the specifications of the c-structure tree, which makes evaluation of grammaticality possible. Under this approach, the VP rule in (246) above can be expanded along the lines of the following:

(258) VP → V (NP   ) (NP   ) (VP'   )

$\quad\quad\quad\quad$ (($\uparrow$ OBJ) = $\downarrow$) (($\uparrow$ OBJ2) = $\downarrow$) (($\uparrow$ VCOMP) = $\downarrow$)

Now an additional rule is needed:

(259) VP' → (to)   VP

$\quad\quad\quad\quad\quad\quad\quad$ $\uparrow = \downarrow$

By their lexical specifications, auxiliaries allow only VCOMP to follow them; what remains is to insure that in any specific instance, the VCOMP to follow is of the specific type required for the particular auxiliary. Take as an example the sentence (260):

(260) A girl is handing the baby a toy.

Here two lexical entries are of crucial importance to the discussion. First, the form for the VCOMP:

(261) handing: V,   (↑ PARTICIPLE) = PRESENT
                    (↑ PRED) = 'HAND ⟨ (↑ SUBJ) (↑ OBJ) (↑ OBJ2) ⟩'

Obviously, if this is to be considered a lexical entry there are redundancies to be captured in terms of the generality of the present participle form for all verbs that allow it, and the relation of the particular form in this case to the verb *hand* and its f-structure features. But of crucial importance in discussion of the auxiliary itself is the association of the form *handing* with the specification that it is a PRESENT PARTICIPLE. Now note the following lexical entry for the specific form for the verb *be* found in the example:

(262)   is: V,   (↑ TENSE) = PRESENT
                 (↑ SUBJ NUM) = SG
                 (↑ PRED) = 'PROG ⟨ (↑ VCOMP) ⟩'
                 (↑ VCOMP PARTICIPLE) = PRESENT
                 (↑ VCOMP SUBJ) = (↑ SUBJ)

Given this specification, the form *is* is identified as being a PRESENT TENSE form; it requires a SINGULAR SUBJECT; its argument is to be passed on to the sentence level as the argument for the PROG subject; it requires that the VCOMP PARTICIPLE form be PRESENT; and it requires that its SUBJECT be that also of the VCOMP. It is the lack of conflict among feature specifications that rules (260) grammatical. In particular, from the lexical entry for the VCOMP *handing* the specification for PARTICIPLE is PRESENT; from the lexical entry for *is* the specification of its VCOMP is specified as being a PRESENT PARTICIPLE, and thus there is a compatible matching and unification is possible. Compare such an outcome now with (263):

(263) *A girl is hands the baby a toy.

The following is the lexical specification for *hands:*

(264) hands: V,   (↑ PARTICIPLE) = NONE
                  (↑ TENSE) = PRESENT
                  (↑ SUBJ NUM) = SG
                  (↑ PRED) = 'HAND ⟨ (↑ SUBJ) (↑ OBJ) (↑ OBJ2) ⟩'

(Again we ignore the redundancies here.) In this case we find an incompatibility—*is* requires that a PRESENT PARTICIPLE follow it, but although *hands* is a PRESENT tense form, its PARTICIPLE specification is NONE rather than the required PRESENT. This incompatibility in f-structure results in a failure of unification and thus identifies (263) as being ungrammatical. Thus, accounting for the grammaticality of the English auxiliary within LFG is handled no differently from accounting for the grammaticality of any other syntactic structures.

As a final comment, note that LFG makes use of lexical information also to capture the multiple functions of single arguments in complex structures. For example, a verb like *persuaded* has a lexical specification requiring that the f-structure of the object is also the f-structure for the subject of the VCOMP; by contrast, a verb like *promised* has a lexical specification requiring that the f-structure of the subject is also the f-structure of the subject of the VCOMP. The appropriate lexical entries will be along the following lines:

(265) persuaded: V, ($\uparrow$ TENSE) = PAST
$\qquad\qquad\quad$ ($\uparrow$ PRED) = 'PERSUADE $\langle$ ($\uparrow$ SUBJ) ($\uparrow$ OBJ)
$\qquad\qquad\qquad\qquad\qquad$ ($\uparrow$ VCOMP) $\rangle$ '
$\qquad\qquad\quad$ ($\uparrow$ VCOMP SUBJ) = ($\uparrow$ OBJ)

$\qquad$ promised: V, ($\uparrow$ TENSE) = PAST
$\qquad\qquad\quad$ ($\uparrow$ PRED) = 'PROMISE $\langle$ ($\uparrow$ SUBJ) ($\uparrow$ OBJ)
$\qquad\qquad\qquad\qquad\qquad$ ($\uparrow$ VCOMP) $\rangle$ '
$\qquad\qquad\quad$ ($\uparrow$ VCOMP SUBJ) = ($\uparrow$ SUBJ)

The result is that the following sentences, though comparable in c-structure, have different interpretations:

(266) A girl persuaded the baby to go.
$\qquad$ A girl promised the baby to go.

6.4 LFG Theorizing

1.   LFG emphasizes two levels of syntactic structure: Constituent Structure (c-structure) and Functional Structure (f-structure). The former deals with syntactic phrase structure and is captured in a series of phrase-structure rules; the latter deals with syntactic function and results from the application of universal principles to the lexical structure of the constituents involved. All these types of information are combined into a composite Functional Description (f-description),

derived algorithmically. There is, in addition, a separate level of Semantic Representation.

2. Primitive symbols include those of argument structure (e.g., [+ restricted], [+ objective], etc.), those of c-structure (typical phrasal categories), those representing syntactic functions (e.g., SUBJ, OBJ), and those of lexical entries (e.g., agent, goal, theme).

3. There is a strong emphasis in LFG on universals. In addition to the selection of various categories from the set of universal primitive symbols, there are universal laws proposed to map argument structure (found in the lexicon) to f-structure. The f-structure is mapped onto c-structure by mapping rules, which though language-specific are undoubtedly heavily constrained universally.

4. LFG makes use of no transformational rules. Structures that might be related transformationally in other models are related in LFG by the association of alternative argument structures for the same entries in the lexicon.

5. At this point in time, LFG is a sentence-based theory of syntax, sharing in common with other models within the generative tradition the notion that accounting for child language acquisition is the primary goal; an important distinction exists between competence and performance; argumentation is expected to evaluate competing analyses.

7

Montague Grammar and Generalized Phrase Structure Grammar

7.1 General ontology, methodology, and world view

In the following discussion of Montague Grammar, we intend to restrict our overt comments to Montague's (1974) "Proper treatment of quantification in ordinary English (PTQ)," although much of what is said would apply to other models with an explicit semantics, e.g., Cresswell (1973) and Keenan (1985), who employ BOOLEAN ALGEBRA-BASED semantics or Hintikka's GAME THEORETICAL semantics.

It is quite evident from reading Montague's work that he was much more interested in the semantics of natural languages than in their syntax. He did, nonetheless, provide a syntax to accompany the rules of interpretation. This syntax, however, does not resemble any of the grammars already discussed. In particular, Montague Grammar employs a CATEGORIAL GRAMMAR for the syntax of English and also for the syntax of a logical language that accompanies the syntax of English. Categorial grammars to some degree and the apparatus of formal logics most certainly are more familiar to philosophers than to linguists. Montague, however, did identify himself in part with linguists more than with philosophers to the extent that he strove to analyze natural language, in particular "...a certain fragment of a certain dialect of English" (1974:247). In general, philosophers and logicians have regarded natural languages as filled with exceptions and imprecision to the point that natural statements cannot be falsified. Instead of trying to work with natural languages, these investigators have preferred to offer treatments of formal languages such as the PROPOSITIONAL CALCULUS, PREDICATE

183

CALCULUS, MODAL LOGICS, etc., which they view as better-behaved. In this regard, Montague sided with linguists.

> There is in my opinion no important theoretical difference between natural languages and the artificial languages of logicians; indeed, I consider it possible to comprehend the syntax and semantics of both kinds of languages within a single natural and mathematically precise theory. On this point I differ from a number of philosophers, but agree, I believe, with Chomsky and his associates. (1974b:222)

As Thomason says in his introduction to *Formal Philosophy*, Montague regards the study of human languages as part of mathematics and not part of psychology. Resultingly, Montague has a different view as to the nature of linguistic universals. He is not interested in universals as the result of language acquisition, as is Chomsky. Rather, he regards UNIVERSAL to mean a theory sufficiently general to be capable of encompassing any logically conceivable grammar in the same way that mathematical topology is a universal theory of geometry (Thomason's 1974a introduction). Universal for Montague thus means 'comprehensive theoretically' not 'psychologically determinative'. This interest in formalization may be unattractive to some. Indeed, Montague's work constitutes a challenge to any but the most canny of logicians. It will for this reason not be possible to expose it in any depth. In fact, we shall avoid its details almost entirely and concentrate instead on its principles. A good introduction to Montague Grammar is provided by Dowty, Wall, and Peters (1981).

If there is a central idea in PTQ (and other work by Montague), it is the structural parallelism of syntax and semantics. Very briefly, the rules that produce the syntactic structure of a sentence play a crucial role in the interpretation assigned to that sentence. The interpretation of a sentence is built up piece-by-piece by recapitulating the syntactic rules used to build up the structure piece-by-piece. Stated another way, the meanings of wholes are derivable from the meanings of parts plus information about how the parts are combined structurally. Following Cresswell (1973), this assumption is called FREGE's PRINCIPLE.[13]

---

[13]As we pointed out earlier in chapter three, Frege's Principle relies on the Russell/Carnap view of meaning of a whole being constructible out of the meaning of its parts. Wittgenstein in his later opus specifically denied this claim, saying that the concept *composition* itself is in need of explication, or wholes are more than the meanings of their parts (even where the whole could be the sum or product or any other functional combination of the meanings of parts).

Montague Grammar uses TRUTH FUNCTIONAL SEMANTICS. This idea found its most rigorous statement in the work of the Polish logician Alfred Tarski, who said that to know what a statement means is to know under what conditions it would be true. Thus, if someone says, 'It's going to rain tomorrow', still it cannot with certainty be established today whether this is, in fact, a truth or falsity. We can still understand it, because we know what things would be like when it is true; we know the statement's TRUTH CONDITIONS. Tarski also found it important to establish two different levels in speaking of meaning, the OBJECT LANGUAGE and the METALANGUAGE or LANGUAGE OF DEFINITION. If this were not done, then a piece of paper on which was written 'The statement on the opposite side of this page is false' and on whose other side was written 'The statement on the opposite side of this page is true' would lead to irreconcilable paradox. To avoid such pitfalls, Tarski would distinguish between the defining language and the language defined. He illustrated this difference with the whimsical example in (267).

(267) *Snow is white* is true iff snow is white.

It is crucial to understand that the material in italics is object language, whereas the remainder is metalanguage. Expressions in the object language must, therefore, be defined and interpreted in terms of a metalanguage, which coincidentally, might contain exactly the same words, as in this special case. Of course, the metalanguage cannot be questioned or doubted, as it is to be considered already interpreted and presupposed. Moreover, what (267) shows is that the statement *snow is white* is defined by the conditions under which it is true (TRUTH CONDITIONS), not whether some statement is, in fact, true. Thus, Montague semantics is truth functional in the sense that each expression of the syntax is associated with a semantic function or a semantic argument that combines to produce just the true sentences from information about the parts. Montague semantics makes use of this sense of 'meaning' and 'interpretation'.

(268) The President of the U.S. died today.

Montague also employs the notion of POSSIBLE WORLD. A statement like (268) contains an expression that could refer to about forty persons, who have lived in partially overlapping time spans. Therefore, the expression *the President of the U.S.* will refer to different persons at different times. In nonhonorific contexts it will refer to a unique person at any given moment. But, in different possible worlds, at different times, or in worlds of our (or another's) imagination, it might refer to yet other people than those it actually has referred to.

7.2 Specific assumptions and problem-solving capacity of Montague Grammar

Instead of beginning with a discussion of Montague Grammar as such, we would like to first present a simpler illustration of the procedure used in an explicit semantic theory. We assume, first of all, that we are creating a possible world over which we have complete control. In the inventory of this world, called world 5332 (W 5332), we have the entities listed in (269).

(269)   ENTITIES IN W 5332

Individuals

a = Abe, b= Betty, c = Carrie, d = Del, e = Ed, f = Fanny, al = Arlington, uta = University of Texas at Arlington

1-place properties of individuals

sleep' = {b,e,f}, snore' = {a,b}, city' = {al}, university' = {uta}, girl' = {b,c,f}, boy' = {a,d,e} (the prime mark indicates the interpretation, not the symbol).

2-place properties

love' = {<a,b>,<b,a>,<c,c>,<f,e>,<e,d>}, date' = {<a,b>, <b,a>}, admire' = {<c,d>,<f,a>,<a,f>}, be located in' = {<uta,al>}

From the list of individuals one can see that W 5332 is characterized mostly by being a pretty lazy, co-ed university situation, probably hopelessly impoverished by comparison to anyone's real world of actual experience. In fact, it is saved from utter boredom only by Fanny's unrequited love for Ed and some other shenanigans among participants. Not only do we have this soap opera microcosm at our disposal before further discussion begins, we also possess a minigrammar as in (270).

(270) a. S   → NP VP   f. N → {Abe, Betty, Carrie, Del, Ed
      b. VP → V   Fanny, Arlington, UTA}

      c. VP → V NP   g. V → {snores, sleeps} /__

      d. NP → Det N   h. V → {loves, dates, admires}/__NP

      e. NP → N   i. V → {is in}/__Arlington

We are, of course, simplifying this minigrammar even beyond what we have already talked about in order to reduce complexity.

Beyond this world and minigrammar, we also have a set of PROJECTION RULES. These are instructions about how to construct the meanings of complex expressions from their constituent parts. Corresponding to each rule of the minigrammar, there is a projection rule. The categories with primes refer to the (semantic) denotations of the syntactic symbols or structures.

(271) a. S'   = VP'(NP')

      b. VP' = V'

      c. VP' = V'(NP')

      d. NP' = Det'(N')

      e. NP' = N'

      f. A'   = a (where a is the value of the terminal symbol)

Moreover, we can evaluate a sentence of the grammar in W 5332.

(272) A sentence S' is true in model W 5332 iff its constituent parts NP' (subject) and VP' (predicate) are related as follows:
$$NP' \in VP'$$

That means the sentence S' is true in our fictional world just in case that the individual in that world picked out by NP' is an element of the set of individuals in that world picked out by VP'. Note that—as we defined them above—VP' represents a set of individuals, namely exactly those that "vp" in this world. In other words, given that we know about the entities in a world and know the sets of individuals that represent a property, then the above rule allows us to induce which sentences will be true in this world from the information about its parts. Most of the work involved in doing the semantics is to devise the projection rules, such as the above rule, and pick the world in a fashion that all the intuitively true sentences will come out being true in the model. To illustrate that we have, in fact, picked correctly we provide a derivation.

(273)   Syntax

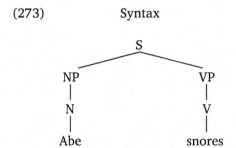

Interpretation

a. snore$_V$ $\Rightarrow$ {a,b}
b. snores$_{VP}$ $\Rightarrow$ {a,b}
c. Abe$_N$ $\Rightarrow$ a
d. Abe$_{NP}$ $\Rightarrow$ a
e. S' = VP'(NP') = ({a,b})(a)

S' is true in W 5332 because a $\in$ {a,b}

This interpretation shows how one can use the information contained in (269) to determine in an algorithmic way whether a sentence is true or not in this world.

An example with a 2-place verb can be seen in (274).

(274)   Syntax

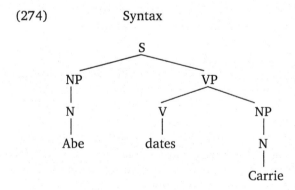

Interpretation

a. dates$_V$ $\Rightarrow$ $\{<a,b>,<b,a>\}$
b. Carrie$_N$ $\Rightarrow$ c
c. Carrie$_{NP}$ $\Rightarrow$ c
d. dates Carrie$_{VP}$ $\Rightarrow$ $(\{<a,b>,<b,a>\})(c)$
e. Abe$_{NP}$ $\Rightarrow$ a
f. Abe dates Carrie$_S$ $\Rightarrow$ $(\{<a,b>,<b,a>\})(c)(a)$
   $= (\{<a,b>,<b,a>\})(<a,c>)$
   by the Theorem that $f(y)(x) = f(x,y)$

Therefore, this sentence is false in W 5332, since the pair $<a,c>$ is not in the function $\{<a,b>,<b,a>\}$.

Montague's PTQ, unlike many aspects of the above oversimplified illustration, uses the method of INDIRECT INTERPRETATION. It is not the syntactic structures of English that are interpreted with the aid of projection rules in a direct fashion. Instead, English syntax is first translated into the syntax of a formal language, called INTENSIONAL LOGIC (IL). IL is, in turn, interpreted with the methods of MODEL THEORY, a way of assigning meaning from parts to wholes via a kind of algebra.

7.2.1 Categorial syntax. Montague Grammar differs from all previous approaches in its syntax as well. Instead of PS rules or transformations, Montague used a CATEGORIAL GRAMMAR. Moreover, context-sensitive and context-free rules are mixed in sequence and not divided into distinct components as in the *Aspects* model. Since an introduction to categorial grammars is a prerequisite to further understanding of Montague, we now turn to that.

Categorial grammars were developed by the Polish logician Ajdukiewicz in the 1930s. They were briefly considered by Bar-Hillel (1960) as alternatives to context-free grammars. Because simple categorial grammars were proven to be weakly equivalent to context-free grammars, and because these grammars were shown to be inadequate for describing natural languages, interest in them waned until Montague's work came along.

The basic notion of categorial grammar is that all categories of the syntax can be divided into two types, BASIC or PRIMITIVE categories and DERIVED or FUNCTOR categories. Referring once again to the formal definition of a grammar, we note that a categorial grammar will have rules relating the vocabulary items, i.e., categories. In Chomsky's conception, a sentence could be represented by a phrase marker as in (275).

(275)

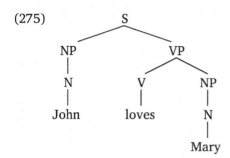

While no complex lexical expression such as *loves Mary* appears explicitly in the phrase marker (only simple lexical items such as *John, loves,* or *Mary*), it is not a great departure from Chomsky's approach to represent sentences with a more explicit graph as in (276).

(276)

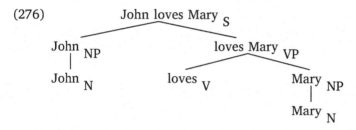

In this categorial grammar representation, the complex string of symbols with its category is written at each level of the phrase marker. Thus, in a categorial grammar, rules relate both categories and expressions; moreover, all categories are derived except for the few (usually two or three) basic categories. For example, if one takes the categories PROPER NAME (N) and SENTENCE (S) as basic, then additional derived categories can be made such as S/N (read: the category that takes a proper name and turns it into a sentence). Usually, we call this category the one-place verb, verb phrase, or predicate. In every case, categories can be constructed that answer the combinatorial description we seek. In a sentence *John ran* the name *John* is an expression in the category N and *John ran* is an expression in the category S, thus *ran* is an expression in the category S/N, because it converts $John_N$ into *John ran$_S$*. This category S/N we commonly refer to as intransitive (one-place) verb. In the sentence *John ran fast* the adverb *fast* belongs to that category turning a one-place verb *run* into another, complex one-place verb *run fast*. Using the notation of PS rules we are familiar with, any acceptable category of a categorial language can be written as in (277).

(277) A → A/B B

In Montague Grammar, only notional equivalents to binary expansion of the PS rule are assumed. Montague defines his primitive and derived categories by means of an inductive definition, saying that: (1) e(ntity) and t(ruth value) are primitive categories; (2) the set of acceptable categories CAT for English is to be the smallest set X such that e and t are in X; and (3) if A and B are in X, then so are A/B and A//B.[14] A//B represents a category that takes the same kind of arguments as A/B and produces exactly the same result but is simply a different function. An analogy from elementary trigonometry are the functions sine and cosine, which have the same domain and range but are, nevertheless, different functions. For Montague t/e is the intransitive verb whereas $t//e$ is the common noun.

In addition to the categories of a categorial grammar, there are also expressions in this grammar. Just as in the case of categories, there are BASIC EXPRESSIONS and COMPLEX or DERIVED expressions. The basic expressions are essentially the same as the lexical entries of a language. The derived expressions should be made to be those strings that have been put together by some rule. So *John, Mary, love* are in the set of basic expressions and *loves Mary, John loves Mary* are derived expressions, one a one-place (VP) and the other a sentence. The unusual thing about a categorial grammar is that once the lexical items (basic expressions) and the categories have been specified, then all the derived expressions are automatically produced. In particular, basic expressions are put together according to a single rule such as (278).

(278) If a is of category A/B and b is of category B, then the complex $(a(b))$ is of category A.

The combination of expressions can be thought of as a kind of cancellation of fractions as in (279).

(279) $(a_{A/B})\ (b_B)$ → (a b_A)
   (Of course, a and b could themselves be complex.)

---

[14]These three steps are essential in an inductive definition: (a) that the primitive symbols are in a set (in this case X); (b) that if two well-formed possibly complex symbol strings, A and B, are in X, then so too is A/B and A//B; and finally, (c) that this X is to be the smallest possible set (called CAT) with these properties (this is to guarantee uniqueness of CAT and is a crucial part of the definition).

Despite this generalization, Montague does write a specific rule for each syntactic linkage of expressions. This is done so that the rules translating English syntax into IL syntax can be stated one-to-one, and, ultimately, so that the rules of semantic interpretation can also be stated one-to-one with the syntax.

Before we turn to the rules, however, let us examine the categories and expressions used by Montague, listed in (280).

(280) Derived categories in Montague Grammar
      IV (intransitive verbs) = t/e
      T (terms, approximates NP) = t/IV = t/(t/e)
      TV (transitive verbs) = IV/T = (t/e)/(t/(t/e))
      IAV (IV modifying adverbs) = IV/IV = (t/e)/(t/e)
      CN (common nouns) = t//e

Some of the basic expressions in Montague's PTQ are given in (281).

(281) B_{IV} = {run, walk, talk, rise}
      B_T = {John, Mary, Bill, he_1, he_2, etc}
      B_{TV} = {find, lose, sat, love, date}
      B_{CN} = {man, woman, park, fish}

Having introduced an adequate but incomplete sample of categories of English and a fragment of the total set of basic expressions needed for English, we must say something in general about combinations of basic expressions into larger units, called phrases. We insist, first of all, that all basic expressions of category A are simultaneously phrases of category A and that terms (subject NPs) combine with an IV to produce a sentence and that TV (transitive verbs) combine with terms (object NPs) to give an IV.

(282) a. $P_A \supseteq B_A$
      b. If $a \in P_{t/IV}$ and $b \in P_{IV}$, then ab (actually ab', where b'
          is the third person singular form of the verb) $\in P_t$
      c. If $a \in P_T$ and $b \in P_{TV}$, then ba $\in P_{IV}$

Briefly, rule (282a) says, "all basic expressions in category A are also phrases of category A." Rule (282b) says, "if a is a term phrase and b is an intransitive verb phrase, then a applied to b as a function gives a t-phrase. Rule (282c) says, "if a is a term phrase and b is a transitive verb phrase, ba is an intransitive verb phrase."

To illustrate the effect of these rules consider a simple sentence in (283).

(283)

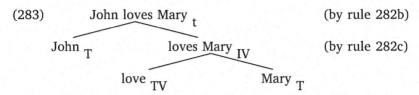

Of particular interest in Montague Grammar is the treatment of quantifier expressions. In order to produce expressions such as *every man, a woman, the unicorn,* Montague employs the notion of SYNCATEGORIMATIC DERIVATION. In the PTQ fragment, English forms like *a, the, every* are not found among the set of basic expressions. Instead, these quantifier words are introduced by rule. In fact, three rules are used. Where P_{CN} is a phrase (including possibly basic expressions of English), we have the rules in (284).

(284) If $\zeta \in P_{CN}$, then A $\zeta \in P_T$, EVERY $\zeta \in P_T$ and THE $\zeta \in P_T$

The effect of these rules is illustrated in (285).

(285)

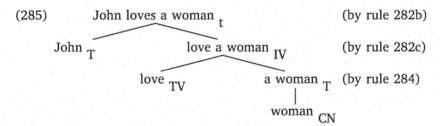

One final but decisive wrinkle of Montague Grammar involves the RULE OF QUANTIFICATION. This rule has no counterpart in traditional or modern grammar. What is intended is that a sentence with a variable, i.e., one of the pronoun forms, he_n is replaced by another term (NP) from outside the sentence.

(286)   John loves a woman $_t$ (by the Rule of Quantification)

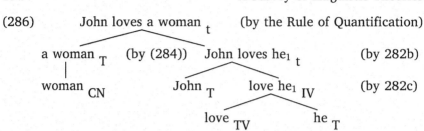

a woman $_T$ (by (284))   John loves he$_1$ $_t$ (by 282b)

woman $_{CN}$ John $_T$ love he$_1$ $_{IV}$ (by 282c)

                        love $_{TV}$ he $_T$

This completes our fragmentary sketch of the syntax of English. It is not intended to do justice to a very large part of the grammar of English. Still, it does have some unusual features worthy of comment. Notice, first of all, that every noun phrase could arise in a number of ways, either by having been produced in the location where it surfaces (285) or by having undergone the Rule of Quantification, which introduces it from a position outside the sentence (286). There is little if any evidence that NPs in English have structural ambiguity. The motivation for dual derivations of NPs is solely semantic. Some sentences of English (and other languages) are said to be semantically ambiguous. These all involve INTENSIONAL VERBS. For example, the sentence *Earnest is hunting a lion* it is claimed, can mean that he's gone lion hunting, maybe in the city park, if he's crazy enough. This sentence can be true without lions existing there or at all. That's why we can say *Earnest is hunting a unicorn* without violating generally accepted beliefs about existent animals. Other verbs are not intensional, however. Therefore, we cannot say *Earnest shot a unicorn* without simultaneously claiming they exist. Now, in the first sentence about Earnest, he might be a keeper from the circus in town out after an escapee from his act named Leo. The object NP of verbs like *hunt, seek, look for,* admit of this two-facedness. In Montague Grammar, the nonintensional reading of the sentence *Earnest seeks a lion* results from that structure having undergone a Rule of Quantification. The intensional interpretation comes from the in-place or internal derivation of the object NP using rule (282c). The two might be illustrated as in (287).

(287) Syntactic derivation   (external derivation)

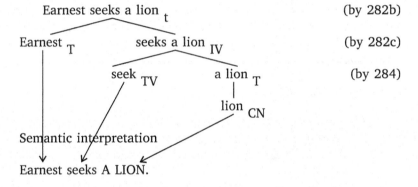

We have written *a lion* and *A LION* in (287) in lower and upper case respectively because they must have different denotations even if the English words seem phonologically and grammatically identical; semantically they are very different. In the first derivation in (287), *a lion* lies outside the SCOPE of the intensional verb *seek* and, therefore, can be a referring expression, i.e., has an extension and denotes an individual in the world of evaluation. In the second derivation in (287), *A LION* is subject only to an interpretation as a set of properties, i.e., {large carnivore, great cat, buff color, brown mane, four legs,...}; it is an intensional concept that may or may not be instantiated by any existing thing. That's why we can say that *Earnest is seeking a cure for cancer, a centaur, a woman with three left feet,* etc. That such intensional concepts are tolerated in natural language is a function of the particular verb. If one changes *seek* to *find*, then the intensional concepts must reduce to an extension. Compare the interpretations with *Earnest found a cure for cancer, a centaur, a woman with three left feet.*

In Montague semantics, unlike the simple-minded semantics of the world of 5332, the denotations of syntactic expressions are intensional throughout. His grand tour de force was to discover a FORMAL APPARATUS in which the denotations of the respective syntactic items fit together constructively like the extensional semantic interpretation of 5332 but that were elevated off the level of extensions (individuals and truth-values) to higher order entities (intensions), which—in the environment of the appropriate verb (or other intensional category)—would then reduce back down to extensions. The mediating level of the language IL performed this function.

7.2.2 Montague Grammar theorizing. An introduction in accordance with the goals we have established here can hardly do justice to the richness of Montague's PTQ machinery and certainly not to the profundity found in his "universal grammar." Such topics are truly for those who wish to specialize. Nevertheless, we hope to have at the very least given a characterization and not a caricature of this difficult theoretical model.

Summary of Montague Grammar

1. Levels. MG does not assume any specific level, abstract or underlying. Still, in the case of the Rule of Quantification, expressions appear at places other than their ultimate locations.
2. Primitive symbols. MG has in its syntax of English only two, in IL only three. The only primitives in the semantics (model) are A (set of individuals); {0, 1} (the truth set, true and false); I (set of possible worlds); and J (set of time points). The basic expressions are just the lexical words of the fragment of the language one is studying.
3. Rules produce a constituent order, structure, distribution, and all the complex syntactic categories.
4. Rules do not produce or reference grammatical relations directly. Nevertheless, subject and direct object terms are treated differently in terms of their function-argument structure, which has been exploited by some to develop a means of describing grammatical relations.

5. Context sensitivity. Context-sensitive and context-free rules are mixed together.
6. The syntax generates structure by rules, which are then re-capitulated in the interpretation of signs.
7. Sentences are related by rules, e.g., something like relativization and a Rule of Quantification.
8. There is no separation of subcomponents in the syntax. There is, however, a second syntax of the intermediate language IL.
9. There is no discussion of directionality. MG probably does not represent itself as a psychological model of actual language production or reception. Nevertheless, it does intend to capture human abilities to induce the meaning of complexes from meanings of their parts.

7.3 Generalized phrase structure grammar

Generalized phrase structure grammar is the product of the fruitful mind of a British linguist named Gerald Gazdar (1980). His starting point is the claim by Chomsky that natural languages exhibit properties in their syntax that resemble context-sensitive languages. In particular Chomsky has stated that the sentence *Tom, Dick, and Harry are a butcher, a baker, and a candlestick maker respectively* shows conclusively this property. If there is, indeed, a syntactic dependency in which branches cross, i.e., *Tom* and *a butcher* are syntactically linked as are *Dick* and *a baker*, etc., then Chomsky's claim is justified, since no context-free grammar could ever produce such interstitial crossed-branched dependency. But, says Gazdar, it is far from evident that such a syntactic dependency exists in this sentence. While it is true that SEMANTICALLY *Tom* is related to *butcher*, etc., no syntactic dependency need be assumed. Therefore, for reasons of explanatory adequacy, it is advantageous to strive for the most constrained theory possible and among the desirable things is to be able to embed natural languages into the set of context-free languages.

Before Gazdar, context-free grammars were never considered serious candidates for the description (and ultimate explanation) of natural languages. But, in order to develop a transformationless context-free grammar—for that is what Gazdar will do—some additional discussion of alternatives to PS rules is in order.

It will be recalled that a grammar is a collection of rewrite rules of the type πxδ → πyδ. In fact, there are sequences of such rules, one applying to the output of the application of others. Notice, however, that only one level of structure is produced at a time with such rules as shown in (288).

(288)

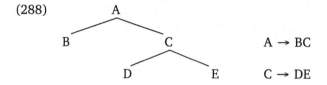

A → BC

C → DE

If, however, we wished to produce the English auxiliary complex without transformations, then rules are needed that depend upon structure at a deeper level. For example, in *little Miss Muffet has sat on a tuffet* the *has* causes the past participle form to appear on the VERB FORM TO ITS RIGHT AND ONE LEVEL LOWER DOWN.

(289)

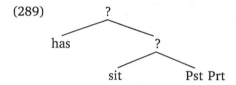

Indeed, many rules of English that are treated transformationally in the *Aspects* model exhibit that CROSS-LEVEL DEPENDENCY. PS rules cannot produce this kind of structure. One can expand the capacity of the notion of grammar, however, if one conceives of it as a sequence of subtrees instead of a sequence of mono-level PS rules. Thus, in place of S → NP VP one employs the subtree [$_S$NP VP$_S$]; for VP → V NP, one can use [$_{VP}$V NP$_{VP}$]. In fact, all rules in GPSG are made up of three parts: (a) a rule number (in order to keep track of the rules), (b) a (possibly multilevel) subtree, and (c) a projection rule for the semantics (one for each subtree or rule of the syntax), basically using Montague Grammar.

Another new feature of GPSG is the SLASH CATEGORY. Up to now we have sketched how rewrite dependency is expressed without transformation. There remain, though, cases of apparent movement to be dealt with. For example, consider the instances of WH-MOVEMENT in chapter five.

(290) The man [$_{S'}$ who Mary loves t $_{S'}$]is here.

Now, we need to produce both the structures *Mary loves the man* as well as *who Mary loves t*, as both occur somewhere in English. The first of these will be generated by the sequence of subtree rules in (291).

(291) a.   <1, [$_S$NP VP],semantic projection rule>
  b.   <2, [$_{VP}$V NP],semantic projection rule>

These two subtree rules produce the tree in (292).

(292)

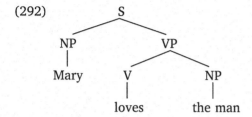

For each of the categories in a subtree, there also exists a corresponding, related but independent subtree, that differs from the original by having a slash category in an NP position and in all the nodes that dominate this NP with the same slash category.[15] So, in addition to (292) we also have (293).

(293)

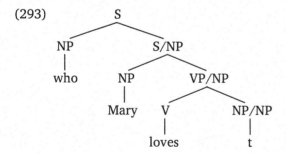

As one can see, a slash category is projected up the tree to the S level, where it appears again. This feature makes the constituents of the relative clause *who Mary loves t* have all the same lexical features (selectional

---

[15]To the best of our knowledge, Gazdar and others have not discussed whether the notion of slash category has any relation to the derived (functor) categories of a categorial grammar such as that found in Montague Grammar. We believe there are some common features shared between slash categories and derived categories. There may also be some points of commonality between slash categories and lambda-conversion in Montague's PTQ and Cresswell (1973).

restrictions and subcategorization) as the full statement form *Mary loves the man* just as it should. On the other hand, there is NO MOVEMENT OF NPs, since only THE GAP where an NP should be is projected up the tree to higher structural levels, and then the NP is 'drawn out of the hole', so to speak.

Another difference between GPSG and other transformational approaches is the notion of METARULE. We have discussed this kind of rule in an earlier context. For Gazdar, metarules are important because they can assume many of the functions formerly fulfilled by transformations. Yet, such metarules do not enrich the size of the language produced.[16] As one saw in the case of stratificational grammar, metarules are rules over rules. Since only the phrase-structure rules produce the structures of the language, the grammar remains within the class of context-free grammar. In general, Gazdar's metarules can be characterized as in (294).

(294) If the grammar contains a rule of the form A, then it also contains a rule of the form B, where B can come from A functionally.

For example, the passive metarule for English is stated in (295).

(295) If there exists a rule:
  $<$n, $[_{VP}$V NP X], F(NP')$>$
  where X can be an empty string and F is some 'semantic' function, then there also exists a rule of the form:
  $<$i, $[_{AP}$A X PP$_1$], H(NP')]$>$
  where $A_i^* = G(V_n^*)$ and G is a function replacing a verb by its passive form, e.g., *loved* for *love*, *given* for *give*, etc. PP1 is connected up by means of the rule:
  $<$36, $[_{PP1}[_{P}$by] NP], NP'
  and H is a 'semantic' function related to F so that the two subtrees receive the same interpretation.

In brief, whenever there is a sentence like (296) there will also be a corresponding sentence like (297). The two sentences are not, however, related by transformation but by metarule.

---

[16]If metarules are so strong as to connect an unlimited number of phrase-structure rules, this may cause the grammar as a whole to burst the bounds of CF-grammar. Thus, it has been suggested that a condition on metarules called FINITE CLOSURE must abide to prevent slipping out of the context-free realm.

(296)

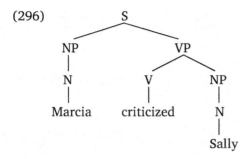

(297)

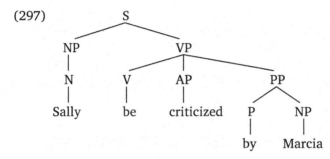

7.4 Conjunction

Sentences such as (298) are grammatical even though they contradict the nearly universally claimed rule that conjuncts must belong to the same grammatical category.

(298) a.   Walk slowly and with a big stick. (Adv and PP)
       b.   His father was well known to the police and a genuine scholar. (AP and NP)

GPSG provides an account for these structures.

As has been discussed above, features of some syntactic categories can be projected to higher or lower levels in a tree structure. For example, the missing NP in a slash category (293) is passed up the tree to higher categorial levels. In a similar fashion, categories of conjunctions can be passed up to higher levels. This grammatical property is known as the HEAD-FEATURE-CONVENTION. In the case of (298b), *well known to the police*, which is an AP, will have the following features: {... <N, + >, <V, + >, <PRD, + >}, where PRD means predicative. The phrase *a genuine scholar* is a noun phrase, which will have the features: {... <N, + >, <V, − >, <PRD, + >}. One of the discoveries of GPSG is that, in conjunction, the head-feature convention passes not the entire set, but only the intersection of the sets of features of all the elements being conjoined to the next higher categorial level. In this instance, this includes only the features: { <N, + >, <PRD, + >}. The copular verb *be* requires only the specification <PRD, + >, so (298b) is correctly predicted to be grammatical. Moreover, sentences such as (299) are predictably ungrammatical.

(299) *The [well-known and a genuine scholar] man was my father.

The conjoined phrase would have an intersection of features { <N, + >, <PRD, + >}, as we just saw; however, a head noun N can be combined only with features of AP, i.e., {...<N, + >, <V, + >, <PRD, + >}. Thus, the modifying construction in (299) contains a phrase with features incompatible with those of the head with which it combines, namely N.

7.5 Dominance/linear precedence and language typologies

In their 1985 book Gazdar, Pullum, and Sag propose a further feature to the GPSG approach. They note that it is possible to gain generalizations if one untangles the Dominance Relations from Linear Precedence. In a Phrase structure grammar the rule A → B C, for instance, requires not only that A is the mother node dominating both B and C, but that B linearly precedes C. But, they argue that the "vertical" or dominance relation and the "horizontal" or linear precedence can be disassociated with profit. They propose to use the formalism A → B, C, where the comma indicates that A dominates B and C to be sure, but that B and C are not ordered left-to-right by the rule. Thus, B C and C B strings are generated. The ordering of constituents must be accomplished at the end by linear precedence rules such as B < C, B occurs to the left of C. By separating these two aspects, one can account for typological difference across languages. For instance, a language with SOV properties such as Japanese would have auxiliaries following the main verb, whereas English would have auxiliaries preceding the main verb, e.g., *wakari-mashi-ta* 'understand-polite-past' versus 'perf understand'.

This proposal resembles in some ways the fixing of the directionality parameter in P&P linguistics; Japanese being a head-last language and English a head-first language. Moreover, it may be possible to deal with recalcitrant problems of word order versus constituency by invoking the division into syntactic dominance versus linear precedence. For example, some Celtic, Austronesian, and Mayan languages are known to have VSO word order. The problem posed by VSO languages rests in the conflict between syntactic dominance and linear precedence. A VP constituent does not permit S to intervene between V and O. However, if one allows that the linear precedence rule for Verb, Subject, and Object, at times, need not attend to syntactic dominance and simply assigns an order, then the problem would disappear.

Generalized Phrase Structure Grammar has refocused attention on categorial grammar of a type like that used by Montague and successors. Therefore, it seems appropriate to put these traditions together in one chapter.

7.6 GPSG theorizing

To conclude, Generalized Phrase Structure Grammar has the traits listed in the following summary.

Summary of Generalized Phrase Structure Grammar

1. Levels. Since there are no transformations, all structure can be surface structure.
2. Primitive symbols. Since EST primitive symbols are employed, the inventory is the same as for this approach. However, we have seen that features can appear in grammar rules, and for that reason, the number of primitive symbols might be larger than EST.
3. Rules produce strings as in the case of EST/REST/P&P but slash categories and metarules allow the abolishment of transformations.
4. There is no reference to grammatical relations.
5. Structures, distributions, and constituents are produced by subtrees. Each subtree is joined to the next higher and the next lower level.
6. Some syntactic processes are expressed indirectly by means of rules on rules, i.e., metarules. There are no transformations.
7. The syntactic component consists of the grammar of subtrees. Since each syntactic rule has its own projection rule, the semantics is separate from but attached to each syntactic rule.

8. This grammar has been used as a starting point both for analysis and for parsing and generation in computational linguistics. Thus, it might be thought of as being bidirectional.

8

Relational Grammar

8.1 Introduction to Relational Grammar (RG)

At the LSA Institute held in the summer of 1974 at the University of Massachusetts, Amherst, Paul Postal and David Perlmutter offered a well-attended class on a new kind of grammar, which came to be known as RELATIONAL GRAMMAR. In subsequent work with David Johnson, a similar approach has been developed called ARC PAIR GRAMMAR (Johnson and Postal 1980); this view is different enough to keep the two separate, but space prevents our discussing more than RG here. Unlike most of the other models discussed, a nearly complete and relatively up-to-date bibliography is available for this body of work (Dubinsky and Rosen 1983, 1987). As the name indicates, the central notion of concern to grammarians in this tradition is the behavior of NPs and predicates in grammatical relations of which SUBJECT, DIRECT OBJECT, and INDIRECT OBJECT are the most discussed (studied in several dozen languages in over 350 papers). In fact RG can be seen as both reaction and simultaneous impetus to weight grammatical relations more heavily in describing syntax. As has been remarked previously, Chomsky's *Aspects* model treats subject as a secondary, configurationally defined category dependent upon the NP immediately dominated by S as in (300). RG makes these notions primary as the target for analysis.

(300)   S

NP

Not only are the grammatical relations themselves of interest to RG, but even more significant are the processes that can be described with

205

them. In particular, such things as a universal theory of PASSIVE, ERGATIVITY, PROMOTION, and other relation-changing operations comes in range once one has an inventory of concepts such as subject, direct object, and indirect object. Much of this work has concentrated on generalizations across languages in addition to the details of particular languages.

8.2 General ontology, methodology, and world view

The most important claim that separates RG from the remainder of generative work is that the grammatical relations must be primitives of the theory, not derivative, and, presumably, existent in every language. Because some rules are shared by many languages, though they may not be universal, grammatical relations must be considered as the basis for such processes. What cannot be considered as, for example, the descriptive basis for passive are: case markers, word order, verb morphology, auxiliary verbs, change of transitivity from transitive to intransitive, constituent structure, and a number of other possible candidates. The major aim is to formulate linguistic universals and to leave the specifics of such things as word order, verb morphology, etc. to the grammars of the individual languages. Since there are different word orders, a grammar that relies on rewrite rules replacing symbols in a left to right order can never be the basis for a universal grammar, only for the grammar of a specific language.

Grammatical relations are, just as their names indicate, relational in nature. For that reason, the primitives are relating in nature and not ground-level primitives. The representation of clauses in a language must, therefore, reflect this property of relations. In this regard, RG bears a resemblance to stratificational grammar by emphasizing relations instead of first-order units. In a sentence such as *Marcia criticized Sally*, the NP *Marcia* stands in the SUBJECT (SU) relation to the clause, the NP *Sally* in the DIRECT OBJECT (DO) relation to the clause, and the verb *criticize* stands in the PREDICATE relation to the clause. These relations are indicated by means of labeled arcs with the TAILS on the clause symbol and their HEADS on the respective NPs *Marcia* and *Sally*. Also, the verb *criticize* heads the predicate arc. This arrow expresses the predicate relation.

(301)

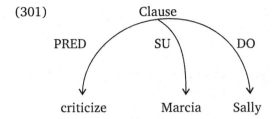

In the corresponding passive variant of this sentence, *Sally was criticized by Marcia,* the relations have changed. *Sally* has become the subject; *criticize,* with some language-specific changes in verb morphology, remains predicate; and *Marcia* has also changed its status. This second relational pattern may be indicated by means of new arrows next to the active clause relations in the network notation.

(302)

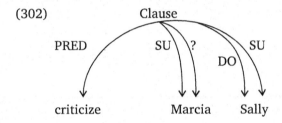

The relations—subject, direct object, and indirect object—since they occur with such frequency, are abbreviated with the digits 1, 2, and 3 respectively. Thus, in (301), *Marcia* heads the 1 arc in the earliest stratum, *Sally* the 2 arc in this stratum, and *criticize* the P (predicate) arc. In the second stratum in (302), however, *Sally* heads the 1 arc and *criticize* the P arc. *Marcia,* though, is not subject, direct object, or any other relation known to traditional grammarians. In English, this new relation is shown by means of the preposition *by.* To indicate that it has changed status, one calls this former subject CHÔMEUR, a French word for 'unemployed'. This relation is abbreviated with the symbol Cho. Now, with these new concepts and notational devices, the network of relations for the passive forms can be represented. Note (303).

(303)
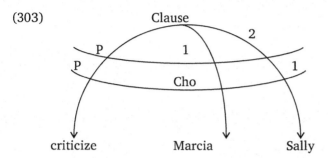

While the passive is taken as a prototypical relation-changing rule, other kinds of such rules are now known. For instance, in German there is not only the PROMOTION (2 → 1 is the relational change) of 2s to subject, there are also cases of 3 → 1 promotion, which English does not have. (English does have a relation-changing rule 3 → 2 as well as 2 → 1. These two can FEED each other to yield a set of three strata: 3 → 2 → 1, as in: *John awarded a medal to Mary* → *John awarded Mary a medal* → *Mary was awarded a medal by John.*)

(304) a. *Mein   Bruder   erzählte   mir   diese   Geschichte.*
          my   brother   told   me   this   story

      b. *Ich   kriegte   diese   Geschichte   von   meinem   Bruder   erzählt.*
          I   got   this   story   by   my   brother   told

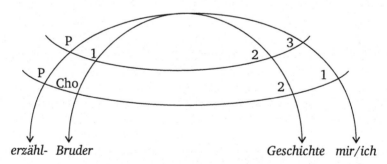

In this example, a pronoun in the dative case, *mir,* is promoted directly to the subject (nominative), *ich,* in this sentence. We know that German does not have a rule 3 → 2, as English does, because a sentence such as **mein Bruder erzählte diese Geschichte mich* in which *mich* is the direct object (accusative) form of the pronoun is ungrammatical.

These examples indicate the representational device. What RG has emphasized is the laws that govern and restrict the change of relations.

Keenan and Comrie (1977 and 1979) demonstrated that not all grammatical relations are equally accessible to grammatical processes. In relativization (formation of relative clauses), for example, the relative clause modifier can most easily be constructed with the subject missing, e.g., *the man [that___loves Mary]*. English also allows the formation of relatives on the object position of the clause, e.g., *the man [that Mary loves___]*. We also can form relative clauses on genitive modifiers, standards of comparison, and perhaps even amounts of comparison as in (305).

(305) a. *the man [whose wife John loves ___]*
　　　b. *the man [Mary is taller than ___]*
　　　c. *the amount [Mary is taller than the man by ___]*

In other languages, only a subset of these positions admit of relative clause construction. In Amis, a VSO, partially ergative Austronesian language spoken in Taiwan, only the subject position can be used to form relative clauses.

(306) a. *mafoti'ay ko　mikalatay to　tamdaw a　waco*
　　　　 sleep　 NOM bite　　ACC person　LINK dog
　　　　 [mafotiay [ko [$_s$mikalatay ____ to tamdaw$_s$] a waco]]
　　　　 The dog that bit the man is sleeping.

　　　b. **mafotiay ko mikalatay ko waco a tamdaw*
　　　　 [mafotiay [ko [$_s$mikalatay ko waco ____ $_s$] a tamdaw]]
　　　　 The person that the dog bit is sleeping.

In the first example, the subject of the relative clause *ko waco* is missing. One might paraphrase this sentence as *the bit the man dog is sleeping*. But the second sentence is unacceptable, paraphrasable as *the the dog bit man is sleeping*. Other languages—such as Indonesian—allow only subjects and direct objects to be relativized upon. Thus, one can see that languages may require the notions of subject and direct object in the statement of a grammatical rule. Nevertheless, universal characterizations of subject and direct object have proven difficult to state in semantic, pragmatic terms. Perlmutter and Postal proposed a taxonomy of grammatical relations that nominals can bear in clauses, which they take as primitive notions. (The assumption that certain categories do not require definition is not an unusual practice in grammatical theory, cf., for example, the use of S, NP, VP in Chomsky 1965.) The categories RG assumes are shown in (307).

(307) a. TERMS, i.e., subject, direct object, indirect object
      b. NONTERMS, i.e., obliques such as benefactives, instruments, directions, etc.

Term relations, of which there are two types—nuclear terms (subject and direct object) and nonnuclear terms (indirect object)—are thought to be more active in relation-changing rules, with the nonterms (including Cho) less active. Among the latter, the obliques correspond closely to the semantic roles of the same name.

8.3 Problem solving in RG

Unlike the previous discussions of solving problems, we will not give a sketch of the English auxiliary system to illustrate RG; RG, to our knowledge, has not treated the auxiliary system of English. We focus our discussion here, instead, on areas in which RG makes significant universal claims.

8.3.1 Revaluations. A particularly revealing example of the machinery of RG can be found in revaluation rules, illustrated briefly in (302)–(304). For example, one of the universal laws of grammar is called THE 1-ADVANCEMENT EXCLUSIVENESS LAW, another THE FINAL 1 LAW. The first of these requires that in the derivation of any one clause there can be an advancement to 1 (subject) only once. In a language that allows both 2 → 1 and 3 → 1 passives, such as Modern German, it is conceivable that both of these rules could apply. Consider the sentences in (308).

(308) a. *Mein Bruder   erzählte mir diese Geschichte*
         my   brother told   me   this   story

      b. *Diese Geschichte wurde mir von meinem Bruder   erzählt*
         this story   was   me   by   my   brother told (2→1)

      c. *Ich kriegte diese Geschichte von meinem Bruder   erzählt*
         I   got   this   story   by   my   brother told (3→1)

The stratal diagram for (308c) is shown in (309).

(309)

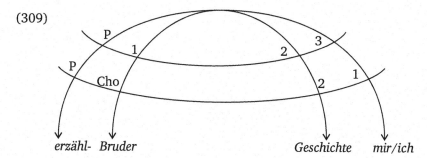

erzähl- Bruder   Geschichte   mir/ich

Notice that in the second stratum *Geschichte* is still a direct object NP and in principle should be promotable to give a sentence **Diese Geschichte wurde von mir von meinem Bruder erzählt gekriegt.*

(310)

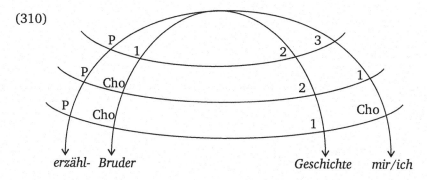

erzähl- Bruder   Geschichte   mir/ich

Such sentences, however, are so unthinkably ill-formed that native speakers are quite astonished when they hear them. They are usually unable even to guess at their meanings. In order to identify as ungrammatical sentences of this type and possibly others in which passivization (or other advancement to 1) has taken place more than once, RG posits the first of these two laws.

The second of these laws (The Final 1 Law) states that in the final stratum of a clause there must be a 1-arc. In other words, surface subjectless sentences are universally unacceptable. Notice that in English we need to say *it rains* with a kind of DUMMY SUBJECT. In other languages one says *rain fell* or *rain rained*. Still, in some languages the phenomenon of dummy subjects will need a closer examination to determine whether such dummies can be justified. Suffice it to say that the overt presence of some special empty form with weather verbs and perhaps with others is widespread.

8.3.2 The Unaccusative Hypothesis. One of the most dramatic claims of RG is that sentences can be intransitive in more than one way. (For discussion of such facts in Principles and Parameters Theory, see §5.4.1.) The traditional view was that a transitive sentence was one that possessed a subject and a direct object, intransitives were ones that had only a subject. A fundamental assumption of RG is that there are strata, i.e., multiple levels of derivation of grammatical relations. As a result, it is possible that a clause could originally have been intransitive by virtue of having only a subject and a predicate in the initial stratum, or that it could have been intransitive by virtue of having only an object in the original stratum. The fact that both final forms possess a subject is a manifestation of the Final 1 Law, which states that every clause must have a subject in its final stratum, if only a dummy.

The reason that differences of this sort hadn't been discovered until recently seems to lie in the fact that unaccusative advancement of 2 to 1 in an intransitive clause masks the original situation. Relational grammarians have found evidence that the two clauses behave differently in some languages. In Amis, an Austronesian language found on Taiwan, there is a systematic difference between intransitive clauses manifested in the form of the prefix on the verb (Edmondson forthcoming); in Choctaw there is a difference in the form of subject agreement in the verb (Rosen 1984:58). Consider the Amis sentences in (311) and the Choctaw sentences in (312).

(311) a. ***ma**-warin-ay k-iya   tamdaw i   lotok*
          ERG-roll-PFT   NOM-the man   LOC mountain
          The man rolled down the mountain.

      b. ***mi**-warin-ay k-iya   tamdaw i   lotok*
          ACT-roll-PFT   NOM-the man   LOC mountain
          The man rolled down the mountain.

(312) a. *an-a-t-o   sa-nayokpa*
          1st-DET-NOM-CONTR 1stACC-happy
          I am happy.

      b. *an-a-t-o   hilha-**li**-tok*
          1st-DET-NOM-CONTR dance-1stNOM-PST
          I danced.

The sentences in (311) do not have exactly the same meaning; (311a) indicates that the action occurred by accident without the control of the subject *kiya tamdaw*, whereas (311b) expresses a situation in which the subject *kiya tamdaw* is playing a game, i.e., lies down and rolls down the hill, or at least controls the situation. In (312a), there is a NOM case agreement marker on the verb, but an ACC case agreement marker appears in (312b). In both the Amis and Choctaw examples, the subject itself is marked with the NOM case, which we take to indicate that *kiya tamdaw* 'the person' and *an-a-t-o* 'I' are subjects in the final stratum of their respective clauses. Perlmutter 1978 has suggested that such structures as (312) will have nonidentical stratal diagrams as in (313).

(313) a.

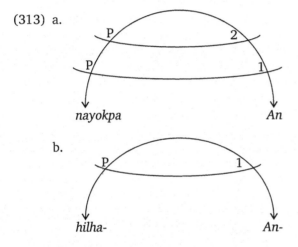

b.

The relational diagram (313a) expresses the fact that an original 2 has advanced to 1; (313b) is simply an intransitive clause with an initial 1. The Unaccusative Hypothesis provides an account for a number of differences of form and behavior among intransitives, some noticed in traditional grammar, some unnoticed before. Further, in many languages there seems to be a semantic difference associated with unaccusative predicates such as (311a) and (312a) versus unergative predicates such as (311b) and (312b).

(314) Unaccusative predicates in English may include: fall, drop, sink, float, seep, ooze, trickle, drown, rot, freeze, exist, transpire, ensue, shine, glow, pop, survive.

(315) Unergative predicates in English may include: work, swim, knock, study, laugh, shout, growl, bark, quack, chirp, cough, belch, sleep, cry.

The Unaccusative Hypothesis is, of course, a universal principle and must be applicable to English as well as to other languages in which there is little if any overt grammatical indication of its presence. Notice that even in Amis and Choctaw the Final 1 Law partly covers up a difference between unaccusative and unergative predicates with the advancement of 2 → 1 (Unaccusative Advancement); specifically, in both languages the overt (final) subject nominal is in the nominative case.

A second kind of argument has been advanced for the Unaccusative Hypothesis on the basis of Italian by Carol Rosen. She reports a cluster of behavioral phenomena too complex to discuss in detail here that separate unaccusative and unergative intransitive verbs. One of the major differences in these two is that unaccusative intransitive verbs require the auxiliary *be* in constructions involving periphrastic tenses, whereas unergative intransitive verbs require the auxiliary *have* in constructions involving periphrastic tenses in this language. We return to this topic and provide examples in our discussion of CLAUSE UNION in §8.3.4.

8.3.3 Antipassive, inversion, and other demotions. Early versions of RG claimed that no term, i.e., 1, 2, or 3, could be demoted; terms can only go *en chômage* by force of being displaced by an advancing nominal. This law proved to be untenable universally. Some of the major kinds of data that show this phenomenon are called RETREATS, i.e., 1 → 2 (antipassive), 1 → 3 (inversion). We will illustrate antipassive from Davies (1984).

As mentioned above, Choctaw possesses both case marking of nominals and agreement marking on the verb. Consider first a monostratal clause in (316).

(316) *is-sa-bashli-tok*
      2NOM-1ACC-cut-PST
      You cut me.

Here 'you' is subject and shows nominative agreement; 'me' is object and shows accusative agreement. Choctaw also possesses clauses of the structure type in (317).

(317) *sa-ttola-tok*
       1ACC-fall-PST
       I fell.

Notice that *sa* is a first-person agreement marker, but it belongs to
the direct object set and not to the subject set of markers, as one can tell
from comparing (317) to (316). Notice also pairs such as those in (318).

(318) a. *shokha   anõpa ish-yimmi   hõ*
          story   2NOM-believe Q
          Do you believe the story?

      b. *shokha anõpa chi-yimmi   hõ*
          story   2ACC-believe Q
          Do you believe the story?

The sentences in (318) have the same meaning, but in (318a) the
verb shows nominative agreement, whereas in (318b) it shows accusative agreement. Davies argues that sentences such as (318b) involve
antipassive, but he notes that not all intransitive clauses arise via
antipassive; some are simply intransitive initially. He proposes that
(318a) and (318b) would have the stratal diagrams in (319) and (320).

(319)

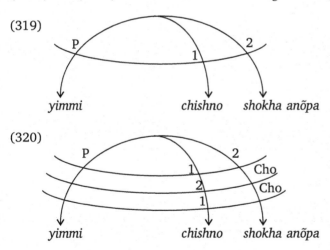

Davies argues that *chishno* (the base form used in the initial stratum,
ultimately to be manifested by a prefix on the verb) is an initial 1 by
virtue of its behavior in regard to the case marking of the nominal, not

identical to agreement and reflexivization. Moreover, we know that *chishno* is a final 1 because of data from equi-NP deletion (not included here). Notice that (319) and (320) differ only in that (320) is a final intransitive clause, possessing a 1 and a Cho, whereas (319) is finally transitive, possessing a 1 and a 2. The agreement in the verb is determined by the grammatical relation of the nominal in a nonfinal stratum, so that NOM appears in (318a) and ACC in (318b).

Another language that possesses an antipassive construction is Eskimo.[17] In the Inupiat variety of this language in the antipassive construction, the verb agrees with the final subject and direct object in person and number and is marked with an antipassive marker *si*. Consider the following data from Nivens (1986).

(321) a. *mari-m   taapkua kamŋ-ich tuni-gai   [saityak-Mun]*
          Mary-ERG those   boots-p   sold-3s/3p Saityak-DAT
          Mary sold those boots (to Saityak).

      b. *mari-ø   kamiŋ-ñik   tuni-si-ruq   [saityak-mun]*
          Mary-ABS boots-2CHO sell-ANTIP-3s
          Mary sold boots (to Saityak).

The stratal diagrams associated with (321a) and (321b) are, respectively, (322) and (323).

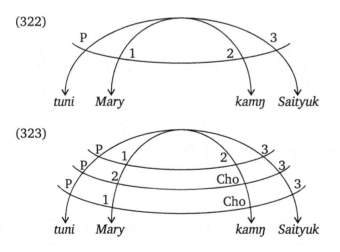

(322)

tuni   Mary   kamŋ   Saityuk

(323)

tuni   Mary   kamŋ   Saityuk

---

[17]We thank Jann Parrish for drawing our attention to this data and analysis.

As these stratal diagrams indicate, the antipassive involves the retreat of the initial subject *Mary* to a 2, thereby forcing the original direct object *en chômage*. In Inupiat, a 2 Cho is indicated with a special case marker *ñik*. In the final stratum, the 2 must have advanced to 1 in order to obey the Final 1 Law; the final 1 in such constructions manifests the absolute case marker, -∅.

8.3.4 Clause Union. As a final area of exemplification of RG, we turn to what has been termed CLAUSE UNION. This is an area of considerable development within RG at the present time; we consider first a standard analysis, then a current proposed modification.

Consider first a French sentence in (324).

(324) *Je ferai aller Jean.*
      I will make Jean go.

Under the standard analysis, there are two clauses involved in such sentences, and, as a result, two sets of grammatical relations. The stratal diagram for the initial stratum of (324) has a clause embedded under a 2 arc as seen in (325).

(325)

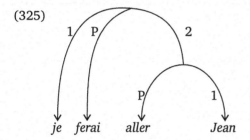

je is subject (=1) of the main clause (dubbed the "upstairs" clause) and *ferai* is predicate; the object (=2) of the predicate is the embedded clause (dubbed the "downstairs" clause), which has its own relations, with a predicate *aller* and a subject *Jean*. After operations relevant to clause union have applied, the result is the diagram in (326).

(326)

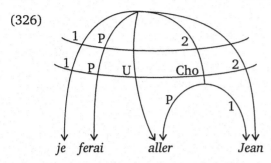

Note that *Jean* is now identified as being the object of the upstairs verb *faire* (correctly, because if a pronoun occurred it would be accusative). Further, the downstairs predicate *aller* bears a UNION (U) relation to the clause as a whole, a relation proposed only for such cases; note that *aller* is not inflected for tense, the proposal of the U relation being in part to distinguish such tenseless predicates from those which are marked for tense.

Davies and Rosen (1988) propose that rather than accounting for sentences like the above through a structure containing a downstairs clause embedded in an upstairs clause, the preferred account is monoclausal. Further, they argue that in terms of operations (and consequently *chômeurs* as well) predicates should be considered to be on a par with terms. The result is that instead of the stratal diagram in (326), the diagram in (327) is proposed.

(327)

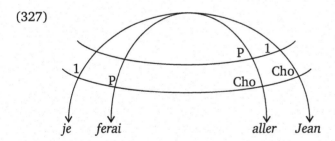

Note that the predicate of the embedded clause becomes a Cho, which will follow naturally if predicates are included in the set of relations subject to the STRATAL UNIQUENESS LAW, i.e., no more than one nominal may head an arc with the same term relation.

A comparison of the two analyses reveals that this proposal, namely that predicates function in a manner similar to that of terms, results in a simpler stratal diagram, but it is a significant modification of the theory and must be supported by argumentation.

One argument is a theory-internal one: if a monoclausal analysis can be supported, the U relation needed for the biclausal analysis can be dispensed with. Because U is a primitive relation, dispensing with U results in a simplification of the inventory of primitive terms, an important claim as to the nature of language. More important than the theoretical simplification, however, it can be demonstrated that the monoclausal analysis is more revealing of the facts of language. Among the arguments which have been set forth is the distribution of the Italian auxiliaries *avere* 'have' versus *essere* 'be' in perfect tenses.

Crucial among the facts to be considered are the following: among intransitive clauses, some verbs require *avere*, some require *essere*; transitive clauses normally take *avere*, but if a reflexive clitic occurs, they obligatorily take *essere*. We have mentioned above how the Unaccusative Hypothesis accounts for the distribution of the auxiliary in intransitive clauses; the relevant Italian data (cf. the German discussion above) is as follows (*ha* is from *avere*, *è* is from *essere*):

(328) *Ugo ha esagerato.*
        Ugo exaggerated.

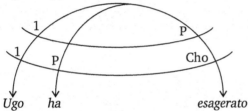

(329) *Ugo è migliorato.*
        Ugo improved.

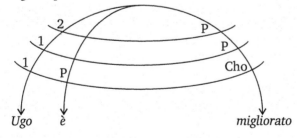

Here, the predicate *esagerato* is a simple intransitive and takes *avere*; *migliorato*, on the other hand, is an unaccusative construction derived via 2 → 1 (Unaccusative Advancement) and thus takes *essere*.

Now compare the following transitive sentences, the first of which has a typical direct object, the second being a reflexive (*se* is the reflexive clitic).

(330) *Ugo ha difeso Pippo.*
       Ugo defended Pippo.

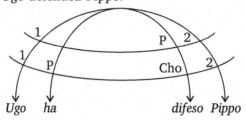

(331) *Ugo se è difeso.*
       Ugo defended himself.

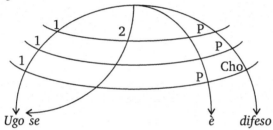

It can be seen that in (331) *Ugo* heads both a 1-arc and a 2-arc (so-called MULTI-ATTACHMENT); when we look at the intransitive sentence in (329) we find the same pattern, except that in this case *Ugo* heads a single arc labeled with both a 1 and a 2, although at different stratal levels. Both sentences take *essere*, in contrast with (328) and (330) which lack such a pattern and take *avere*. What is desirable here is a single generalization which will define the distribution of the auxiliary *essere* in Italian. This can be captured through a monoclausal analysis like that of (331) by means of the following (Davies and Rosen 1988:63): Auxiliary Selection in Italian. The perfect Aux is *essere* in any clause containing a 1-arc and a 2-arc with the same head. Otherwise, it is *avere*.

Now note a further set of constructions containing the verb *dovere*.

(332) a. *Ugo ci **ha** dovuto collaborare.*
           Ugo had to collaborate in it.

b.   *Ugo ci è dovuto intervenire.*
     Ugo had to intervene in it.

c.   *Ugo mi **ha** dovuto difendere.*
     Ugo had to defend me.

d.   *Ugo si è dovuto difendere.*
     Ugo had to defend himself.

Again, we see a distribution of *avere* in (332a) and (332c), and *essere* in (332b) and (332d). The difficulty of accounting for the distribution of the auxiliaries here is that in each case the verb which is determining the construction is not the one with which the auxiliary itself occurs, but rather the infinitive. Under a biclausal analysis, the stratal diagrams for (332a) and (332b) are diagramed in (333) and (334), respectively.

(333)

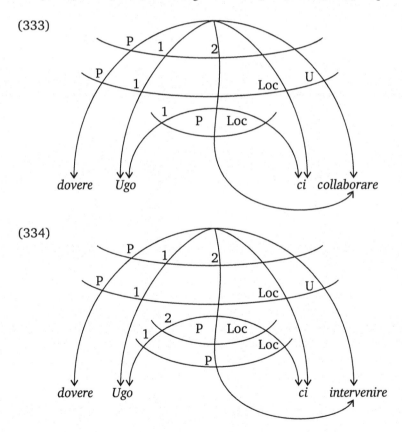

(334)

That is, in neither case is there an NP which heads both a 1-arc and a 2-arc in the main clause, so the generalization predicts (incorrectly) that *avere* will occur in both. A monoclausal analysis, however, can account for the distribution of the auxiliaries in these cases too by means of the same generalization, by making use of the fact that the auxiliary heads one of the arcs, the modal a second, and the main predicate a third, as shown in the diagram in (335).

(335)

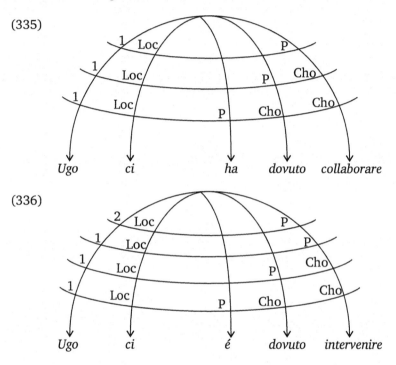

(336)

The auxiliary distribution rule can be modified as follows to capture the distribution of Italian auxiliaries in (328)–(334).

AUXILIARY SELECTION IN ITALIAN: The perfect Aux is *essere* iff the tail and head of its P-initial 1-arc are also the tail and head of a 2-arc.

That is, at whatever place in the relational network the auxiliary is chosen (that being the P-initial stratum for the auxiliary), if the tail and head of the 1-arc is also tail and head of a 2-arc, *essere* is found. The monoclausal analysis, then, allows a single generalization to account for all of these sentences, a fact not possible under the biclausal analysis.

8.4 Mapping theory

Relational grammar has been used to study a wide variety of languages and language types. Carol Rosen 1985 presented solutions in the RG paradigm to some very difficult problems of agreement found in Southern Tiwa, a language of New Mexico. These solutions have turned out to be of wider relevance, because they point out that it might be possible to avoid reference to strata other than the final stratum, if there are restrictions on the mapping of GR's to surface forms. While the problem in its full form is too complex to present here, Rosen's solution is worthy of a brief examination. Basically, she suggests that SU—DO—IO and the persons first person, second person, and third person must be aligned in Southern Tiwa, a characteristic sometimes called the ANIMACY HIERARCHY. Thus, we would construct a linear system, SU-1st-3rd-DO, with SU and 1st to be connected by a line drawn up from SU and down in v-shape to 1st.

$$\bigwedge \quad \bigwedge$$
SU 1st 3rd DO

Notice that first person can be subject and third person can be direct object, but if first person is to be direct object and third person is to be subject, then the lines of mapping would cross and such crossing is in Southern Tiwa a violation.

SU 1st 3rd DO

We may thus conclude that in some languages mapping of GR's onto morphosyntactic arguments can be subject to restrictions. This problem suggests that GR's and categories of surface form such as person or case may be on different tiers or planes in the manner of autosegmental phonology. This insight has led to some new work called Mapping Theory that we now briefly introduce.

The work on Mapping Theory was initiated in Gerdts 1992, 1993 and Burgess, Dziwirek, and Gerdts 1995. Simply stated, there are basically four modules of Mapping Theory and two of these involve parts of RG.

1. Thematic Relations—semantic roles of a type similar to those proposed by Gruber 1970 and P&P's θ-roles.

2. Grammatical Relations—identical to the initial stratum of Relational Grammar ordered according to the hierarchy of RG 1 > 2 > 3 > oblique.
3. MAPs—Morphosyntactically licensed Argument Positions, which correspond approximately to the final Grammatical Relation in RG. Nominals associated with a MAP are direct arguments, not obliques.
4. Presentation—the morphosyntactic correlates of a MAP, such as case, agreement, word order, etc.

Thus, for example, an English sentence such as

(337) I saw you.

would have the analysis:

(338) Thematic Relations   Agent   Theme
            | |
      GR   1   2
            | |
      MAP   A   B
            | |
      Presentation   nom. case   acc. case

In any clause the number of MAPs assigned depends upon: (a) the lexical semantic valence of the verb; (b) MAP-reducing or MAP-building morphology; and (c) the threshold set for a language (i.e., some languages allow only two MAPs, some three, and some even four, cf. Gerdts 1992, 1993) in the instance of unmarked or "vertical" association (represented in (338)). It is crucial in the passive *You were seen by me* that the first GR is unlinked and one MAP will be canceled:

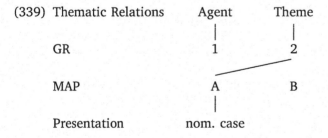

(339) Thematic Relations   Agent   Theme
            | |
      GR   1   2

      MAP   A   B
            |
      Presentation   nom. case

In antipassives, see above discussion of Eskimo, the B MAP will be canceled and the association will be vertical or unmarked to the 1.

(340) Thematic Relations   Agent   Theme
                                   | |
        GR   1   2
                                   |
        MAP   A   B
                                   |
        Presentation   nom. case

According to Gerdts 1993 there are universal principles to link GRs to MAPs:

> SATURATION—every MAP must be linked to a GR or canceled
> BIUNIQUENESS—every MAP is linked only to a single GR and
>   every GR to at most one MAP
> NO DELINKING—there are no delinkings

In the passive (339) the agent must be presented as a non-argument, usually as an oblique, whereas in the antipassive (340) the theme must be presented as a non-argument.

Gerdts shows that morphological constraints on the number of allowed MAPs are, to some degree, independent of the number of GRs in a given clause, nevertheless there are universal rules of association of the two aspects. She claims that a purely "syntactic" account based on GRs alone is inadequate. So, for example, some languages may allow as many as four MAPs per clause while others allow only two or perhaps three. Thus, the alignment between GRs and morphology is not invariant across languages.

Map theory is an attempt to develop principles that express linguistic universals but that also predict language specific manifestations of these principles. This development can be regarded as an answer to critics of RG who have criticized the "abstractness" of RG, since the laws of RG can be seen only through the glass of final stratal forms of real language sentences.

8.5 Relational grammar theorizing

As we have indicated, RG is interested primarily in the grammar of grammatical relations. This being the case, such topics of contemporary interest as INVERSION (1 → 3 retreat) and the behavior of multipredicate structures in a wide range of typologically diverse languages are currently being subject to extensive investigation.

Summary of Relational Grammar

1. Levels: RG assumes that various syntactic strata exist in the clause.
2. Primitive symbols include a small number of grammatical relations, i.e., the TERMS: subject, direct object, indirect object; and nonterms such as predicate, *chômeur*, oblique object, POSS (genitive of possession relation).
3. Rules produce no constituent structure or distribution. Only the linkages between networks of grammatical relations are derived.
4. Rules reference grammatical relations directly.
5. The rules seem to be largely context-free. Relational grammarians propose analyses for specific languages that can refer to grammatical relations of certain nominals at different stratal levels, stratally nonlocal rules.
6. Generative capacity is not discussed.
7. Other components of grammar, i.e., phonology, are not discussed.
8. A set of universal laws serves to identify or define the set of permissible relational networks in any human language. Grammatical phenomena from specific languages are used to support or modify these universal principles.

9

Functional Models of Grammar

9.1 Introduction

In this chapter, we consider three different points of view that share several common features: the nature of language as seen in its functional aspects, with lesser attention paid to its formal characteristics. These three trends in today's functionalism we will characterize with the statements: (1) Functional forces in language that come to bear in the domain of discourse/texts or use of language in communicative situations; (2) Functional forces in language that come to bear in social uses of language (the giving and saving of face); and (3) Functional forces in language that are found at all levels and are instrumental in the formation of language signs (iconicity in language). As an example of the first we present a brief summary of Functional Typological Grammar as developed in Givón (1984 and 1990) to establish the basic perspective. Then we examine Paul Hopper's notion of Emergent Grammar, the claim that grammar rules for sentences emerge from discourse use. The second area is exemplified by the work of Brown and Gilman (1970) reprint. The third area is illustrated by a brief look at the features of iconicity in linguistic discussion. While the theories considered here differ significantly, their shared emphasis on the functional aspects of language allows them to be considered together here as representative of the general orientation.

9.2 Functional Typological Grammar

9.2.1 Ontological primitives. In his book *Syntax: A Functional-Typological Introduction,* Givón (1984) outlines his approach to linguistic

227

theorizing. In the first chapter of this work, the author goes into some detail about the weaknesses of others and presents his views on the nature of linguistic investigation. Not surprisingly, he especially criticizes the generative-transformational tradition. Givón's assumptions are:

1. INTERDEPENDENCE OF LANGUAGE SUBPARTS—the components of language are not independent of one another; i.e., syntax, semantics, pragmatics, and phonology are not autonomous. The structure of language must be linked with the functions of language.

2. INNATENESS OF GENERAL COGNITIVE ABILITIES—language and communication are viewed as being maturational phenomena and part of general, Piagetian cognitive abilities; this is in contrast with the view that takes language structural constraints, e.g., Subjacency, MOVE ALPHA, and X-Bar Syntax, as being innate.

3. DEVELOPMENTALISM—the FTG approach is basically developmental in the sense that it considers how language acquisition, language change, and language evolution affect language behavior.

4. LANGUAGE AS AN OPEN RATHER THAN CLOSED SYSTEM—human languages are best described in terms of (a) categories that are defined not as discrete, but rather based on proto-types with fuzzy boundaries, and (b) with rules that are not exceptionless, but contingent and pragmatically based.

5. BALANCE OF DATA AND THEORY—an attempt is made to prevent theory from being extremely underdetermined by data.

6. THE CROSS-LINGUISTIC NATURE OF GENERALIZATIONS—unlike the transformational generative paradigm with its deep structure universals that have received their greatest impetus from the detailed study of one language, FTG directs its main effort toward universals holding across languages, especially universals at the level of function/meaning with surface structure forms being variables.

7. THE PROTO-TYPICAL NATURE OF LINGUISTIC CATEGORIES—unlike almost every grammatical tradition since Aristotle's Metaphysics, FTG stresses that categories lack sharp boundaries; e.g., adjectives shade off into verbs in regard to some properties and shade off into nouns in regard to others.

8. There is a FUNCTIONAL BIND because syntax has to code both propositional semantic information and discourse-pragmatic function; these two can interfere with each other. (1984:5–23)

Of course, lists such as the above are too vague to provide more than a general idea of the differences between this approach and others we have studied in this volume. In order to make these ideas somewhat clearer, we now examine Givón's description of information-theoretic preliminaries to discourse pragmatics (1984:239–67).

Since the primary aim of language is the transfer of information, and since this information must be delivered as a sequence of information packets, called PROPOSITIONS, it stands to reason that these propositions in a discourse must be organized into a structure with a beginning, end, and central part. Moreover, there must be a linkage among these parts, called COHERENCE. Without coherence one would not have a text or discourse but only a motley collection of propositions. To put it in terms of the old saw, the two sentences, *The King died. And the Queen died.* are just two raw sentences. But, *The King died. And the Queen died of grief.* makes a coherent discourse.

The notion of coherence can vary between two extremes, TAUTOLOGY and CONTRADICTION. Tautology represents the extreme of REDUNDANCY in which absolutely no new information is added to an existing discourse.[18] Contradiction, on the other hand, represents adding absolute incompatibility to an existing discourse. Informationally, both of these end points are dysfunctional; we expect real discourses to show propositions that contain both some old information and some new information.

There is also another dichotomy of information type to consider, namely the two poles called FOREGROUND and BACKGROUND.[19] Almost certainly, the hearer's background information is relatively large, and it may be generic and general or specific to that discourse. Large amounts of it are in organization HYPERTEXTUAL, i.e., retrievable globally from any arbitrary information location. If these conditions were not fulfilled, then understanding new information would simply be too slow, and would require too much overt preparation and rehearsing for verbal

---

[18]Tautologies in the form of repetitions and paraphrases may, however, have other functions than the transfer of information in a longer piece of discourse. These other functions (for example, the use of repetition as a mechanism for persuasion, irony, or emphasis) may override considerations of information in certain discourses. One example of this use might be Mark Anthony's repetition of "And Brutus is an honorable man" in Shakespeare's *Julius Caesar*.

[19]These notions seem similar in principle to those of Longacre, who refers to such things as the narrative cline of information being relatively on or off the storyline.

exchanges to be informationally effective. The reliance on hypertextual background can in some discourses become quite extreme with the result that those lacking the long term and short term storage of needed specific or general information (lexicon and world knowledge) fail to understand or draw unintended inferences. Children, nonnative speakers, and those with neurolinguistic disorders may thus be comparatively less communicatively competent than adult native speakers. Givón (1984:405) sees a relationship between various components in regard to referential accessibility.

(341)

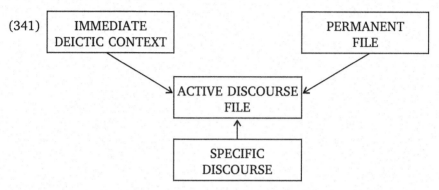

There also appears to be an informational continuum of discourse types that Givón calls INFORMATIVE versus MANIPULATIVE. The discourses of young children, he says, are prototypically manipulative, mono-propositional, with immediate deictically obvious context, impoverished code, closed social circle, low cultural complexity, and slow cultural change. That of adults, by contrast, is multi-propositional, informative, with less predominantly immediate deictically obvious context, elaborate code, open social circle, high cultural complexity, and rapid cultural change.

Some languages have specific grammatical devices to code some of these pragmatic categories. Longacre and others have found extensive evidence that particles usually ascribed mysterious functions are, in fact, markers of informational, that is to say, pragmatic categories. One thinks in this connection of Japanese *wa* and the focus markers found in Philippine languages in which the existence or nonexistence of a form is governed not by considerations of sentence structure, but of information structure.

9.3 Emergent Grammar

9.3.1 Ontological position. Givón's work about information structuring in natural language might be thought of as establishing a different plane of analysis from proposals about the form-structure—e.g., P&P syntax—and the meaning structuring effects of semantics—à la Montague and allied traditions. Givón has brought up issues of what speakers know, when and how (i.e., from what source) they know it, and how they use that information to shape their communications. Theories such as Functional-Typological Grammar have chosen not especially to stress the core issue about speakers' knowledge of sentence forms (i.e., the idea that the forms of language are like molds into which content is poured and the form or mold is known because speakers know rules of grammar before they speak or understand). The position that most directly confronts this a priori character of Chomskian grammars was set forth by Paul Hopper and those that follow his Hypothesis of Emergent Grammar.

In 1985 Paul Hopper made a very unorthodox proposal about the origins and nature of grammar, by challenging the basic notion of generative transformational grammar that our grammatical knowledge was a given in advance and that the acquisition process is merely well-known work-in-progress toward the necessary goal of a complete set of grammatical rules (cf. Hopper 1988). Dr. Susan Herring, one of our colleagues at the University of Texas at Arlington, has described the ideas of Hopper, Givón, and others by contrasting them with the ideas of the generative formalists on this issue. We take over this grid of discussion from her. In the following we use FUNCTIONALIST to signify investigators such as Paul Hopper and FORMALISTS to describe the followers of Chomsky and to an extent linguists in the tradition of Montague and other formal semanticists.

	Formalists	Functionalists
1. OBJECTS OF STUDY	decontextualized sentences	sentences and units in larger (discourse) context
2. METHODS OF STUDY	Introspection of "grammatical" and "ungrammatical" sentences	Empirical examinations of real speech; often statistical evaluation of results is employed

3. SOLUTIONS TO PROBLEMS	Formalization of rules, principles, or parameters with sharp boundaries	Solutions remain informal or are stated as trends or tendencies with NONSHARP BOUNDARIES
4. GRAMMAR	Rule sets producing "platonic" ideals that are immutable and given a priori as a result of linguistic universals and shared language experience in acquisition	Rules are incomplete and partial, only EMERGENT from discourse patterns by processes called GRAMMATICALIZATION, tendencies that become conventionalized as morpho-syntax
5. TIME	Grammars, at least in part, are fixed in time as are ideal laws of nature	Grammars are emergent in time and and are (partly) universally developmental in tendency

GTG investigators assume that a grammar is a fixed body of information in the form of rules and until one possesses this grammar, then the output of the rules may be less than well-formed sentences. This body of rules is necessary and sufficient to produce all but only the grammatical sentences. This body of rules, moreover, produces absolute judgments of grammaticality. Sentences are rule-governed and thus they are part of the language in question or they are not; *tertium non datur;* there are no third alternatives. Data for theory construction are sentences removed from any surrounding context. The important aspects of grammar produce ideal sets of sentences not subject to the forces of language change in time or context. Hopper uses the term A PRIORI GRAMMAR to described Chomsky's conception. As for discourse, grammarians in the tradition of GTG and successors have generally felt that features of sentence grammar are governed by principles of Universal Grammar, whereas discourses are governed by principles of pragmatics. For example, pronouns obviously can have antecedents across sentence boundaries. But, so the GTG analyst, the principles determined within sentences—e.g., binding condition B, a pronominal is always free in its governing category—will result in an interpretation which will be extended in trans-sentential linguistics. This position might be called the BOTTOM-UP HYPOTHESIS.

> We suppose...that the ideal speaker-hearer has a finite gram-
> mar, internally represented in some manner, generating a
> language that consists of an infinite number of sentences,
> each with specific properties. He knows the language gener-
> ated by the grammar. This knowledge of language
> encompasses a variety of properties of sentences. The gram-
> mar must deal with the physical form of a sentence and its
> meaning. Furthermore, the person who knows a language
> know the conditions under which it is appropriate to use a
> sentence, knows what purposes can be furthered by appropri-
> ate use of a sentence under given social conditions. For
> purposes of inquiry and exposition, we may proceed to distin-
> guish "grammatical competence" from "pragmatic
> competence," restricting the first to the knowledge of form
> and meaning and the second to knowledge of conditions and
> manner of appropriate use...
>
> Linguistic knowledge, of course, extends beyond the level of
> the sentence. We know how to construct and understand dis-
> courses of various sorts, and there are no doubt principles
> governing discourse structures. (Chomsky 1980:224ff.)

The most startling idea in Hopper 1988 is that, contra Chomsky,
grammars may not be fixed in advance in a manner that allows knowledge of sentence structure to extend to discourses, nor are these grammars complete, immutable, nor do they have sharp edges with
black-white distinctions between grammatical and nongrammatical sentences. His position is that human language grammars are only sets of
incomplete partials.

> ...the name [emergent grammar stands] for a vaguely de-
> fined set of sedimented (i.e., grammaticalized) recurrent
> partials whose status is constantly being renegotiated in
> speech and which cannot be distinguished *in principle* from
> strategies for building discourses. (Hopper 1988:118)

Grammars are negotiated among interlocutors within discourse.
Grammars cannot be constructed from decontextualized sentences, but
only from the function of language in larger and informationally rich
and real discourse. Grammars are dynamic and developmental, changing over time, and there is in principle no real difference between rules
of discourse that have emerged by grammaticalization and rules of sentences that once were rules of discourse. This position might be called
the TOP-DOWN HYPOTHESIS; the negotiated and informationally-based ad

hoc rules of discourse can in time be projected down to the sentence level.

Once example may serve to illustrate Hopper's position. It is often been observed that certain tense/aspect markers or sentence-final particles are associated with storytelling. In English typically the tense that is found in narration is the epic preterite, the simple past time. As in English, in many other languages there are special tense-aspects of the verb used with discourse functions in narration. The usual assumption is that the syntactico-semantic notion of past is elaborated to special auxiliary functions in discourse as a narrative marker. This is, in fact, the idea underlying the name *epic preterite*, in the sense that in recounting past occurrences in sequence a special form for narration developed that required a modifier to explain this use. However, one might equally well, so Hopper, take the inverse position, namely that from narrating stories the concept of completed action emerged and in time that sense of completed action was *grammaticalized* into a simple past tense that did not need the narrative context.

9.3.2 Problem-solving capacity. To illustrate how emergent grammar would go about solving problems, let us again take an example from Chinese discourse as portrayed in Chu (1998).

Much has been written about the perfective aspect marker *-le*. Its use has been described as indicating a bounded situation focusing on the endpoint. The use can be illustrated by the sentences:

(342) a. *Wo zai nali   zhu-LE   liangge yue.*
        I   at there live-PFV two-M months
        I lived there two months.

    b. *Wo pengdao-LE   Lin Hui.*
        I   bump-into-PFV Lin Hui
        I ran into Lin Hui.

    c. *Wo wang-LE   tade   dizhi.*
        I   forgot-PFV her/his address
        I forgot her/his address.

    d. *Wo kanwan-LE   bao,   jiu   shui.*
        I   read-finish-PFV newspaper then sleep
        When I have finished reading the newspaper, I'll go to sleep.

However, Chu tells us that -*le* in Chinese may be used with a discoursal function too. In fact, it is used to mark the peak, a sentence of particular semantic importance within a discourse, cf. Longacre on peak as well as Hinds 1979. Consider the discourse:

(343) a. *Jinnian   lai   suizhe   Zhongwai wenhua*
         recent-year come follow-DUR Chinese   foreign^culture

         jiaoliu   shiye   de fazhan
         exchange business DE development

      b. *Beijing kaoya   he   'Quanjude' dianhao   ye   piao Ø*
         Beijing roast^duck and Quanjude store^name also float

         yang   guo   Ø   hai
         ocean gross   sea

      c. *chuandao   Ø   guowai*
         transmit-arrive country outside

      d. *zhe jiu   shi   gengduo   de   ren   changdao-LE*
         this then make even   more DE people taste-reach-PFV

         wei-xiang-se-mei   de   Beijing kaoya   LE
         taste-sweet-color-pretty DE Beijing roast^duck LE

Recently, along with cultural exchanges between China and other countries, Beijing roast duck and the store named *Quan-Ju-De* went abroad, crossing the seas and oceans. This made it possible for more people to (be able to) taste the delicious and splendid-looking Beijing roast duck.

Notes: DE is an attributive particle.
       Taken from Chu 1998:68–69.

The locations marked with Ø are places where a -*le* could potentially appear but does not. The reason that it does not—according to Chang (1986:88)—is that these locations are NONPEAK clauses and the occurrence of -*le* at the end is exactly because this clause is the peak. The discoursal use of -*le* will solve a lot of problems about the non-use of -*le* in places it would otherwise be expected and its use in some places where it is not expected.

A person espousing the emergent grammar theory of Hopper might want to interpret the case of aspectual -le as the grammaticalization of the discourse peak marker that in time has become a part of Chinese sentence grammar.

9.4 The formative role of language in the social context

Many aspects of language are difficult to analyze in terms of form and meaning without considering language use, specifically the attitude one wishes to express or engender. Saying *Hello,* for instance, cannot be said to have a meaning in the narrow sense. Rather, the idea is to extend a greeting and acknowledge the presence of an acquaintance, friend, family member, or other person.

In a similar vein speech can be a kind of countersign to indicate that one is a member of a particular group. This use is as old as the 13th century BC for it says in Judges 12:6 that the Gileadites tested a captive Ephraimites by asking him to pronounce the Hebrew word *shibboleth* 'an ear of corn'. If he answered *sibboleth,* then they took him and slew him at the passages of Jordan. Also in modern times, drug dealers in South Africa employed some years ago a special form of the Zulu language to authenticate a potential customer. And again, discjockeys employ extreme forms of vernacular English to show they are *hip,* older *hep,* that is, informed (from *hep* a drill sergeant's call to step in line). Thus, we can learn from these examples that certain lexical items, phonology, or sentence pattern can be markers or forms to which strong attitudes are attached.

Forms of address are also indications of how to do things with words. In their famous paper, The pronouns of power and solidarity, Brown and Gilman claim that at the bottom of what they call the V pronoun (from Latin *vos*) and the T pronoun (from Latin *tu*) of address are 'power' and 'solidarity', respectively. By power they mean that control one person has over another. The non-symmetrical relationship is incarnated in the forms of address that encode this power semantic, in point the superior says T and receives V. The crucial concept is symmetry in the relationship and this feature figures into the genesis of the T form use in symmetrical relationships, reaching an ideal peak among twin brothers or a person's soliloquizing address to himself or herself. As Brown and Gilman point out, the T form has experienced several centuries of growth at the expense of the V form, as the value systems of the Middle Ages have been displaced with a social system of greater equality among people.

9.5 The formative role of the sign user in language

9.5.1 The conceptual basis of constructional iconicity. Among the most time honored concepts in linguistics is the division of communications systems into *sign, signified,* and *sign user*. Similarly, the study of the relationship of signs is syntax, the study of the relationship between signs and signified is *semantics,* and the study of the relationship among signs, signified, and sign user is *pragmatics*. Signs themselves can be divided into three ideal types: (1) *images,* which are reproductions of all or most features of the object signified; (2) *icons,* which are reproductions of only a few features of the object signified; and (3) *symbols,* which are not reproductions of the signified at all, but instead arbitrary and conventional representatives of the signified. The symbolic nature of language has always been emphasized. Earlier investigators have argued that natural languages do not demonstrate phonetic symbolism. Prominently, there is the most famous dictum in linguistics ascribed to Ferdinand de Saussure that the linguistic sign is arbitrary. And aside from the onomatopoeia of the barnyard and the whistles and howls of the weather, the words of English do seem very different from those in languages unrelated to it. The lexical shapes of words around the world are different.

(344)

English	Chinese	Kiswahili	Hausa
woman	nüren	mwanamke	màcè
elephant	çaŋ	tembo	giiwaa
two	er	-wili/mbili	biyu

But when one turns to the construction of linguistic forms in paradigms—the variation from singular to plural, from nominative to accusative, from first person to third person—then some of the apparent arbitrariness disappears. There is a surprising amount of correlation. Sapir in 1929 conducted experiments with nonsense words of the CVC type. Newman 1933 related tongue position and size. This feature was studied by Brown, Black, and Horowitz under the name *phonetic symbolism,* who conclude that

> For the present we prefer to interpret our results as indicative of a primitive phonetic symbolism deriving from the origin of speech in some kind of imitative or physiognomic linkage of sounds and meanings. We forsake conservatism on this occasion for the excellent reason that the thesis proposed is so alien to most thinking in psycholinguistics that it needs to be

brought forward strongly so that we may see that its unpopularity has not been deserved. (1955:272)

Here we will suggest that the user of signs, usually a human using a natural language, comes especially in focus. The signs of a language may be modeled on the user of those signs. Iconicity in human languages it is suggested is an example of how form follows function.

Nearly all linguists agree that a natural language possesses form, meaning, and function. The disagreements are about the relationships among these. In the case of plurality, for instance, we could say that the meaning of a plural is approximately that the thing denoted by the singular form exists in countable amounts equal to or greater than two. There is a semantic manifoldness expressed in *boys* not found in *boy*. If there were true arbitrariness in the encoding of singular *s* and plurals, then there would be no correlation across languages. That means that ADDITIVE STRATEGIES for expressing plurals, informally stated as in English *singular + s,* would be no more common that SUBTRACTIVE STRATEGIES for expressing plurals, say *singular minus last segment of the word base.* Subtractive strategies do occur in some languages, but they are exceedingly rare. Surveys of plurals show that the additive strategy is the most common, e.g., *boy:boy + s,* followed by MODULATORY STRATEGIES, e.g., *foot:feet,* followed by ZERO STRATEGIES, e.g., *sheep:sheep,* cf. Mayerthaler 1981, 1986.

It is also a feature of human experience that some kinds of objects occur most commonly in groups. The most important work in the area of human experience, cognition and categorization, has been done by Eleanor Rosch, cf. Varela, Thompson, and Rosch 1991 and Rosch 1978. Thus, eyes, ears, breasts, legs, arms, hands and, for that matter, kidneys and lungs exist in pairs in the natural state. English does not recognize the existence of such naturally occurring groups by having special ways of dealing with their plurals; some languages have special dual forms for body parts. Still, in some or all kinds of English we do say *the police, the government, my family...have come/voted/are visiting;* these are cases of plurals according to sense *(constructio ad sensum).* The word *police* even has a singulative, e.g., *police* (pl): *policeman/police officer.* In these cases form follows meaning and it follows it in the direction away from arbitrariness. Form also follows function and it is these cases that we now turn to.

Willi Mayerthaler of University of Klagenfurt has spoken of the LINGUISTIC DOPPLER EFFECT. If one examines the vowels in the paradigm of deictic forms for proximal and distal demonstratives, then with a far greater than chance probability proximals are formed with high vowels, whereas distals are formed with low vowels. A good examples of the Doppler Effect is French *ici* 'here' vs. *là-bas* 'there' or Chinese *zheige* 'this' vs. *nage* 'that'. The form is constructed iconically in proportion to the user's perception; close space is reflected as a close gap between tongue and palate and distant space is reflected as a large gap between tongue and palate. If speakers don't proprioceptively associate tongue position to distance, they may associate distances with the acoustic properties of sounds.

9.5.2 Markedness in category; markeredness in construction.
One way to express the relationship between points on a scale such as *near* vs. *far, here* vs. *there, now* vs. *then, I* vs. *he, singular* vs. *plural,* is markedness. The usual tests to recognize markedness are: (1) the unmarked is acquired first by children; (2) the marked is most apt to change over time; (3) the marked tends to occur less frequently across languages and tends to be used less frequently within a language that possesses it; (4) the marked item occur more often in speech errors. Thus, most believe that singular is less marked as a category than plural, Greenberg 1966. In other words, the semantic category, the signified, plural, is more marked than the singular category. As we spoke of above though, we need to consider how plurality is encoded in a particular language, its signifier in a particular language. In English the only productive way to construct plural today is additive *s: boy:boys; stem:stem + s.* We retain a few idiosyncratic examples of plural that employ a modulatory strategy, e.g., *foot:feet; mouse:mice; goose:geese.* Constructionally, the additive encoding is the least marked, as an additive sign is closest to the "moreness" of the signified. So we can say that an additive *s*-plural is *markered* (has a non-zero sign) and that a markered additive *s* is better than a markered modulatory vowel; and that a modulatory vowel is better still than a completely unmarkered plural, as in *sheep.*

9.5.3 Markedness reversal.
Humans apparently assign values to things in terms of their everyday world of experience, giving paired values with the less marked value equal to that term more easily accessible, cognitively nearer, culturally more important, weightier, more significant, the figure as opposed to the ground, etc. The principle of alignment of markedness and markeredness in constructions does not always accurately predict the morphological forms one finds. Often though the exceptions to these rules are only apparent. To use Mayerthaler's metaphor in today's world wearing clothes is the norm, the *unmarked case.* Individuals in a state of (relative) undress are *marked,* subject to censure, arrest, wonderment, verbal abuse or, in some cultures, severe sanctions. Occasionally and exceptionally, there is markedness reversal, as occurs on a nudist beach. In the marked environment of a colony of sun worshipers the clothed are

marked and the unclothed the norm. In our example above police, apparently, in English are as a type more likely to occur in groups. Thus, the plural form *police* becomes the base and the singulative *police officer* is then a predicted form. In some languages plural or dual terms for body parts occurring naturally in pairs are taken as the base form and a single hand, eye, etc., is treated as a derived singulative. A single eye is then a marked setting and calls for a reversal of the usual rule singular < plural (where < means less marked than).

9.5.4 Freezes and the linguistic homunculus.

Haj Ross of the University of North Texas and Willi Mayerthaler have also talked about the role of cognitive accessibility, the cognitively unmarked in freezes. Freezes are sequences of conjuncts whose order is fixed or conventional. For example, by a far greater than chance margin languages around the world prefer the ordering *this and that* to *that and this*. Similarly, we find freezes such as:

(345) a.   here and there
       b.   now and then
       c.   here and now
       d.   today and tomorrow
       e.   where and when
       f.   now and again
       g.   once and for all
       h.   now and later
       i.   hither and thither

which may indicate that the proximal is more accessible than the distal and the spatial more accessible than the temporal. Ross speaks in this connection of LINGUISTIC MYOPIA; humans see better close up than far away. That is also why the set of proximal deictic forms is typically richer than the distal set.

Haiman 1985 in his famous collection on iconicity in syntax has called the phenomena described above in §§9.5.1–9.5.3 as *motivation* or ways in which the linguistic form is a diagram of conceptual structure and homologous with it in interesting ways. Beyond motivation, however, he also notes that there are other cases of iconicity in syntax such as, for example, the question of *isomorphism* or the tendency to associate a single invariant meaning with each invariant form, the classic dictum "one meaning, one form." For instance, the English system of marking plurality was much more complex in Anglo-Saxon with several distinct paradigms for plural, but this one-to-many relation in Middle English has since mostly evolved into a single system of s-plurals with few residues and thus more consistent with the desideratum one meaning, one form. Finally, he says a third issue in iconicity is *apparent arbitrariness* in language as a result of "the limited good" of linguistic expression. These issues bear on the question of functionalism in the sense that grammaticalization is seen as a force that shifts "relatively freely constructed utterances in discourse" or the system external world of discourse to "relatively fixed constructions in grammar" (Du Bois in Haiman 1985:346). Du Bois says that these external (discourse) and internal (grammatical) forces can, at times, be in competition and require a kind of linguistic theory that studies both discourse and grammar and how the two resolve conflicts when they arise and how each interacts to the dictates of the other.

Freezes in other cases seem to be reflections not of cognitive abilities as much as of physiological abilities.

(346) a. light and dark
      b. day and night
      c. right and left
      d. front and rear
      e. sight and sound

Humans are visually dominant and, furthermore, not nocturnal creatures, seeing better in the light than in the dark, seeing in front better than behind. About 90% of us are right-handed or lateralized to the left hemisphere of the brain. These features are manifested in our preference for basic abilities.

There is no doubt that cultural traditions and prejudices may also enter into freezes. These features may thus determine the orderings:

(347) a. man and boy
      b. husband and wife
      c. north and south
      d. east and west
      e. young and old
      f. men, women, and children
      g. he and she, him and her; his and hers, Mr. and Mrs.
      h. tall and slender
      i. meat and potatoes
      j. gin and tonic

What lies behind all these cases is that some aspects of nature's languages are blueprints of the sign users themselves, their limits, and experiences. The symbolic and arbitrary choice of language signs is modulated with projections of our bodies, our brains, and our prejudices. We might name this force to model ourselves in our speech the LINGUISTIC HOMUNCULUS, who could be described as adult, male, right-handed, with eyes in the front, who sees better in daylight objects that are close. This idea is similar to the ideas in George Lakoff's *Women, Fire, and Dangerous Things* and Mark Johnson's *The Body in the Mind.*

9.6 Functionalist theorizing

It is somewhat difficult to generalize about the features of the three traditions we have spoken about in this chapter. Many contemporary functionalists would subscribe to all three directions since the basic shared notion is that communicative, informational, and cognitive functions drive linguistic forms.

1. Levels. The functionalist approach has emphasized contextualization more than level per se. For sentences, that means studying them in a discourse context. As the Chinese examples showed, the information structure in some languages as manifested in a sequence of several sentences is important.
2. Categories. Generally there are fewer categories in this approach. They often possess fuzzy boundaries, scales, or continua and represent prototypes.
3. Rules. Since the form of sentences is not an issue, rules tend to be about meaning or information or what is appropriate rather than what is allowed. Rule violations are often tested by canvassing opinion of many speakers. For Hopper, grammar emerges from discourse and a priori there are only partials, applets and applications (to use a software metaphor) that can be combined by calling on them.
4. Context sensitivity. Context is all important, but since we are not concerned here with a grammar generating or enumerating all the well formed sentences, considerations of context free vs. context sensitivity, etc., are not in focus.

References

Algeo, John. 1973. Stratificational grammar. In Adam Makkai and David G. Lockwood (eds.), Readings in statifical lingusitics. University of Alabama Press.

Asongwed, Tah and Larry M. Hyman. 1976. Morphotonology of the Ngamambo noun. In Larry M. Hyman (ed.), Studies in Bantu tonology. Southern California Occasional Papers in Linguistics 3. Los Angeles: Department of Linguistics, University of Southern California.

Bailey, Charles-James N. 1982. On the yin and yang nature of linguistics. Ann Arbor: Karoma Press.

————. 1985. English phonetic transcription. Dallas: Summer Institute of Linguistics and the University of Texas at Arlington.

Ball, W. W. Rouse. 1906. A short account of the history of mathematics. New York: Dover Publications. Reprinted in 1960.

Bar-Hillel, Yehoshua. 1960. Information and control. Reading: Addison-Wesley.

Bloomfield, Leonard. 1933. Language. New York: Holt, Rinehart, and Winston.

Bresnan, Joan. 1978. A realistic transformational grammar. In Morris Halle, Joan Bresnan, and George A. Miller (eds.), Linguistic theory and psychological reality, 1–59. Cambridge, Mass.: MIT Press.

————, ed. 1982. The mental representation of grammatical relations. Cambridge, Mass.: MIT Press.

————. 1990. Monotonicity and the theory of relation changes in LFG. Paper presented at the Seoul International Conference on Natural Language Processing, Seoul, Korea.

———— and Jonni M. Kanerva. 1989. Locative inversion in Chichêwa: A case study of factorization in grammar. Linguistic Inquiry 20:1–50.

Also in Tim Stowell and Eric Wehrli (eds.), Syntax and Semantics 26: Syntax and the lexicon, 53–101. New York: Academic Press.

——— and Lioba Moshi. 1990. Object asymmetries in comparative Bantu syntax. Linguistic Inquiry 21:147–85.

Brown, Roger and Albert Gilman. 1970. Pronouns of power and solidarity. In Psycholinguistics: Selected papers, 302–35. New York: The Free Press.

———, Abraham H. Black, and Arnold E. Horowitz. 1955. Phonetic symbolism. Journal of Abnormal and Social psychology, 388–93; Psycholinguistics, 258–73.

Burgess, Clifford S., Katarzyna Dziwirek, and Donna Gerdts, eds. 1995. Grammatical relations: Theoretical approaches to empirical questions. Stanford, Calif.: CSLI Publications.

Chang, Vincent Wuchang. 1986. The particle LE in Chinese narrative discourse. Ph.D. dissertation. University of Florida Gainsville.

Chapman, Charles F. 1942. Piloting, seamanship and small boat handling. New York: Motor Boating.

Chomsky, Noam. 1956. Three models for the description of language. IRE Transactions in information theory. IT-2:113–24. Reprinted in Robert Duncan Luce, Robert R. Bush, and Eugene Golanter (eds.), Handbook of mathematical psychology 7. New York: Wiley and Sons.

———. 1957. Syntactic structures. The Hague: Mouton.

———. 1959. Review of B. F. Skinner. 1957. Verbal behavior. Language 35:26–58.

———. 1965. Aspects of the theory of syntax. Cambridge, Mass.: MIT Press.

———. 1971a. Topics in the theory of generative grammar. In John R. Searle (ed.), The philosophy of language. London: Oxford University Press.

———. 1971b. Recent contributions to the theory of innate ideas. In John R. Searle (ed.), The philosophy of language. London: Oxford University Press.

———. 1972. Studies on semantics in generative grammar. The Hague: Mouton.

———. 1980. Rules and representations. New York: Columbia University Press.

———. 1982. Some concepts and consequences of the theory of government and binding. Cambridge, Mass.: MIT Press.

———. 1984. Lectures on government and binding: The Pisa lectures. Dordrecht: Foris Publications.

———. 1986. Barriers. Cambridge, Mass.: MIT Press.

—— and Morris Halle. 1968. The sound pattern of English. New York: Harper and Row.

—— and Howard Lasnik. 1977. Filters and control. Linguistic Inquiry 8:425–504.

—— and ——. 1991. Principles and Parameters Theory. In J. Jacobs, A. von Stechow, W. Sternefeld, and T. Vennemann (eds.), Syntax: An international handbook of contemporary research. Berlin: de Gruyter.

Chu, Chauncey Cheng-hsi. 1998. A discourse grammar of Mandarin Chinese. Berkeley Models of Grammars 6. New York: Peter Lang Publishing.

Cooper, William E. 1979. Speech perception and production. Norwood, N.J.: Ablex.

Cowpers, Elizabeth A. 1992. A concise introduction to syntactic theory: The government and binding approach. Chicago: The University of Chicago Press.

Cresswell, Max J. 1973. Logics and languages. London: Methuen.

Culicover, Peter W. 1976. Syntax. New York: Academic Press.

Darden, William. 1974. Introduction. In Anthony Bruck, Robert A. Fox, and Michael W. LaGaly (eds.), Papers from the parasession on natural phonology. Chicago: Chicago Linguistic Society.

Davies, William. 1984. Antipassive: Choctaw evidence for a universal characterization. In David Perlmutter and Carol G. Rosen (eds.), Studies in relational grammar 2. Chicago: The University of Chicago Press.

—— and Carol Rosen. 1988. Unions as multi-predicate clauses. Language 64(1):52–88.

Donegan, Patricia J. and David Stampe. 1979. The study of natural phonology. In Daniel A. Dinnsen (ed.), Current approaches to phonological theory. Bloomington: Indiana University Press.

Dowty, David, Robert Wall, and Stanley Peters. 1981. An introduction to Montague semantics. Dordrecht: Reidel.

Dubinsky, Stanley and Carol Rosen. 1983. A bibliography on relational grammar through April 1983 with selected titles on lexical functional grammar. Bloomington: Indiana University Linguistics Club.

—— and ——. 1987. A bibliography on relational grammar through May 1987 with selected titles on lexical functional grammar. Bloomington: Indiana University Linguistics Club.

Du Bois, John. 1985. Competing motivations. In Haiman, 342–65.

Dwyer, David. 1978. What sort of tone language is Mende? Studies in African Linguistics 9:167–208.

Edmondson, Jerold A. forthcoming. A grammar of Hsiukuluan Amis. ms.

Esau, Helmut. 1981. Conversational turn-taking: Assessment and overview. Journal of the Linguistic Association of the Southwest
  4(1):9–16.

Feyerabend, Paul. 1978. Against method: Outline of an anarchistic theory of knowledge. London: Verso.

Fillmore, Charles. 1968. The case for case. In Emmon W. Bach and Robert T. Harms (eds.), Universals in linguistic theory. New York: Holt,
  Rinehart, and Winston.

Fleming, Ilah. 1967. Omission of the determined element: A type of
  aphasic error. Paper presented at the Linguistic Society of America,
  Ann Arbor, Michigan.

————. 1986. Some basic concepts and constraints for a stratified communication model. ms.

————. 1988. Communication analysis: A stratificational approach 2. A
  field guide for communication situation, semantic, and morphemic
  analysis. Dallas: Summer Institute of Linguistics.

————. 1990. Communication analysis: A stratificational approach 1.
  An introductory text. Dallas: Summer Institute of Linguistics.

Foley, William A. and Robert D. Van Valin, Jr. 1984. Functional syntax
  and universal grammar. Cambridge: Cambridge University Press.

Friedlander, Gerhart, Joseph W. Kennedy, Edward Macias, and Julian
  Malcolm Miller. 1981. Nuclear and radiochemistry. New York: John
  Wiley and Sons.

Gazdar, Gerald. 1980. Context free grammar. Unpublished.

————, Geoffrey Pullum, and Ivan Sag. 1980. A phrase structure grammar of the English auxiliary system. Bloomington: Indiana University Linguistics Club.

————, ————, and ————. 1982. Auxiliaries and related phenomena in
  a restrictive theory of grammar. Language 58:591–638.

————, Ewan Klein, Geoffrey Pullum, and Ivan Sag. 1985. Generalized
  phrase structure grammar. Cambridge, Mass.: Harvard University
  Press.

Gerdts, Donna B. 1992. Morphologically-mediated relational profiles.
  BLS 18:322–37.

————. 1993. Mapping Transitive Voice in Halkomelem. BLS 19S:22–34.

Givón, Talmy. 1984. Syntax: A functional-typological introduction 1.
  Amsterdam: Benjamins.

————. 1990. Syntax: A functional-typological introduction 2. Amsterdam: Benjamins.

Gleason, Henry A. 1973. Contrastive analysis in discourse structure. In
  Adam Makkai and David G. Lockwood (eds.), Readings in
  stratificational linguistics. University of Alabama Press.

Goffman, Erving. 1959. Presentation of self in everyday life. New York: Anchor Books.

Goldsmith, John. 1976. Autosegmental phonology. Bloomington: Indiana University Linguistics Club.

———. 1979. The aims of autosegmental phonology. In Daniel A. Dinnsen (ed.), Current approaches to phonological theory. Bloomington: Indiana University Press.

Greenburg, Joseph H. 1966. Universals of language. Cambridge, Mass.: MIT Press.

Gruber, Jeffrey. 1970. Studies in lexical relations. Bloomington: Indiana University Linguistics Club.

Gussmann, Edmund. 1980. Studies in abstract phonology. Cambridge, Mass.: MIT Press.

Haegeman, Liliane. 1994. Introduction to government and binding theory, 2nd edition. Oxford, England: Blackwell.

Haiman, John, ed. 1985. Iconicity in syntax: Proceedings of a symposium on iconicity in syntax, Stanford, June 24–26, 1983. Amsterdam/Philadelphia: John Benjamins.

Halle, Morris, Joan Bresnan, and George A. Miller, eds. 1978. Linguistic theory and psychological reality. Cambridge, Mass.: MIT Press.

Halmos, Paul R. 1960. Naive set theory. Princeton, N.J.: Van Nostrand.

Hinds, John. 1979. Organizational patterns in discourse. In Talmy Givón (ed.), Discourse and syntax: Syntax and semantics series, Vol. 12. New York: Academic Press.

Hintikka, Jaakko. 1974. Quantifiers vs. quantification theory. Linguistic Inquiry 5(2):153–77.

Hofstadter, Douglas R. 1980. Gödel, Escher, Bach: An eternal golden braid. New York: Vintage Books.

Hooper, Joan B. 1976. Introduction to natural generative phonology. New York: Academic Press.

Hopper, Paul J. 1988. Emergent Grammar and the a priori grammar postulate. In Deborah Tannen (ed.), Linguistics in context: Connecting observations and understanding, 117–134. Lectures from the 1985 LSA/TESOL and NEH Institute. Norwood, N.J.: Ablex Publishing.

——— and Sandra A. Thompson. 1980. Transitivity in grammar and discourse. Language 56(2):251–99.

Hyman, Larry M. 1975. Phonology: Theory and analysis. New York: Holt, Rinehart, and Winston.

Jackendoff, Ray S. 1972. Semantic interpretation in generative grammar. Cambridge, Mass.: MIT Press.

Johnson, David E. and Paul M. Postal. 1980. Arc pair grammar. Princeton: Princeton University Press.

Johnson, Mark. 1987. The body in the mind. Chicago: University of Chicago Press.

Jones, Linda. 1980. A synopsis of tagmemics. In Edith A. Moravcsik and Jessica R. Wirth (eds.), Syntax and semantics 13: Current approaches to syntax. New York: Academic Press.

Kaplan, Ronald M. and Joan Bresnan. 1982. Lexical-functional grammar: A formal system for grammatical representation. In Joan W. Bresnan (ed.), The mental representation of grammatical relations. Cambridge, Mass.: MIT Press.

Katz, Jerrold and Paul M. Postal. 1964. An integrated theory of linguistic description. Cambridge, Mass.: MIT Press.

Keenan, Edward L. 1985. Boolean semantics for natural language. Dordrecht: Reidel.

—— and Bernard Comrie. 1977. Noun phrase accessibility and universal grammar. Linguistic Inquiry 8:63–99.

—— and ——. 1979. Data on the noun phrase accessibility hierarchy. Language 55:333–51.

Kuhn, Thomas S. 1962. The structure of scientific revolutions. International encyclopedia of unified science 2(2). Chicago: The University of Chicago Press. Reprinted in 1970.

Labov, William. 1972a. Sociolinguistic patterns. Philadelphia: University of Pennsylvania Press.

——. 1972b. Language in the inner city. Philadelphia: University of Pennsylvania Press.

Lakatos, Imre. 1976. Proofs and refutations: The logic of mathematical discovery. Cambridge: Cambridge University Press.

Lakoff, George. 1971/1975. Presupposition and relative well-formedness. In Leon A. Jakobovits and Danny D. Steinberg (eds.), Semantics: An interdisciplinary reader in philosophy, linguistics, and psychology. Cambridge: Cambridge University Press.

——. 1972. Linguistics and natural logic. In Donald Davidson and Gilbert Harman (eds.), Semantics of natural language, 545–665. Dordrecht: Reidel.

——. 1975. Pragmatics in natural logic. In Edward L. Keenan (ed.), Formal semantics of natural language, 253–86. Cambridge: Cambridge University Press.

——. 1990. Women, fire, and dangerous things: What categories reveal about the mind. Chicago: University of Chicago Press.

Lamb, Sydney. 1966. Outline of stratificational grammar. Washington, D.C.: Georgetown University Press.

———. 1989. Some differences between two branches of linguistics. Lecture given at the International Linguistics Center, Dallas, Texas in July 1989.

Laudan, Larry. 1977. Progress and its problems: Towards a theory of scientific growth. London: Routledge and Kegan Paul.

Lieberman, Philip. 1977. Speech physiology and acoustic phonetics: An introduction. New York: Macmillan.

Lockwood, David G. 1972. Introduction to stratificational linguistics. New York: Harcourt Brace and Jovanovich.

———. 1973. Readings in stratificational linguistics. University of Alabama Press.

Longacre, Robert E. 1964. Grammar discovery procedures. The Hague: Mouton.

———. 1976. An anatomy of speech notions. Lisse: de Ridder.

———. 1981. A spectrum and profile approach to discourse analysis. TEXT 1:337–59.

———. 1983. The grammar of discourse. New York: Plenum.

———. 1985. Interpreting Biblical stories. In Teun A. van Dijk (ed.), Discourse and literature. Amsterdam: Benjamins.

———. 1987. The semantics of the storyline in east and west Africa. Journal of Semantics 5:51–64.

———. 1989. Two hypotheses regarding text generation and analysis. Discourse Processes 12:413–60.

———. 1996. The grammar of discourse, 2nd edition. New York: Plenum.

Mayerthaler, Willi. 1981. Morphologische Natürlichkeit. Wiesbaden: Athänion Verlag.

———. 1986. Morphological naturalness. Ann Arbor: Karoma Press.

McCarthy, John. 1982. Prosodic structure and expletive infixation. Language 58:574–90.

McCawley, James D. 1972. A program for logic. In Donald Davidson and Gilbert Harman (eds.), Semantics of natural languages. Dordrecht: Reidel.

———. 1980. An un-syntax. In Edith A. Moravcsik and Jessica R. Wirth (eds.), Syntax and semantics 13: Current approaches to syntax. New York: Academic Press.

Michelmore, Peter. 1962. Einstein, profile of the man. New York: Dodd, Mead and Co.

Nagel, Ernest and James R. Newman. 1958. Gödel's proof. New York: New York University Press.

Nivens, Richard. 1986. Grammatical relations in Eskimo: A response to Kalmar. In Desmond C. Derbyshire (ed.), Work papers of the

Summer Institute of Linguistics, University of North Dakota session 30:77–88.

Pais, Abraham. 1982. "Subtle is the Lord—": The science and the life of Albert Einstein. New York: Oxford University Press.

Partee, Barbara H. 1971. Linguistic metatheory. In William O. Dingwall (ed.), A survey of linguistic science. University of Maryland, Linguistics Program.

Pepper, Stephen C. 1942. World hypotheses: A study in evidence. Berkeley: University of California Press. Reprinted in 1970.

Perlmutter, David. 1971. Deep and surface structure constraints on syntax. New York: Holt, Rinehart, and Winston.

———. 1978. Impersonal passives and the unaccusative hypothesis. Berkeley Linguistics Society 4:157–89.

Peters, P. Stanley and R. W. Richie. 1972. On the generative power of transformational grammars. Information Science.

Pike, Eunice V. 1976. Phonology. In Ruth Brend and Kenneth Pike (eds.), Tagmemics 1: Aspects of the field. The Hague: Mouton.

Pike, Kenneth L. 1971. Language in relation to a unified theory of the structure of human behavior. The Hague: Mouton.

———. 1976/1947. Phonemics: A technique for reducing languages to writing. Ann Arbor: University of Michigan Press.

———. 1982. Linguistic concepts: An introduction to tagmemics. Lincoln: University of Nebraska Press.

———. 1987. The relation of language to the world. International Journal of Dravidian Linguistics 76(1):77–98.

——— and Evelyn G. Pike. 1974. Rules as components of tagmemes in the English verb phrase. In Ruth Brend (ed.), Advances in tagmemics. Amsterdam: North-Hollard.

——— and ———. 1982. Grammatical analysis. Dallas: Summer Institute of Linguistics and the University of Texas at Arlington.

——— and ———. 1983. Text and tagmeme. London: Francis Pinter.

Popper, Karl R. 1950. The open society and its enemies. Revised edition. Princeton, N.J.: Princeton University Press.

———. 1962. The logic of scientific discovery. London: Hutchinson. Reprinted in 1974.

Radford, Andrew. 1981. Transformational syntax: A student's guide to Chomsky's extended standard theory. Cambridge: Cambridge University Press.

Reich, Peter. 1970. The English auxiliaries: A relational network description. Canadian Journal of Linguistics 16:18–50.

————. 1973a. Competence, performance, and relational networks. In Adam Makkai and David G. Lockwood (eds.), Readings in stratificational linguistics. University of Alabama Press.

————. 1973b. Symbols, relations and structural complexity. In Adam Makkai and David G. Lockwood (eds.), Readings in stratificational linguistics. University of Alabama Press.

Rosch, Eleanor. 1978. Cognition and categorization. Hillsdale, N.J.: L. Erlbaum Associates.

Rosen, Carol G. 1984. Interface between semantic roles and initial grammatical relations. In David Perlmutter and Carol G. Rosen (eds.), Studies in relational grammar 2. Chicago: The University of Chicago Press.

Ross, John R. 1969. Auxiliaries as main verbs. In W. Todd (ed.), Studies in philosophical linguistics 1. Evanston, Ill.: Great Expectations Press.

Russell, Bertrand. 1910. Mysticism and logic and other essays [first published as "Philosophical essays"]. London: Allen and Unwin.

Sagan, Carl. 1980. Cosmos. New York: Random House.

Sapir, Edward. 1933. The psychological reality of phonemes. In David G. Mandelbaum (ed.), Selected writings of Edward Sapir on language, culture, and personality, 46–60, (1958/1949). Berkeley: University of California Press.

Schachter, Paul. 1980. Explaining auxiliary order. Bloomington: Indiana University Linguistics Club.

Sommerstein, Alan H. 1977. Modern phonology. Baltimore: University Park Press.

Stampe, David. 1979. A dissertation on natural phonology. New York: Garland.

Stegmüller, Wolfgang. 1969. Hauptströmungen der gegenwärtigen Philosophie. Eine kritische Einführung. Band 1. Stuttgart: Alfred Kröner.

————. 1975. Hauptströmungen der gegenwärtigen Philosophie. Eine kritische Einführung. Band 2. Stuttgart: Alfred Kröner.

Sullivan, William. J. 1980. Syntax and linguistic semantics in stratificational theory. In Edith A. Moravcsik and Jessica R. Wirth (eds.), Syntax and semantics 13: Current approaches to syntax. New York: Academic Press.

Tesnière, Lucien. 1969. Eléments de syntaxe structurale. Paris: Editions Klincksieck.

Thomason, Richmond, ed. 1974. Formal philosophy: Selected papers of Richard Montague. New Haven: Yale University Press.

Trudgill, Peter. 1974. Sociolinguistics. Harmondsworth: Penguin Books.

Van Riemsdijk, Henk and Edwin Williams. 1986. Introduction to the theory of grammar. Cambridge, Mass.: MIT Press.

Varela, Francisco J., Evan Thompson, and Eleanor Rosch. 1991. The embodied mind: Cognitive science and human experience. Cambridge: MIT Press.

Vennemann, Theo. 1974. Words and syllables in generative grammar. In Anthony Bruck, Robert A. Fox, and Michael W. LaGaly (eds.), Papers from the parasession on natural phonology. Chicago: Chicago Linguistics Society.

Von Kutschera, Franz. 1975. Philosophy of language. Synthese Library 71. Dordrecht: Reidel.

Waldrop, M. Mitshell. 1984. Before the beginning. Science 84(5):45–53.

Wall, Robert. 1972. Introduction to mathematical linguistics. Englewood Cliffs, N.J.: Prentice-Hall.

Wittgenstein, Ludwig. 1961. Tractus-logico-philosophicus. New York: Humanities Press.

―――. 1971. Philosophische Untersuchungen. Frankfurt: Suhrkamp.

Index

CPSIA information can be obtained
at www.ICGtesting.com
Printed in the USA
LVOW13s1444100117

520453LV00011B/1139/P

9 781556 710681